W9-BIG-553

THE BEST
GRADUATE BUSINESS
SCHOOLS

"I believe the approach to examining and evaluating MBA programs in *The Best Graduate Business Schools* is going to set the standard and become the new, more intelligent way for candidates to select the best programs for them."

Peter Veruki, Director
Career Planning and Placement Services
The Owen School of Management
VANDERBILT UNIVERSITY

THE BEST
GRADUATE BUSINESS
SCHOOLS

THOMAS BACHHUBER, Ed.D

MACMILLAN • USA

Macmillan General Reference
A Prentice Hall Macmillan Company
15 Columbus Circle
New York, NY 10023

An Arco Book

MACMILLAN is a registered trademark of Macmillan, Inc.
ARCO is a registered trademark of Prentice-Hall, Inc.

Library of Congress Cataloging-in-Publication Data

Bachhuber, Thomas D.
      The best graduate business schools / Thomas Bachhuber.
          p.   cm.
     ISBN 0-671-88541-3
      1. Business schools—United States—Handbooks, manuals, etc.
    2. College choice—United States—Handbooks, manuals, etc.
    I. Title.
    HF1131.B33   1994   94-31300
    650'.071'173—dc20   CIP

Manufactured in the United States of America

10 9 8 7 6 5 4 3 2 1

TABLE OF CONTENTS

THE BEST GRADUATE BUSINESS SCHOOLS

ACKNOWLEDGEMENTS

A book of this nature is a puzzle with many pieces. I believe they have come together to make *The Best Graduate Business Schools* the most valuable resource of its kind. The work and conributions of many people made it happen; I am indebted to them all.

Executive Editor, Linda Bernbach, and Vice President/Editor in Chief, Chuck Wall, were superb. They demonstrated excellence in editing--which is the art of increasing the readers' understanding of the author's ideas while preserving the integrity of the ideas themselves.

The designer/typesetter for the book, Janet Stumper, deserves a medal of honor and a purple heart. Her accomplishments and skills were heroic.

William Glover (MBA and small business executive) designed, implemented and wrote the valuable research study on the employer view. His expertise on past and present research also helped set the tone for this book's innovative approach.

Cathy Sandford and Lauren Florczak did an excellent job writing significant portions of the school profiles. Their work was critical to the book's success. Lauren deserves credit for keeping Janet away from sharp objects during the final months of the project.

Dr. William Sedlecek, Professor of Education at the University of Maryland, provided valuable consultation on research design and application--as well as a droll sense of humor at all the right moments.

Thanks to Robin Greene for developing a useful format and an original look at "womens issues".

I'm thankful for superior advice on the MBA market and job market from Dr. Karen Dowd, former Director of Career Services at Virginia-Darden, Peter Veruki, Director of Career Planning and Placement at Vanderbilt-Owen and Dr. Christopher Shinkman, former Director of The Career Center at Georgetown Graduate Business.

I have great respect for the solid research and effective communications with 66 business schools from good friends Jean Merikle, Ethel Kienz and Melinda Bellafronte. Ehtel and Jean also accomplished exemplary, first-rate proofreading.

Appreciation is extended to all the Deans, Career Services Directors, Associate/ Assistant Deans and Employers for their cooperation and insights. Their contributions make the "inteligence" candidates need to identify, apply to and be accepted at the best graduate business school for them.

And finally...thanks to Les, Lib, Em and Jay for their love in this and all my work.

Thomas Bachhuber

ADVICE FROM THE EXPERTS

"Over the past few years, business schools have undergone more change than at any other time in the past 30 years. We think we are through. We are not. Rapid change will continue for at least another five years. All of this change calls for graduates who understand market forces, who can manage across blurred boundaries, who can accomplish aims through people, who can communicate effectively and who have been effectively taught. Business classrooms which do not adapt to this new reality will lose both students and recruiters—in a word, they will disappear."

> J.D. Hammond, Dean
> Smeal College of Business Administration
> PENNSYLVANIA STATE UNIVERSITY

"Employers are sending fewer recruiters to fewer schools. Many others are shifting to 'just-in-time' recruiting since they cannot pre-plan their staffing needs to use the traditional on-campus interviewing model.

What does this mean for today's MBA student? In a nutshell:

1] Be focused and know what you want [the days of shopping for the best job are over].

2] Work hard and consistently on your career search over the entire 2-year program.

3] 'Target' an industry, city or geographic region, a functional area where you can bring some immediate skills.

4] Be aggressive and learn how to interview well; learn how to sell yourself.

5] Finally, Network, Network, Network. Learn what this really means and how to do it. It is one of the most valuable skills you can learn during your MBA program."

> Peter E. Veruki, Director
> Career Planning and Placement
> Owen Graduate School of Management
> VANDERBILT UNIVERSITY

"Don't let MBA rankings drive your decision about where to go to school. Even a top MBA program could be a bad choice for you. As you decide which one is right for you, look at more than just the surface of the program. Make a check list of what you expect from your graduate experience. Ask enough questions to make an educated decision. You have to feel comfortable with the total environment, or nothing else matters."

>Deborah F. Booker, Director of
>MBA Admissions
>John M. Olin School of Business
>WASHINGTON UNIVERSITY IN ST. LOUIS

"The MBA, as we have known it, is at risk. Unless it can be demonstrated that the MBA experience unambiguously provides value to students and employers, it will be reduced to a meaningless certification. This means that in addition to breadth of content and managerial skills, the MBA for the 21st century must have the depth of understanding necessary to be a contributing member of the management team in the first week of employment. The learning key will be greater focus of study and a bona fide relationship with industry."

>Louis S. Corsini, Graduate Dean
>The Wallace E. Carroll School of Management
>BOSTON COLLEGE

"At a recent meeting, a psychologist colleague labeled the type of behavior that makes students successful in interviews a "narcissistic personality disorder." Historically, MBAs, with their natural ability to brag and inflate accomplishments, have been especially prone to this disorder. As employers of late seem to be emphasizing team accomplishments more than individual initiative, MBA programs which encourage a little humility and stress group process may be producing a new breed of MBA who is more employable."

>Sally M. Watson
>Director of MBA Placement
>THE COLLEGE OF WILLIAM AND MARY

The Best Graduate Business Schools

"This customer focus is not a temporary fad. Schools that do not maintain this emphasis on relevancy to their marketplace will fall aside. If the schools that you evaluate are living on a previous reputation and not continuously trying to create, innovate, and involve multiple constituencies, you best look elsewhere.

Because of these pressures, anyone contemplating attendance at a top school better get into a mode for learning that will literally consume massive amounts of time. Gone are the days of reading a book and parroting it back on a test to prove that you have mastered the material.

The new mode of learning involves sharing, teamwork, massive reading, quick distillation, technology use, case discussions, and real world involvement."

> Dr. C. Randall Powell, Director of
> Placement Services
> School of Business
> INDIANA UNIVERSITY

"Placement considerations are critical throughout the MBA experience, even during the application process. Prospective applicants should carefully research the employers who frequent a school to determine whether the typical employer's interests are in line with their own. In a tough job market, this can make a huge difference in placement success. Applicants should also ask about job search training. If the school offers comprehensive training for independent job search, the odds for placement success are greatly enhanced."

> Alan Ferrell, Director of
> Management Placement
> Krannert Graduate School of Management
> PURDUE UNIVERSITY

"The business environment has become increasingly global, with many large US based companies, for example, generating over 50% of their gross revenues from outside of the United States. Starting employment assignments for graduates interested in international business, however, are likely to be located in the graduate's home country. International assignments are most likely to be found several years into a career, once you have learned your employer's business and have proven your value. If you are interested in global business, consider including language and cultural study in your graduate study so you will understand the context within which you will be working."

> Jim Case, Assistant Vice President
> for Employer Relations and Career Services
> THUNDERBIRD,
> THE AMERICAN GRADUATE
> SCHOOL OF INTERNATIONAL
> MANAGEMENT

Advice From the Experts

"What is the ideal 'profile' for a graduating MBA? According to one technical MBA recruiter, the most desirable candidate has three to five years engineering experience coupled with a graduate business degree. Strong communication and interpersonal skills are crucial for the candidate to be effective on the job, which includes cross-disciplinary work teams. This recruiter also places a priority on ethnic and gender diversity among new hires."

> Lois A Meerdink, Director,
> Commerce Placement Office
> College of Commerce and
> Business Administration
> UNIVERSITY OF ILLINOIS
> AT URBANA-CHAMPAIGN

"Select a business school that has close ties to the business world. This will ensure that the curriculum is practical and state-of-the-art. A relevant program will meet your needs by meeting the needs of your future employers. When a graduate school has close ties to the business world, it facilitates access to the career that you choose and opens the door to the best jobs."

> Dr. Jonathan B. Welch
> Associate Dean & Professor
> Graduate School of Business
> NORTHEASTERN UNIVERSITY

"The best advice I can give is spend as much time as possible on your first year internship search. This is especially true if you are making a career change through your MBA program. Concentrate on alums as your key networking sources especially those who have just graduated. They are a fountain of knowledge and contacts, and can give you shortcuts based on first hand experience."

> Dan Nagy, Director
> Career Sevirces and Placement
> The Fuqua School of Business
> DUKE UNIVERSITY

The Best Graduate Business Schools

CHAPTER ONE

WHAT ARE THE KEY ISSUES?

As the 1980's turned to the 1990's, many graduate business schools became serious about change. At places like Duke-Fuqua, UCLA-Anderson, NYU-Stern, Chicago and Yale, both curricula and deanships had new faces. Associate Deans and Career Services Directors were shuffled as well at Georgetown, Cornell, UNC-Kenan-Flagler, Duke-Fuqua, USC and Maryland. The picture was not unlike that in the ranks of Division I football or basketball coaches. Some teams were perceived as not winning enough, so "heads rolled." The flurry of activity and profound changes in programs continue today.

Magnificent facilities are built and renovated, capital campaigns started and completed, top faculty recruited (or "stolen") and curricula redesigned to meet new standards. Marketing is the game, and for this competitive marketplace, all the players have their "game faces" on. The Harvards, Stanfords, Tucks, Kelloggs, Whartons and Chicagos want to stay in the lead; everyone else wants to move up.

Pick up the slick public relations materials from graduate business schools and it's easy to see what's going on. Everyone is trying to be all things to all people. Media kits are replete with sailboats on lakes (that are often miles from campus); smiling faces respond to questions in corporate-appointed classrooms; the shiniest technology is everywhere; students and faculty walk together down oak-lined paths discussing the latest econometric model and words upon words describe how this program differs from the rest.

As you read, you'll notice there are no pictures of students studying at night for bone-crushing finals; no chagrined faces after verbal shellackings from demanding professors over a poor case presentation. You won't find editorials on the serious challenges of going to school here, things to watch out for, where and why students fail and succeed, the substance and nuances of programs and services, or descriptors of what the campus is really like.

Information is muffled on percentage of graduates who are satisfied with their initial jobs or on how many are still looking and how they feel. No answers are given to the big questions: how will this school meet my needs? Is it really worth $50,000 in cash and loans as well as $80,000—$120,000 in foregone income? These are the questions that only you can answer. As you investigate different schools, you'll want to consider how each one addresses the following ten issues considered crucial by the American Assembly of Collegiate Schools of Business (AACSB):

1. INTEGRATED CURRICULUM—emphasis on "cross-functional" skills; rather than specialization in a single business area.

2. TEAMWORK—like apple pie, it's hard to knock; the question is whether it is actually a part of the classroom and extracurricular experience.

3. DIVERSITY—the hot topic in business today; it must be addressed by every business school.

4. ETHICS—all schools promote their own high standards as well as business ethics through the curricula.

5. SKILLS DEVELOPMENT—not competencies, abilities or knowledge, but skills. Soft, technical, career and functional skills are what the MBA is about.

6. TOP FACULTY—every place has its stars and they really are good, combining keen business insights with "David Letterman" pizazz.

7. MANAGER AS GENERALIST—emphasis on being able to see the big picture while running day-to-day affairs effectively and sensitively, using the leading business tools.

8. GLOBALISM—see "teamwork," "ethics" and "diversity" above; it's just as hot. What organization isn't promoting the international view?

9. PLACEMENT/CAREER SERVICES—it's crucial to reassure prospective students that the school is committed to making job contacts in the business world, bringing employers to campus for interviews and offering educational and counseling programs for MBA candidates.

10. CORPORATE PARTNERSHIPS—links forged on academic, employment, internship, consultative, faculty, advisory and financial fronts that enhance the position of the school in the business world. These links define success.

The next section will consider each of these important issues in detail. It will also suggest ways to measure how well different schools handle each issue.

ASSESSING THE ISSUES

All of the issues just listed can be vital in choosing a graduate business school. Let's consider each issue in turn. For each one, you'll learn what you can do to evaluate its importance at a given school.

CURRICULUM

The study of business covers a variety of functions including finance, accounting, marketing and human resources. A top manager needs some understanding of all these functions and in-depth understanding of select ones, depending on personal and career goals. Terms such as *integrated curriculum* and *cross curricula skills* describe a philosophy of educating students broadly in the business disciplines.

YOU MUST... examine specifically how each school attempts to impart this general business education. Investigate required or "core" courses, electives, opportunities to take courses in other university divisions, experiential models, competitions, internships, and other extracurricular opportunities. Check out the opportunities to apply theoretical concepts in the real-world workplace. The number of credits required for an MBA degree is normally between 60 and 70; question any program that requires many more or many fewer. Also, ask about the number of faculty contact hours for a two-year program; 750 is about average.

TEAMWORK AND COMMUNICATIONS

Good managers today rely on teamwork and effective communications. Both are essential in the modern business world, where management situations often require excellent interpersonal skills.

YOU MUST...first assess your own communication skills, on paper, in person or in front of a group. Determine what opportunities the school provides for developing these skills. Examine specific courses as well as programs offered by Career Services and other offices, institutes and centers at the school. Ask how the school promotes small group learning and team projects.

DIVERSITY

It's relatively easy to assess the extent of diversity in the student body; check faces when you visit and note the statistics, always readily available. There may be courses with the term *diversity* in the title. These are a good sign that the school takes diversity seriously.

YOU MUST...explore any courses that have *diversity* in their titles. Question the issues addressed and methodology for addressing them. Also ask about diversity on the faculty and in the administration. Explore how diversity is addressed across the curriculum. Inside and outside the classrooms, what opinions do you hear expressed on campus? What do those opinions say about the school's attitude toward diversity?. Inquire about innovative services and programs for minority recruitment. Ask the honest, tough questions about those diversity issues that concern you.

ETHICS

Ethics, like diversity, are a major concern of business schools today. Every school seeks to address ethics both in lessons and by example.

YOU MUST...consider your own ethics and whether they match those of your chosen school. Listen to the values expressed in campus debates--especially those involving legal matters.

FACULTY

At top business schools, there are many "star" professors and few slouches. But how much contact will you really have with leading faculty members?

YOU MUST...determine whether top faculty interact with students, or merely lecture. Check course and faculty evaluation publications. Ask also about non-faculty personnel--Career Services staff, Exchange Program staff, and the like. Will you have access to the most capable among them?

EMPHASIS ON MANAGER AS GENERALIST

Business leaders need to be generalists as well as experts in a particular field. How well does a school prepare students for this dual role?

YOU MUST...determine what opportunities the school provides for you to learn overall management theory, ideas and techniques as well as develop a specific expertise. Look at required courses and electives as well as courses available outside the Business School. Examine opportunities, competitions, internships, jobs, games and volunteer experiences beyond the curricula.

SKILLS DEVELOPMENT

Business education used to be concerned with knowledge; now it's skills. All kinds of skills. And you want a business school that teaches them all.

YOU MUST...determine the extent to which critical thinking and problem-solving skills are stressed in the curriculum. Are skill-building techniques employed in the classroom? Are skill-building workshops and training sessions offered?

GLOBALISM

Everyone talks about global business, but which schools offer serious preparation for it? Which ones will truly prepare you to compete in a worldwide marketplace?

YOU MUST...determine how much of the school's curriculum is devoted to international concerns. For starters, count the courses with *international* or *global* in the title. Look for exchange programs with other countries and top international business schools—how many, which countries and, most importantly, how many students participate? Also, consider the number of international faculty and students in the program. Finally, determine the extent to which international studies are integrated into the general curriculum. Are they a part of every subject, or studied separately?

The Best Graduate Business Schools

PLACEMENT/CAREER SERVICES

In the past, little attention was devoted to placement services. There was always an abundance of companies coming to campus to woo MBAs. But not anymore; even the elite schools now tout the achievements of their Career Services or Career Planning and Placement Services.

YOU MUST...request complete Placement Reports from the Admissions Office or from Career Services. Inspect follow-up surveys of graduates covering starting positions, salary ranges and percent of graduating class in full-time career positions at different times such as three months before graduation, at graduation, three months out, and six months out.

A high percentage of graduates placed in jobs soon after graduation doesn't necessarily mean a lot. Most surveys do not address the vital issue of job satisfaction. Ask what percentage of graduates by business concentration get their jobs through on-campus interviews. Ask how many graduates change fields or change employers within 5 years.

Also, don't judge the effectiveness of the Career Services office by its placement record only; that record can depend more on the school's overall reputation than on other skills.

Ask good questions about Career Services programs—how many students participate, how these programs are integrated with curriculum, and what kinds of special services there are for first-year students. There should be seminars on goal-setting and internships that shape career direction and build employment skills.

Finally, assess those all-important, hard-to-measure and harder to find intangible qualities of the Career Services staff: personal care and commitment. Do the people in the office want to work with you, support you, teach you, listen to your hard-knock stories? Are they the kind of people you can talk with and exchange ideas with? What kinds of innovative programs and resources do they have to help you set goals and connect to jobs?

PARTNERSHIPS WITH BUSINESS

Business schools are bullish on partnerships with businesses. Successful ones result in money for the school and jobs for the students. Partnerships also help to attract top students.

YOU MUST...find out whether a school actively pursues business partnerships. If it does not, it risks being trapped in an "ivory tower"; the curriculum gets stagnant, faculty don't consult, capital campaigns go flat, and students lose contact with employers on campus. With partnerships, everything works—and you'll know, too, that the business world values the school and seeks out its graduates.

Find out if there are innovative ways for students to participate in business partnerships, e.g., executive mentoring, courses taught by executives (sometimes in residence), executive-student teams in cases and competitions, opportunities for students to sit on advisory groups. Executive education brings top managers to the campus for continuing professional development—and students can benefit from these contacts.

Each of the issues just discussed may be more or less important to you depending on your personal goals. It may be helpful to assign each one a priority; then you can see how your priorities compare to those of each school you are considering. You can begin by completing the following charts.

SETTING YOUR PRIORITIES

Assign a priority to each issue according to the following key.

4—Highest priority   2—Moderate priority   0—No priority
3—High priority   1—Low priority

SIGNIFICANT ISSUES FOR YOUR MBA EDUCATION	PRIORITY
1. Curriculum (name concentrations or core areas of interest)	
1a. Integrated Curriculum (preparing manager as generalist)	
2. Teaching Methods	
3. Faculty—credentials and reputation	
3a. Faculty—experience and business partnerships	
4. Skills Development—technical/quantitative	
5. Skills Development - management - leadership - teamwork - communications (verbal) - diversity training - communications (written)	
6. Skills Development —career planning/job search	
7. Internships/Experiential Learning	
8. Career Services/Placement	
9. Costs	
10. Financial Assistance	
11. Partnerships with Business/Companies	
12. Location—geography	
13. Environment—facilities, technology	
14. International/Global Emphasis	
15. Climate conducive to Women	
16. Climate conducive to Minorities	
17. Other	
MAIN PRIORITIES:	
THEMES:	
NEXT STEPS:	

COMPARING CRITERIA ACROSS MBA PROGRAMS

Use this chart to record how well each business school addresses the issues that are important to you. Use the following key.

> 5—Highest quality—no one on my list is better
> 4—High quality—better than most on my list
> 3—Competitive with most on my list
> 2—Below quality of most on my list
> 1—Below quality of all others on my list
> 0—Impossible to compare

SIGNIFICANT ISSUES FOR YOUR MBA EDUCATION	MBA PROGRAMS CONSIDERING (NAME)					
1. Specific Curriculum (concentrations/core areas)						
1a. Integrated Curriculum (preparing manager as generalist)						
2. Teaching Methods						
3. Faculty—credentials and reputation						
3a. Faculty—experience and business partnerships						
4. Skills Development— technical/quantitative						
5. Skills Development— - teamwork - diversity training - leadership - communications (verbal) - communications (written)						
6. Skills Development—career planning job search						
7. Internships/Experiential Learning						
8. Career Services/Placement						

Chart continues on next page

COMPARING CRITERIA ACROSS MBA PROGRAMS

SIGNIFICANT ISSUES FOR YOUR MBA EDUCATION	MBA PROGRAMS CONSIDERING (NAME)					
9. Costs						
10. Financial Assistance						
11. Partnerships with Business/Companies						
12. Location—geography						
13. Environment—facilities, technology						
14. International/Global Emphasis						
15. Climate conducive to Women						
16. Climate conducive to Minorities						
17. Other						
TOTALS						

POTENTIAL BEST SCHOOLS FOR ME: _____

_____

_____

NEXT STEPS: _____

_____

_____

CHAPTER TWO

SPECIAL ISSUES FOR WOMEN BUSINESS STUDENTS
BY ROBIN GREENE

This chapter is designed to address some questions relevant to women business students. To answer these questions, it may be necessary to dig beyond the standard information provided by the admissions personnel and the administration. The following are questions that you may want to ask when deciding which school is the right one for you.

ISSUE: WHAT IS THE PERCENTAGE OF WOMEN STUDENTS IN THE PROGRAM?

One of the most important ways to tell if a school is successful at providing high-quality educational and career-boosting employment opportunities is to look at the percentage of women it enrolls each year. Schools that do not satisfy their women students eventually lose the ability to attract new ones. Consider trends over recent years. Is the proportion of female students stable? Rising? Declining? Why?

HOW TO GET ANSWERS

Somewhere in the brochures that the schools send is demographic data on the previous year's classes, including the percentages of women students enrolled. For trends, call the admissions office, which should be able to supply the figures for the past couple of years.

Compare numbers from different schools to determine which ones have high percentages of women. Also consider the fields in which women graduates are placed. For example, a school with 5% women that graduates most of its students into traditionally male fields (such as finance and manufacturing) might be considered more progressive than a school with 30% women that graduates its students into the least male-dominated industries (say, marketing).

ISSUE: WHAT IS THE PERCENTAGE OF WOMEN FACULTY IN THE PROGRAM?

Women faculty members are extremely important to women students. Women professors and instructors make invaluable mentors and generally possess a wealth of personal insight and business experience. Further, the success and proportion of women on the faculty can be indicative of how well the school serves the needs of women students. The presence of women on the faculty contributes to the quality of MBA education for all students.

What percentage of the professors are women? What percentage of those are tenured or have reached a high level of standing at the school? More specifically, what are these proportions in the career fields that you are considering? Has the school successfully recruited and promoted women professors in such traditionally male fields as finance, manufacturing and accounting?

HOW TO GET ANSWERS

Examine the brochures for sections on professors, the administration, the career services office and executive advisory boards. For each school, figure out what percent of the total are women. Look at what courses they teach. The titles after the names can also be informative. Just like employees in any other profession, professors are periodically reviewed for promotion. There are generally four hierarchical levels of professors: Instructor/Lecturer, Assistant Professor, Associate Professor and (full) Professor. Full Professors are tenured, as are some Associate Professors. You may want to compare the percentages of women at each of these different levels at the various schools you are considering. Most schools publish faculty directories, providing biographies and professional backgrounds.

ISSUE: IS THERE AN ACTIVE WOMEN'S GROUP IN THE PROGRAM?

An active women's group in an MBA program can be a source of opportunities for women students. If there is such a group at a school you're considering, does it sponsor a lot of activities? Does it bring women executives to campus? Does it provide professional network contacts for its members? Finding out how much support the group gets from the faculty and other students can tell you about the general attitudes among and towards women. Does the group have faculty advisors? Are the group's events well-attended? Are there any men members? Do men support the group's events (speakers, panel discussions, etc.)? What is the focus of the group (political activism, career advancement, academic excellence, social networking, etc.)? You also may want to keep in mind the leadership opportunities that exist to start a women's group.

HOW TO GET ANSWERS

Contact the admissions office and request information and/or contact names/numbers. Call the officers of the groups. Find out what kind of activities they sponsor. Ask them questions about their membership and the support that they receive from students, professors and administration.

ISSUE: ARE WOMEN STUDENTS TREATED DIFFERENTLY FROM MEN STUDENTS?

Finding out whether women are treated differently from men in an MBA program can help you assess the program. In the classroom, do professors call on men more or less often than they do on women? Do professors pay more, less or different attention to points made by men than those made by women? Are women graded any differently? Are there special programs, scholarships or other opportunities for women? Research shows that women are treated differently in many classrooms. What is the school doing to raise overall awareness of these issues?

The only way to get real answers to most of these questions is to talk to the students and the faculty at the schools; visit the schools and visit classes. Since opinions about these issues are very subjective, it may be a good idea to talk to several different people at each school.

ISSUE: JOBS

For most, the reason to go to business school is for a rewarding job at the end of the program. This is the area in which average data is least meaningful to women. In a school with 70% men, the average placement data is of use only to men. Unfortunately, most schools are loath to reveal career placement data for their women students alone. After graduation, do women get the same caliber jobs as men? Do they receive comparable salaries? Are women graduates concentrated in certain industries or job functions?

Some schools will release summary placement data broken down by sex; most do not. In most cases, there is a gap between the average salary of men and women graduates of the same program. You should also know that there are no studies that control for previous work experience/accomplishments, making these comparisons even less meaningful.

For most of the best business schools, the average starting salaries between schools are very close to one another. On the other hand, average starting salaries within schools vary widely. The primary reason is that different career fields have dramatically different salary ranges and students come from wide-ranging backgrounds. For example, starting salaries in management consulting and investment banking might be from $15,000 to $25,000 per year higher than the starting salaries in human relations and marketing. Generally, students with technical backgrounds will earn more than those without.

HOW TO GET ANSWERS

To get answers about career placement services, speak to recent alumnae as well as to current students. However, since salaries vary according to area of specialization, the single most important placement issue for women applicants is the choice of business specialty. It is also helpful to develop a chart of graduate salaries by business function with numbers of employers interviewing on campus. How do your business interests line up?

ISSUE: HOW SAFE IS THE SECTION OF TOWN WHERE THE SCHOOL IS LOCATED?

It is important to know and understand the neighborhood in which the campus is located. Is it an area where you would feel safe walking alone after studying until 1:00 A.M.? How extensive and effective is the campus security? Does the school offer any kind of escort services to get you home late at night? How about public transportation? Is it easy and is it safe to get a cab outside the library at night? Do women students worry about walking around campus alone? Do the students make efforts to insure that fellow students get home safely (e.g., walk each other home or make phone calls)? Is the campus well-lit? Are there security phones along walkways?

HOWTOGETANSWERS

The best way to get information is to talk to people you know who have lived in the cities being considered. In general, safety is an area in which rural schools have an important advantage over city schools. Remember to check the exact location of the business school. At some schools, the business school is located in a different part of town from the main campus. Most schools promote extensive safety programs. They vary in effectiveness, however, principally because of widely varying community crime rates.

ISSUE: WHAT KIND OF STUDENT HEALTH CARE FACILITIES ARE AVAILABLE?

Full-time students are eligible for coverage under the school insurance plan. Availability of medical services is often a more important issue for women than for men. What kind of OB-GYN services can student health provide? If the school is affiliated with a church, will that affect the services available? How many nurses, nurse practitioners and doctors are available to you? Are women doctors available when requested?

HOWTOGETANSWERS

Many admissions offices provide a specific brochure on health services. If not, or to go beyond the standard information, ask admissions and health service officials. To get inside information, ask women students.

ISSUE: WHAT IS THE IMAGE OF WOMEN'S ISSUES AT THE BUSINESS SCHOOL?

How are women's issues viewed on campus? Are they just now being addressed? Do they remain controversial, or is that old news? Some students will enjoy an environment where there is a sense of pushing frontiers. Other students will prefer an environment where gender is completely irrelevant, in fact as well as theory.

HOWTOGETANSWERS

Pick up copies of the student newspaper and business school periodicals. They are likely to give you a good idea of what issues are important on campus. Are any of them women's issues? What opinions are expressed? Who is expressing them? What are your views and concerns?

CHAPTER THREE

THE MBA JOB MARKET TODAY

The MBA job market today is a challenging one. In 1992, more than 75,000 MBA degrees were granted by the nation's 700-plus business programs, but as computer and industrial giants trim the ranks of middle management and investment and commercial banks downsize, the demand for MBAs has been falling.

It seems everything about MBAs is downsizing, even the job interview programs at top business schools. Dr. Karen Dowd, former director at Virginia's Darden School, says that on-campus recruitment while not yet extinct, is going the way of the dinosaurs. She is consistently seeking new and innovative ways to hook up employers—of every size, from any industry—with Darden students. The top business schools like Harvard, Wharton, Stanford, Chicago and Kellogg market their students using resume database systems that employers can load and search right in their own offices.

Meanwhile, graduate business education is changing dramatically. Dean J.D. Hammond at Penn State's Smeal College of Business says, "Rapid unprecedented change will continue for at least another five years, driven by many of the forces which continue to buffet the private sector."

Many MBA programs lost sight of employer needs in the 1980's, turning out specialists with narrow expertise in single functions like marketing or finance. Today, most programs are seeking to produce generalists. Some schools have even dropped their required courses in accounting and statistics and are looking "across the curriculum" at new interdisciplinary courses such as Socio-economic and Political Implications in a Global Economy. The "Total Quality Management" movement has also hit MBA curricula. The University of Tennessee has designed its whole program around TQM. Students run hypothetical companies where meeting quality standards in all management areas is the goal. Personal development and communication skills courses are also gaining importance in most curricula; students know it takes more than just technical knowledge to succeed today.

A NEW KIND OF EMPLOYER

Until recently, the job market for MBAs was dominated by corporate giants that frequently held out the promise of a long-term career with a single company. Today, however, as corporations down-size and lay off white-collar workers, this picture is changing. The corporation of the future will likely consist of a core of in-house employees who set goals and strategies and a group of outside organizations which are retained to handle both on-going and temporary assignments. This can be great news for smaller firms that specialize in supporting larger ones in management and production areas. But the people who run these smaller companies will have to be a special breed of manager—one who can operate without the services of a sales staff, personnel department or advertising agency. Successful managers will be the well-rounded generalists who also can handle the technical aspects of business with speed and accuracy.

MBAs are also increasingly likely to find jobs with the small and emerging companies that have begun to dot the landscape from Route 128 outside Boston to The Silicon Valley area of California—and numerous places in between. In fact, business schools located close to these start-up business "hotbeds"—near places such as Provo, Utah; Sante Fe, New Mexico; Rochester/Corning, New York; Hunt Valley, Maryland (outside of Baltimore); and the "golden triangle" of Durham, Chapel Hill and Raleigh, North Carolina—may offer their graduates unparalled access to tomorrow's best employment opportunities.

What does all this mean for prospective business students? Plenty! Students will want to choose schools with programs attuned to the new MBA employment pattern. They will want to look for programs that meet the following conditions:

- The MBA program should help graduates function in an uncertain, insecure and ever-changing environment. Simulations, experiential learning, and specific courses should address this need.

- The program should offer formal training in career and life planning skills through a collaboration of career service and academic programs.

- Courses and seminars should be available on such topics as Succeeding on the Job, Success Skills in the Employment Market, Assessing a Company's Organization and Plans, Determining How Your Position Fits with the Bigger Picture Now and in the Future, Relationship Skills, and Working as a Consultant. As companies change, only proven managers will be asked to stay.

- The program should offer concentrations in "Small Business Entrepreneurship" and "Corporate Venturing." That's where the economy is going—and managers need special skills and knowledge to perform well in this area.

- Courses and experiences should be available in...
    - becoming a consultant,
    - personal and business financial planning,
    - working for a foreign owned company,
    - gender issues in the workplace,
    - moving from a larger to a smaller employer,
    - approaches to up-grading skills in the workplace.

These program offerings all demonstrate that a school understands the nature of the market—and recognizes what the future holds for most managers.

CHANGES IN RECRUITING PRACTICES

In today's economy, employers have the upper hand when recruiting MBAs. Some follow the "cooperative education model" filling full-time positions with students who have already proved themselves by working on a temporary or part-time basis. Other employers do the same with summer interns. In either case, everyone benefits; employer and prospective employee have more and better information on which to base successful employment decisions.

Today too, fewer employers conduct traditional on-campus interviews. Peter Veruki, Director of Career Services at Vanderbilt's Owen School, says that many companies are shifting to "just-in-time" recruiting in order to fill new positions. They may visit nearby business schools, but they are more likely to rely on resume referrals, resume books, personal recommendations from contacts at a school or a resume database system that can be accessed on the office computer.

Another change in recruiting practices is the increase in job and career fairs. Instead of the thirty-minute campus interview, employers are choosing candidates based on five-minute contacts that occur at these events. The old adage, "you never get a second chance to make a first impression" is certainly true in these situations. Personal appearance, enthusiasm and a concise, well-spoken goal statement are all essential. At some of these job/career fairs, employers schedule traditional interviews for the next day; nevertheless, that first contact is crucial to getting on the interviewer's list.

All MBA schools are increasing their reliance on alumni for employment contacts and information. Creative Career Service offices seek ways to bring together prospective students, current students, alumni and corporate recruiters.

Many schools have banded together to create consortia which sponsor major Job/Career Fairs. Some of the better known MBA Consortium Job/Career Fairs include:

ATLANTA and NEW YORK

Emory
Florida State
Georgetown
Georgia Tech
Rice
Rochester
Rollins
SMU
Tulane
Vanderbilt
Wake Forest
Washington (St. Louis)
William and Mary

CHICAGO

SUNY at Buffalo
Case Western Reserve
Florida
Georgia
Iowa
Maryland
Michigan State
Minnesota
Ohio State
Penn State
Pittsburgh
Tulane
Washington (Seattle)
Wisconsin

WEST COAST
MBA CONSORTIUM

WEST COAST
MBA CONSORTIUM
(in San Fransisco)

Brigham Young
Claremont Graduate School
Pepperdine
Santa Clara
Thunderbird -The American
  Graduate School of International
  Management
U.C. Davis
U.C. Irvine
U.C. Riverside
University of Arizona
University of Utah
University of Washington
Willamette University

Carnegie Mellon GSIA
Dartmouth-Tuck
Virginia-Darden

Don't look for Harvard or Wharton, et.al. to participate in these collective efforts. These highly selective schools count on their reputations and resources to attract employers.

Career Services needs to be about teaching, counseling and coaching in new ways. Workshops on lightweight topics like "dressing right for interviews" may help some, but leading offices address critical issues like "self-marketing" and problem-solving in interviews in order to beat the competition. Consulting firms like Bain, McKinsey, and Boston Consulting Group demand that candidates speak well in response to questions like, "How many blades of grass are on the RFK Stadium Football field?" or "How many taxicabs are in New York City?" There are no right answers, of course, but creativity counts and there are certainly good—and bad—ways to frame a response.

Major banks like Chase, Chemical and Citicorp as well as public accounting firms like Deloitte Touche, Ernst & Young, and Arthur Anderson still send multiple recruiters to most of the top echelon business schools. So, too, do Booze-Allen, Price Waterhouse and Coopers as well as major manufacturers and technical giants like AT&T, G.E. and Motorola. The number of companies recruiting on campus is a sign of the regard in which a particular school is held. Check for the "non-*Fortune* 500" employers too. Such connections indicate a Career Services office that hustles and is likely to provide an extra measure of assistance when job-hunting time comes around..

The Best Graduate Business Schools

CHAPTER FOUR

EMPLOYERS RANK THE TOP BUSINESS SCHOOLS
BY WILLIAM GLOVER

Chapters 1 and 2 present the key issues in graduate business education and suggest ways for candidates to evaluate various programs in light of their own particular goals and needs. This chapter offers another perspective on graduate business education-- the perspective of the employers who hire MBAs.

THE IMPORTANCE OF RECRUITER RANKINGS

How recruiting employers evaluate a school can be a significant factor in the decision-making process of the prospective MBA. Recruiters visit campus; interact with faculty, administrators and students; and after interviewing many students, refer a select few for further consideration, perhaps resulting in actual job offers.

Because recruiters interview and select candidates from multiple schools, they see the differences between the programs, and observe first hand the strengths and weaknesses of each school. Clearly, most students pursue the MBA in order to have it impact markedly on their careers and to be hired by one of the recruiting employers who visit campus is just the sort of impact most students seek.

HOW THE RANKINGS WERE OBTAINED

To elicit feedback from recruiting employers at the major business schools in the United States, the following steps were taken:

1. Career Services Offices at 61 recognized business schools were asked to provide a list of the top 10 recruiting employers who have been most successful in recruiting and retaining their graduates. Figure 1 shows the schools surveyed.

2. Questionnaires were sent to over 300 employers asking each one to rank as few or as many of the 61 schools as possible on the basis of the "value of the graduates to the business function they recruited." Employers were asked to rank the schools with which they had either direct or indirect recruiting experiences.

DETERMINING THE TOP 20

A list of the top 20 Graduate Business Schools was determined by recruiting employers as follows:

1. First, all schools listed by two or fewer employers were eliminated.

2. For all schools ranked by three or more employers, a "quality score" was derived. Ranking orders (1, 2, 3, etc.) were totaled and a mean score/ranking was developed for each school.

3. The "quality score" also considered the size of the school and the number of recruiters who ranked the school.

4. A margin of error was used to determine whether adjacent schools in the ranking of 1 through 20 were close enough to be ties. Tied schools were arranged in alphabetical order under the mean quality score of the group. Because of the number of ties, the top 20 schools are ranked 1 through 12 as shown in Figure 2.

FIGURE 1
SCHOOLS PROVIDING RECRUITER CONTACTS
AND RANKED BY RECRUITING EMPLOYERS

American Graduate School of International
  Management/Thunderbird
Univ. of Arizona/Eller
Boston College
Boston Univ.
U.C. Berkeley/Haas
U.C. Irvine
U.C.L.A./Anderson
Carnegie Mellon Univ.
Case Western Reserve Univ./Weatherhead
Univ. of Chicago
Cornell Univ./Johnson
Dartmouth/Tuck
Duke Univ./Fuqua
Emory Univ.
Univ. of Florida
Univ. of Georgia
Georgetown Univ.
George Mason Univ.
George Washington Univ.
Harvard Univ.
Hofstra Univ.
Univ. of Illinois
Indiana Univ.
Univ. of Iowa
Univ. of Maryland
Univ. of Mass.
Michigan State Univ.
Univ. of Michigan
Univ. of Minnesota
CUNY Baruch
NYU/Stern
SUNY Buffalo
Northeastern Univ.
Northwestern Univ./Kellogg
Univ. North Carolina/Kenan-Flagler

Univ. of Notre Dame
Ohio State Univ.
Penn State Univ./Smeal
Univ. Penn/Wharton
Univ. Pittsburgh/Katz
Univ. Purdue/Krannert
Rensselear (RPI)
Rice Univ.
Univ. of Rochester/Simon
M.I.T./Sloan
Univ. South Carolina
SMU/Cox
USC
Stanford Univ.
Univ. of Tennessee
Texas A&M Univ.
Univ. of Texas
Tulane Univ.
Wake Forest Univ./Babcock
Wash. Univ./Olin
Univ. of Virginia/Darden
Vanderbilt/Owen
Univ. of Washington-Seattle
William and Mary
Univ. of Wisconsin
Yale Univ.

The Best Graduate Business Schools

FIGURE 2
THE TOP SCHOOLS AS RANKED BY
RECRUITING EMPLOYERS

1. Northwestern University-Kellogg
2. University of Pennsylvania-Wharton
3. University of Michigan
4. Indiana University
    MIT-Sloan
5. Duke University-Fuqua
    Harvard University
    Stanford University
    University of Virginia-Darden
6. Carnegie Mellon University
7. Cornell University-Johnson
8. University of Chicago
    Dartmouth College-Tuck
    University of Florida
9. University of Maryland
10. Georgetown University
11. Vanderbilt University-Owen
12. University of Arizona
    University of Pittsburgh-Katz
    University of North Carolina-Kenan-Flagler

CHAPTER FIVE

THE ADMISSIONS PROCESS

In evaluating candidates for admissions, all graduate business schools consider the following criteria:

- Your undergraduate record regardless of major

- The quality of your undergraduate institution and rigor of your academic program

- Your accomplishments and experience in business that demonstrate managerial success and potential

- Your score on the Graduate Management Admissions Test (GMAT) (except for Harvard)

- Letters of recommendation

- The quality of your responses to key questions and essays on the application

- The strength of your personality, motivation and leadership as conveyed through the application and your interview, if you interview

All graduate business schools emphasize that there is no formula for admission and that each applicant is viewed individually. Nevertheless, the schools have minimal standards for GPAs and GMAT scores. You should be aware of these numbers and know how your scores compare to those of successful applicants in the past. If your numbers are in the lower percentiles, you need to do (or have done) something extraordinary in some other area to offset that deficiency.

It's advisable to apply to from four to six schools. You need some backups for your top choices. Go for the best school you can, given your qualifications, scores and needs. Maybe even try for one or two that are a little above your qualifications, especially if you have unique business accomplishments or experiences. A general rule of thumb:

- Schools a little above qualifications—apply to one or two
- Schools well matched to your qualifications—apply to two or three
- Schools a little below your qualifications—apply to one or two

This assumes that all the schools have the programs, curricula and opportunities you need. Decisions for acceptance are made usually from March through June on a rolling basis. This means that as applications come in, schools act on them. Classes can fill up early, so don't delay submitting your applications.

Some schools will give you specific application deadlines, which means that all applicants will be considered at once. Find out how your target schools make admissions decisions and plan accordingly.

ENCOURAGING A MORE
DIVERSE STUDENT BODY

Most graduate business schools are seeking greater diversity in their student body. They encourage applications from Black, Hispanic, Asian-American, Pacific Island and Native American students, as well as students from unique backgrounds with interesting stories to tell. They also provide many of these students with financial assistance and scholarships.

The Graduate Management Admission Council co-sponsors with the National Society of Hispanic MBAs and the National Black MBA Association a series of meetings called "Destination MBA." These conferences are held annually September through December in cities such as Boston, Atlanta, Washington D.C., New York, Chicago, Los Angeles and San Francisco. These meetings offer panels, workshops and opportunities to meet with graduate business school representatives. For more information, contact: National Director, Destination MBA, GMAC, P.O. Box 6106, Princeton, New Jersey 08541-6106.

For additional general information contact:

National Society of Hispanic MBAs
P.O. Box 862651, Terminal Annex Station
Los Angeles, CA 90086-2651

National Black MBA Association, Inc.
180 North Michigan Ave.
Chicago, IL 60601

Destination MBA is also offered in smaller cities such as Nashville and Charlotte on a rotating basis.

The GMAC also sponsors forums that bring together admissions representatives from over 100 MBA programs in most major cities.

ACCREDITATION AND THE AMERICAN ASSEMBLY OF
COLLEGIATE SCHOOLS OF BUSINESS (AACSB)

The American Assembly of Collegiate Schools of Business (AACSB) is a "not-for-profit corporation comprised of member organizations and institutions devoted to the promotion and continuous improvement of higher education for business administration and management." (AACSB, 1993) The association is recognized as the accrediting agency for business administration and accounting by the Council on Postsecondary Accreditation and by the Office of Postsecondary Education of the U.S. Department of Education.

AACSB accreditation is not the only thing to look for when evaluating business schools—but it's an important criterion. Currently, there are 280 AACSB-accredited institutions out of over 700 MBA programs representing about 50% of all business degrees awarded (undergraduate and graduate).

THE GRADUATE MANAGEMENT
ADMISSION TEST (GMAT)

The Graduate Management Admission Test (GMAT) is a four-hour exam that is required for admission at almost all graduate business schools. The GMAT measures general mathematics and verbal abilities that are required for success in graduate business school. The verbal portion includes reading comprehension and general English usage, while the quantitative portion focuses on analytical problem-solving, quantitative reasoning and interpreting data.

GMAT scores are reported in three ways—verbal, quantitative and composite. Most MBA programs will take the average score if an applicant takes the GMAT more than once.

The average composite GMAT score for all those admitted to graduate business school is about 490; 600 is often a cutoff for the better programs. The importance given to the GMAT score varies from school to school. Schools also put different emphasis on the quantitative or the verbal score depending on the program. Many of the better programs have cutoff scores.

Comparing your GMAT score to those of students admitted by a particular graduate business program is a good way to measure your chances for acceptance by that program. For example, if your composite score is 595 and the business school you are considering reports that 80% of last year's enrolled students scored between 580 and 620, your chances look good—as long as you are competitive in GPA and other categories. Don't count yourself out if a majority of students scored above you; you may have something else that tips the scales in your favor. Remember, GMAT scores are only one factor considered in the admissions process.

PREPARING FOR THE GMAT

Preparing for the GMAT is more than just a good idea. It's a must these days. Several courses and guides are available. Test-taking strategies can help and knowing the test format in advance can build important confidence. Mathematics competence is mandatory.

The format of the GMAT undergoes periodic changes. The latest change is the addition of a one-hour essay section that is graded by business faculty. For the latest GMAT information, contact the Graduate Management Admission Council, the official information and testing organization for graduate business schools. Be sure to request the latest GMAT bulletin. You may write to the following address:

The Graduate Management Admission Council
11601 Wilshire Blvd., Suite 760
Los Angeles, CA 90025-1746

ARCO Publishing, the publisher of this guide, offers the following GMAT preparation materials:
—*GMAT: Graduate Management Admission Test*
—*GMAT Super Course*
—*GRE-GMAT Math Review*

All of these books are available at bookstores everywhere.

THE APPLICATION ESSAY

Many graduate business school applications also require essay responses to questions such as "Identify your three most important accomplishments and explain why you consider them to be important" or "What is your biggest professional weakness and how do you think that a business school education will correct it?" The short-answer questions help admissions officers learn what applicants have done and the essay questions help them learn why those accomplishments are significant.

Essay answers should be well-considered and thoughtful. Most essay questions do not have right or wrong answers in that they must have a certain content in order to please the admissions committee. But answers should have a certain style. A well-considered and thoughtful response will express the applicant's general philosophy on some issue as illustrated by concrete examples; it will sound honest and sincere because it is a reflection of the applicant's true feelings; and it will be well presented, which means that written responses will be carefully edited and typed. A well-written essay can be very important, especially for a marginal candidate.

INTERVIEWS

If the school you are considering requires an interview, be sure to prepare. Go in to the interview with concise points to make in your answers to questions—and specific questions that demonstrate that you know something about the school's program.

The interviewer's questions will be the standard ones found in most job interview guides: What are your plans and what can you do for us? Why do you think you can succeed here? How do you think our program differs from others you are considering? Tell me about your undergraduate successes. What are your career plans? Where do you think this market is going and how do you plan to prepare for it?

Your answers must be thought through and rehearsed in advance. Prepare with a colleague or mentor. But, of course, you shouldn't sound rehearsed. It's tricky—but doable. Practice.

Your questions to the interviewer should be specific and should pertain to the program's curricula, teaching methods, placement services and recruiting record. You can also ask about the program's commitment to certain ideas, ethics, philosophies and business issues. You might want to refer to ideas in current best-selling business books. However, don't cite an idea and quote a source just to show off. It won't work. Be genuine and integrate the ideas into the discussion.

RECOMMENDATIONS

The most important criteria for choosing a recommender are (1) the recommender must know the purpose of an MBA program, (2) the recommender should know you well, and (3) the recommender should specifically describe the connection between (1) and (2). If it happens that the recommender is also a prominent person, so much the better, but prominence alone does not qualify a person as a recommender. It's important to talk to your recommender first; insure that he or she knows to recommend rather than evaluate you. Negative or critical information can screen you out.

The Best Graduate Business Schools

WORK EXPERIENCE

Work experience can count significantly in the admissions decision, but schools vary in the weight they give it. For the schools you are considering, check the profile of enrolled students for the types of experience represented. You will likely find that most students have had three to five years of work experience. However, if you have less experience, you won't necessarily be ruled out.

FINANCING THE MBA

The financial aid situation for MBAs is about the same as for undergraduates.

- Resources are tight.

- Scholarships are few and go to the very brightest and best.

- Your best resource is the business school's financial aid office.

- Teaching and research assistantships as well as part-time jobs are available, but you have to have some special qualification to get the best ones.

  For example, perhaps you worked in the Placement Office as an undergraduate and you know how to staff a career library; sell this skill to the MBA Career Services director. Perhaps you are familiar with the language and procedures of government budgets; sell this skill to the faculty who write federal grant proposals or to the Financial Aid director who communicates with the U.S. Office of Education.

- Loans are a major way of financing the MBA; you may remember the Stafford and the Perkins federal programs from undergraduate days. You can borrow up to $18,000 total from "Mr. Perkins" (less your undergraduate loans, if applicable) and $54,000 from "Ms. Stafford" ($7,500 per year). Interest rates are 5 and 8%, respectively. Repayment begins when you have a job.

- You'll need to apply for financial aid (including grants, loans work-study jobs) through a "need analysis" service called Graduate and Professional School Financial Aid Service (GAPSFAS) or the Financial Aid Form administered by the College Scholarship Service. The new free application for federal student aid is required as well. Forms and information are available in any financial aid office.

SOME USEFUL RESOURCES INCLUDE:

Financing Your Graduate Management Education
Destination MBA
GMAC
P.O. Box 6108
Princeton, NJ 08541-6108

Corporate Executive Fellows
National Urban Fellows, Inc.
55 West 44th Street, Sixth Floor
New York, NY 10036

Consortium for Graduate Study in Management
200 South Hanley Road
Suite 616
St. Louis, MO 63105

The Official Guide to Financing Your MBA
GMAC
P.O. Box 6108
Princeton, NJ 08541-6108
1-800-759-0190

The Best Graduate Business Schools

CHAPTER SIX

THE BEST MBA PROGRAMS

Americans are obsessed with lists and rankings. From vacation spots to beers, movies and of course business schools, we always want to know which is the "best."

When it comes to ranking business schools, the formulas used and criteria evaluated provoke endless criticism. However, becoming familiar with the issues will assist you in making more intelligent judgments about the programs that are best for you.

In general, those institutions that have always been considered "elite" continue to be so, as measured by GPA and GMAT scores of entering students, reputation of faculty members (based on research, publications, speaking fees, etc.) and starting salaries of graduates. There is little dispute about which schools are in the top five or six. However, from there on, there is much disagreement. The picture is further complicated by variations in departmental quality within schools.

In this book, we have selected 66 programs. They have been chosen for a variety of reasons, including the standard indices of quality listed above. Some are included because they offer programs that are innovative or particularly well suited to a specific audience.

Based on our research, we have categorized the programs into three groups: Thirty "Outstanding" Programs, Twenty "Distinguished" Programs and Sixteen "Recommended" Programs. The programs in the first group are given more detailed profiles than those in the second and third groups.

Our aim has been to deliver the kind of information you need to decide which programs best match your qualifications and goals. The schools have provided extensive data on their academic offerings, including functional areas (concentrations), teaching methods, unique programs/resources and career and placement services.

One of the most significant elements of the profiles is the ratings of individual concentrations within the curriculum. These are self-ratings—the schools themselves, knowing best their own strengths, provided them. The letter grade assigned to each area <u>describes</u> it (as indicated in the key) rather than evaluates it.

A word of warning, however. You may want to take some of the schools' self-ratings with a grain of salt. If you have doubts about any ratings, base your judgment on the quantifiable data provided for that school.

THIRTY OUTSTANDING PROGRAMS

AMERICAN GRADUATE SCHOOL OF INTERNATIONAL MANAGEMENT- THUNDERBIRD

15249 North 59th Avenue
Glendale, AZ 85306-6000
Tel: 602-978-7210
Fax: 602-439-5432

AT A GLANCE

First-Year Students:	699	Employer Ranking:	—
Second-Year Students:	726	Student/Faculty Ratio:	14:1
Location:	Suburb	Annual Tuition:	
No. of Employers		in-state:	$15,000
Recruiting on Campus	250	out-of-state:	$15,000

Strengths: Master of International Management; tradition and history of emphasizing global business ideas and international contacts.

Distinctions: Diverse and large alumni network. Unique one-year program option. Project internship assignments offer valuable learning experience. Partnerships with many international businesses.

Words From the President: Roy A. Herberger   Tenure: NA
"Our students often tell me that Thunderbird is one of the few places where they have found people who think like we do. These students are truly "citizens of the world", and theirs is a global perspective."

OVERVIEW

"Globalization" is a very overused word in graduate management education. Everyone knows you have to have it. Thunderbird (named after the former Thunderbird Field, a WWII training facility for pilots) knew it 45 years ago. How Thunderbird differs from the "elite" tier of MBA schools in its application of globalization is the question. For one thing, Thunderbird stresses total command of written and spoken language and its language labs are unrivaled. For another, Thunderbird is more truly international than most other business schools, with a student body that represents many countries and many cultures. Loyalty runs high here as in 156 cities around the world, alumni observe "the first Tuesday" tradition through monthly get togethers. Arizona's favorable climate is a big selling point for students.

ACADEMIC BRIEF

Thunderbird is accredited by the North Central Association and offers the Master of International Management. The M.I.M. program may be completed in three to four terms. The Executive M.I.M. degree is an accelerated program for professionals who wish to complete their degree without interrupting their careers.

1-minimal 2-somewhat 3-significant

CRITERIA	IMPORTANCE	OTHER CONSIDERATIONS
GPA	3	
GMAT Scores	3	Special consideration to
Quality of Undergraduate Inst.	Considered	non-native English speakers,
Quality of Undergrad. Major	Considered	multi-cultural backgrounds,
Years Experience	3	and those with international
Recommendations	2	immersion/exposure.
Activities	2	
Essay	2	
Interview	-	

PROFILE OF ENROLLED STUDENTS

Number Applicants:	1400	Mean GPA Enrolled:	3.3
Number of Offers:	-	Median GMAT Enrolled:	570
Number Enrolled:	402		

Percentile GPA ranking		Percentile ranking by GMAT	
30 % 3.5+		30 % 600+	
53 % 3.0-3.49		53 % 500-599	
17 % 3.0-		17 % 499	

DEMOGRAPHICS

First-Year Students	699	Women	499
Second-Year Students	726	Men	926
International Students	467	Minorities	120
		African American	10
Mean Age	26	Native American	2
Mean Class Size	25	Asian American	68
Mean Years Experience	1-6	Hispanic American	40

% UNDERGRADUATE MAJOR		% HOME REGIONS	
Arts/Humanities	19%	New England	
Business/Management	47%	Mid-Atlantic	
Natural/ Physical		Southeast	
Sciences	2%	Southwest	N/A
Technical/Engineering,		Mid West	
Computer Science	10%	Rocky Mountain	
Language	9%	Far West	

ACADEMIC STRENGTHS/FEATURES*

KEY	REPUTATION	RESOURCE COMMITMENT NEXT 2 YEARS
K E Y	A-exceptionally well known; national reputation B-well respected C-building; targeted as key area D-standard program E- not provided	+ increase = same - less **RELATIONSHIP TO CORE PROGRAM** 1=Required 4=Not offered 2=Elective 5=Plan to 3=Part of offer other courses

BUSINESS FUNCTION	REPUTATION	RESOURCES COMMITTED
Consulting	B	+
Marketing	A	+
Management/Strategy	B,C	+
Operations-Service	D	=
Operations-Production	D	+
Finance/Accounting	A	+
HR/ILR/Organizational Behavior	B,C	+
Technology/Information Systems	C	+
International Trade Strategies	A	+

SPECIAL INTERESTS	REPUTATION	RESOURCES COMMITTED	RELATIONSHIP TO CORE PROGRAM
International	A	+	1
Small Business	B	=	3
Entrepreneurial	A	+	2
Diversity	A	+	3
Communications	A	=	2,3
Manufacturing	D	=	2
Emerging Business	A	+	2,3
Family Business	E	N/A	4
Health Care	C	=	2
Public Administration	C	=	2
Ethics	C	+	3
Technology Management	C	+	2

TEACHING METHODOLOGIES	PERCENTAGE OF ALL COURSES	SKILLS DEVELOPMENT	PERCENTAGE OF ALL COURSES
Case Study	20%	Quantitative/	
Lecture	25%	Technical	
Experiential	15%	Managerial	
Combination	35%	Communication	N/A
Computer-Assisted		Other	
Multi-Media	5%		

*Reported by Dean's Office

CAREER SERVICES

Thunderbird's Career Services Center (CRC) is "user-friendly"; it's even open on Saturday. How many other schools can boast that type of concern for students? Also, director Jim Case is an Assistant Vice President, which allows him to play a significant role in school affairs, thereby making career services more effective. Workshops are run by select students who are a part of the Graduate Associate Program Committee. Thunderbird distributes a well-written *Placement Manual* to all of its students and has recently developed a new career-planning publication to use with workshops.

DISTINGUISHED PROGRAMS/RESOURCES

Career Services Student Committee. Working with the student legislative body, this group plans and supports events that bring students and employers together in a variety of academic, social and professional ways.

CAREER SERVICES

CAREER MANAGEMENT		RECRUITMENT	
Career Planning Program for First Year Students	Yes	Employers Interviewing at School	252
Career Presentations in the Curricula	Yes	Interviews Conducted at School	2,769
Alumni Network	Yes	Marketing to Employers	Yes
Summer Jobs Program/ Internships	Yes	Resume Books	Yes
Employer Associates Program	Yes	Resume Database to employers	Yes
Job Search Course	Yes	Resume Database/ Referral System	Yes
		Career Fairs	Yes

CAREER SERVICES STAFF

Professional	8	Graduate Assistants	6
Support	7	Peer Advisors	4

FIRST JOB STATISTICS AND SALARY DATA

	1993	1992	1991
Mean no. of Job Offers/Graduate	N/A	N/A	N/A
STARTING SALARY	MEAN	MEAN	MEAN
Acct/Finance	$44,230		
Marketing	41,253		
Operations/Services	—		
Management/Strategy	—		
Health Care	—		
Consulting	37,922		
Operations/Production	53,000	N/A	N/A
Tech/Info Systems	—		
HR/LR/O. Dev.	—		
Public Admin.	44,951		
Other	—		
Small Business	—		
International	—		

TOP TEN EMPLOYERS BY HIRES

1. Citibank
2. Pepsi Co.
3. Cabletron Systems
4. Deloitte, Touche & Tohmatsu
5. Goldman Sachs
6. Intel
7. U.S. Government
8. Federal Express
9. Federal Mogul
10. Nomura International

STUDENT LIFE

It comes as no surprise that many of the over 60 clubs on campus focus on international interests. In addition, with fluency in a second language a requirement for graduation, many clubs are formed by students studying various languages. Clubs range from the Africa Club and the China Club to the Women in International Trade and International Wine Tasting Clubs. Students also enjoy the social events of Europe Night, Africa Night, and Asia Night. Students publish a weekly newspaper called *Das Tor*, which means "The Gate" in German, that carries campus news and information about coming events.

Interfest is a popular annual event put on by Thunderbird students for local elementary school children. Games, souvenirs and displays are aimed at stimulating the children's interest in international matters.

With the excellent weather in this area, students take advantage of outdoor athletic activities. Utilizing the facilities on campus, students can participate in team sports such as softball, soccer and rugby, as well as recreational activities such as tennis, basketball and swimming.

FACILITIES AND TECHNOLOGY

On its 89 attractively landscaped acres, the Thunderbird campus features five new Southwestern-style buildings, with red-tiled roofs and white stucco trim. Buildings such as the William Voris Hall of Modern Languages and the International Studies building reflect the focus on International issues. In 1993, a new entrance to the school was opened, with the word "Welcome" etched into the granite in every one of the languages taught at Thunderbird. A newly remodeled student center features lounges, student offices and a European-style coffee house. The current main library, the Barton Kyle Yount Memorial Library, offers access to over 600 databases through the Data-Star and DIALOG systems. Language studies are reinforced by over 9,000 books in languages taught at Thunderbird. Upon completion, the Merle A. Hinrichs International Business Centre will house library services, as well as the International Studies Research Center (ISRC). The ISRC contains an extensive collection of current clipping and document files on over 200 countries. The Joan and David Lincoln Computer Services Center supports both academic and administrative requirements via a campus-wide local area network. Over 100 microcomputers are available for student use, most of which are IBM-compatible.

SCHOLARSHIPS AND FINANCIAL ASSISTANCE

Separate assistance is available for entering and continuing students. Entering students may apply for scholarships from Arizona University and major corporations, including Coors, Coca-Cola and Citicorp. Continuing students may apply for grants (65% receive an award), partial assistantships and student loans.

COMMUNITY/CITY LIFE

Glendale, Arizona Population: 97,000
Phoenix, Arizona Population : 790,000
Weather: Sunny with a year-round average temperature of 70°.

Thunderbird is located in Glendale, Arizona, a suburb of Phoenix, the ninth largest city in America. The Phoenix metropolitan area is home to approximately two million people, who enjoy the cultural and social opportunities of a typical large city. With sun shining 85% of the year, students can enjoy many recreational opportunities such as horseback riding, golf and camping. Within a three- or four- hour drive to the north are numerous ski resorts and the world-famous Grand Canyon. To the south, students can drive through the desert to the city of Tucson and the Mexican border.

HOUSING AND LIVING COSTS

Approximately 35% of the students live on campus in 412 single residences with shared baths. A mandatory meal plan is included for those who live on campus. Room and board for a single semester can average approximately $2,200. There is no housing for married students. Off-campus rent for one semester can average approximately $1,100.

UNIVERSITY OF CALIFORNIA AT BERKELEY

HAAS SCHOOL OF MANAGEMENT

350 Barrows Hall
Berkeley, CA 94720
Tel: 310-206-5726
Fax: 310-206-9830

AT A GLANCE

First-Year Students:	218	Employer Ranking:	—
Second-Year Students:	224	Student/Faculty Ratio:	N/A
Location:	Suburban	Annual Tuition:	
No. of Employers		in-state:	$3,000
Recruiting on Campus	240	out-of-state:	$11,000

Strengths: Management of Technology, International Management and Entrepreneurship. State-of-the-art facilities opened in 1994. Access to the Pacific Rim and the surrounding business community, including Silicon Valley.

Distinctions: Student initiated and run courses for credit. Country Risk and Project Assessment course which includes three-week field exercise in developing country.

Goals: Continue leadership in areas of international, technological and entrepreneurship management.

Words From the Dean: William A. Hasler   Tenure: 3 years
"...while running worldwide consulting and professional education for KPMG Peat Marwick...I had respected for years the influence of 23,000 Berkeley business alumni who extend the school's reach far into the world of management practice."

OVERVIEW

Haas's brand-new high-tech facilities, a superb blend of form and function, are scheduled to open in 1995. Research and management of technology are the best known strengths of the program. Other strengths include being a part of a world-class university and having easy access to San Francisco. The school encourages outside studies and has a number of joint programs. Involvement with local and entrepreneurial business is a part of most students' studies. Berkeley's history of counterculture remains influential; most students are involved in service and charity work.

ACADEMIC BRIEF

Students are required to complete 30 hours of core courses and ten hours of electives. Core courses are completed in the first two semesters and the second-year students take all electives. This arrangement allows students to tailor their education to meet specific career goals. The average class size is 35 students, and each student is supervised by an individual faculty member on the Applied Management Project, usually during the last two semesters.

KEYS TO ADMISSIONS AND APPLICATION

1-minimal   2-somewhat   3-significant

CRITERIA	IMPORTANCE	OTHER CONSIDERATIONS
GPA	2	
GMAT Scores	2	
Quality of Undergraduate Inst.	3	
Quality of Undergrad. Major	2	
Years Experience	3	N/A
Recommendations	3	
Activities	2	
Essay	3	
Interview	2	

PROFILE OF ENROLLED STUDENTS

Number Applicants:	1977	Mean GPA Enrolled:	N/A
Number of Offers:	454	Mean GMAT Enrolled:	450-800
Number Enrolled:	218		

Percentile GPA ranking			Percentile ranking by GMAT		
N/A	%	N/A	N/A	%	N/A
N/A	%	N/A	N/A	%	N/A
N/A	%	N/A	N/A	%	N/A

DEMOGRAPHICS

First-Year Students	218	Women	150
Second-Year Students	224	Men	292
International Students	126	Minorities	79
		African American	18
Mean Age	27	Native American	3
Mean Class Size	72	Asian American	31
Mean Years Experience	-	Hispanic American	15

% UNDERGRADUATE MAJOR		% HOME REGIONS	
Arts/Humanities	9%	New England	16%
Business/Management	12%	Mid-Atlantic	4%
Natural/ Physical		Southeast	2%
Sciences	7%	Mid West	7%
Technical/Engineering,		Southwest	4%
Computer Science	25%	Rocky Mountain	5%
Social Sciences	40%	Far West	35%

ACADEMIC STRENGTHS/FEATURES*

KEY	REPUTATION	RESOURCE COMMITMENT NEXT 2 YEARS	
K E Y	A-exceptionally well known; national reputation B-well respected C-building; targeted as key area D-standard program E-not provided	+ increase = same - less	
		RELATIONSHIP TO CORE PROGRAM	
		1=Required 2=Elective 3=Part of other courses	4=Not offered 5=Plan to offer

BUSINESS FUNCTION	REPUTATION	RESOURCES COMMITTED
Consulting	A	=
Marketing	A	=
Management/Strategy	A	=
Operations-Service	A	+
Operations-Production	A	+
Finance/Accounting	A	=
HR/ILR/Organizational Behavior	A	=
Technology/Information Systems	A	+
Other		

SPECIAL INTERESTS	REPUTATION	RESOURCES COMMITTED	RELATIONSHIP TO CORE PROGRAM
International	A	+	2,3
Small Business	E	N/A	4
Entrepreneurial	A	+	2
Diversity	A	+	2,3
Communications	A	=	1,2
Manufacturing	A	+	1,2
Emerging Business	A	+	2
Family Business	E	N/A	4
Health Care	E	N/A	4
Public Administration	A	=	2
Ethics	A	=	2
Real Estate	A	=	2

TEACHING METHODOLOGIES	PERCENTAGE OF ALL COURSES	SKILLS DEVELOPMENT	PERCENTAGE OF ALL COURSES
Case Study	30%	Quantitative/ Technical	25%
Lecture	20%	Managerial	45%
Experiential	10%	Communication	10%
Combination	40%	Teamwork	20%
Other	—	Other	—

*Reported by Dean's Office

CAREER SERVICES

Taking advantage of the school's numerous partnerships, the Career Center administers a number of worthwhile programs utilizing top business talent from the San Francisco area and beyond. True to its mission statement, the office has "acted as a catalyst for exploration, development and decision-making" in its comprehensive career management services. Its job posting, job faxing and telephone tape service are also helpful.

Michael, a second-year student concentrating in non-profit management, reported that his peers were top-drawer academically and that 90% of the second-year students consult with local businesses.

DISTINGUISHED PROGRAM/RESOURCES

Non-credit Career Planning and Management course, innovated by new director, Martin Levine. New marketing brochure to reach employers not recruiting at Haas.

CAREER SERVICES

CAREER MANAGEMENT		RECRUITMENT	
Career Planning Program for First-Year Students	Yes	Employers Interviewing at School	240
Career Presentations in the Curricula	No	Interviews Conducted at School	N/A
Alumni Network	Yes	Marketing to Employers	Yes
Summer Jobs Program/ Internships	Yes	Resume Books	Yes
Employer Associates Program	Yes	Resume Database to Employers	Yes
Job Search Course	Yes	Resume Database/ Referral System	Yes
		Career Fairs	Yes

CAREER SERVICES STAFF

Professional	4	Graduate Assistants	0
Support	2	Peer Advisors	0

FIRST-JOB STATISTICS AND SALARY DATA

	1993	1992	1991
Mean no. of Job Offers/Graduate	1.5	1.7	N/A
STARTING SALARY	MEAN	MEAN	MEAN
Acct/Finance	$59,400	$50,000	
Marketing	54,583	55,823	
Operations/Services	—	—	
Management/Strategy	—	—	
Health Care	—	—	
Consulting	65,750	70,138	
Operations/Production	—	59,314	N/A
Tech/Info Systems	61,000	—	
HR/LR/O. Dev/	—	—	
Public Admin.	—	—	
General Mangement	—	60,767	
Other	—	—	
Small Business	—	—	
International	—	—	

TOP TEN EMPLOYERS BY HIRES

1. Citibank
2. Coopers & Lybrand
3. Hewlett Packard
4. Intel
5. Kaiser Permanente
6. Clorox
7. Procter & Gamble
8. McKinsey & Co.
9. Montgomery Securities
10. Nestle'

STUDENT LIFE

Involvement is a key word when discussing Haas student life. From the day students enter the MBA program, they become involved in a number of the 19 MBA clubs, intramural sports, community service, and the student government. Students who participate in the MBA Associates (MBAA), the Haas student government organization, influence and even develop curriculum offerings such as a non-credit course in communications and a course on corporate responsibility.

Sports activities are popular with many Haas students. Several campus clubs provide low-cost access to such sports activities as sailing, windsurfing and scuba diving in San Francisco Bay and skiing at Lake Tahoe. Other on-campus activities include a Spring Banquet, Friday afternoon "Consumption Functions," a talent show, Wednesday night happy hour study breaks, and the Challenge for Charity Fun Run.

FACILITIES AND TECHNOLOGY

Situated on a 1,200-acre campus, the University of California at Berkeley is a mix of neoclassical, brown shingle and modern buildings among picturesque creeks and stands of historic redwood trees. The latest addition to the campus is the Haas School Building scheduled for completion in 1995. This state-of-the-art complex, a mini-campus of three pavilions set around a central courtyard, features four floors of classrooms, computer labs, a student lounge, a career development center and a business and economics library. The building, designed by a committee of Haas students, faculty, alumni and business executives, encourages business and educational interaction and, as Dean Hasler states, "... is the foundation of our -Berkeley's-future plans."

Students and faculty are eager to leave the current cramped facilties in Barrows Hall. The Business and Economics Library, currently located in Stephens Hall, will also move to the new Haas building when it opens. Computer facilities, including Macintosh, IBM and UNIX systems, are available at Haas, with communications to other U of C systems. E-mail accounts are assigned to incoming students. All students are introduced to computer and management information systems through several core courses.

SCHOLARSHIPS AND FINANCIAL ASSISTANCE

The school offers various scholarships, including one from the Price Institute for Entrepreneurial Studies. Graduate Minority Fellowships are awarded on the basis of need and academic promise.

COMMUNITY/CITY LIFE

Berkeley Population: 100,000
San Francisco Population: 678,000
Weather: Mild, 59° average temperature in summer and 51° in winter.

Located less than 30 minutes from San Francisco, Berkeley is an active college town, with quiet residential areas to the north and east and a lively retail area to the south. In their off-campus time, students frequent local eateries, which include a diversity of such ethnic restaurants as Thai, Ethiopian and Indian. There are plenty of coffee houses, theaters and some of the best bookstores in the world. Weekend outings to such nearby sites as Napa Valley, Lake Tahoe, and Yosemite National Park are popular, as are frequent trips into San Francisco via the Bay Area Rapid Transit (BART) system, which has a station one block from campus

HOUSING AND LIVING COSTS

Berkeley has on-campus dorms, but most students live off campus. There are many apartments and houses available within walking distance of the school. On-campus living accomodations for the academic year average $5,390. A shared house or apartment averages $3,307.

UNIVERSITY OF CALIFORNIA-LOS ANGELES

JOHN E. ANDERSON GRADUATE SCHOOL OF MANAGEMENT

405 Hilgard Ave. Suite 3371
Los Angeles, CA 90024-1448
Tel: 310-206-5726
Fax: 310-206-9830

AT A GLANCE

First-Year Students:	305	Employer Ranking:	—
Second-Year Students:	346	Student/Faculty Ratio:	9:1
Location:	Major City	Annual Tuition:	
No. of Employers		in-state:	$7,000
Recruiting on Campus:	110	out-of-state:	$16,000

Strengths: Finance, Marketing and Strategy; Emphasis on teamwork. Access to Los Angeles, Southern California and Far East business.

Distinctions: Management Complex to be completed in 1995; Finance faculty ranked tops by professional journals. Management consulting club is outstanding.

Goals: Internationalize curriculum; teach role of information technology, move toward privatization of some program aspects.

Words From the Dean: William Pierskalla   Tenure : 1 1/2 years
"Los Angeles, eclectic and heterogeneous population and its strong international relationships are powerful elements in the school's entrenched position as a leader in issues of diversity and globalization."

OVERVIEW

With a new Dean at the helm—William P. Pierskalla, former Deputy Dean at Wharton—and a new seven-building academic village, to be completed in 1995, Anderson's future is as bright as the California sun. Anderson is well connected to L.A. and California business and has solid programs overseas. The MBA Field Study Program, Management Communications Program, International Management Fellows Program and Entrepreneurial Studies Center are also exemplary programs. UCLA is a beautiful campus located in Westwood, a pleasant suburb just a few miles from all the Hollywood/Beverly Hills "dazzle" and from spectacular beaches.

ACADEMIC BRIEF

Anderson provides an innovative, research-based education in management. The management core is a program of twelve courses from which students must take eleven. These courses prepare students to address critical management issues.

Students are encouraged to put theory into practice. A professor described how four second-year students combined their field study program with the Super Bowl's proximity to campus. Working with the Los Angeles Convention and Visitors Bureau, they wrote a field study entitled, "A Comprehensive Guide to Hosting a Super Bowl."

53

KEYS TO ADMISSIONS AND APPLICATION

1-minimal   2-somewhat   3-significant

CRITERIA	IMPORTANCE	OTHER CONSIDERATIONS
GPA	3	Community and professional
GMAT Scores	3	development - 3
Quality of Undergraduate Inst.	3	
Quality of Undergrad. Major	3	
Years Experience	3	
Recommendations	3	
Activities	3	
Essay	3	
Interview	2	

PROFILE OF ENROLLED STUDENTS

Number Applicants:	2668	Mean GPA Enrolled:	3.5
Number of Offers:	623	Mean GMAT Enrolled:	642
Number Enrolled:	302		

Percentile GPA ranking		Percentile ranking by GMAT		
90 %	3.5-4.0	90 %	650-699	
70 %	3.0-3.49	70 %	600-649	

DEMOGRAPHICS

First-Year Students	302	Women	196
Second-Year Students	346	Men	452
International Students	132	Minorities	110
		African American	36
Mean Age	27.7	Native American	4
Mean Class Size	60	Asian American	41
Mean Years Experience	4-6	Hispanic American	—

% UNDERGRADUATE MAJOR		% HOME REGIONS	
Arts/Humanities	9%	New England	11%
Business/Management	24%	Mid-Atlantic	6%
Natural/ Physical		Southeast	4%
Sciences	4%	Southwest	2%
Technical/Engineering,		Mid West	7%
Computer Science	20%	Rocky Mountain	1%
Social Sciences	17%	Far West	49%

ACADEMIC STRENGTHS/FEATURES*

KEY	REPUTATION	RESOURCE COMMITMENT NEXT 2 YEARS	
	A-exceptionally well known; national reputation	+ increase = same - less	
	B-well respected	RELATIONSHIP TO CORE PROGRAM	
	C-building; targeted as key area	1=Required	4=Not offered
	D-standard program	2=Elective	5=Plan to
	E-not provided	3=Part of other courses	offer

BUSINESS FUNCTION	REPUTATION	RESOURCES COMMITTED
Consulting	A	=
Marketing	A	+
Management/Strategy	A	+
Operations-Service	A	+
Operations-Production	A	+
Finance/Accounting	A	+
HR/ILR/Organizational Behavior	A	+
Technology/Information Systems	A	+
Other		

SPECIAL INTERESTS	REPUTATION	RESOURCES COMMITTED	RELATIONSHIP TO CORE PROGRAM
International	A	+	3,1
Small Business	B	=	2
Entrepreneurial	A	+	2,3
Diversity	A-	=	2,3
Communications	—	=	2
Manufacturing	A	+	1
Emerging Business	A	+	2
Family Business	B	=	2
Health Care	—	+	2
Public Administration	B	=	2
Ethics	—	=	—
Arts Management	A	=	2

TEACHING METHODOLOGIES	PERCENTAGE OF ALL COURSES	SKILLS DEVELOPMENT	PERCENTAGE OF ALL COURSES
Case Study	30%	Quantitative/ Technical	40%
Lecture	50%	Managerial	30%
Experiential	20%	Communication	30%
Combination	—	Other	—
Other	—		

*Reported by Dean's Office

CAREER SERVICES

Like many Career Services operations in the MBA world, UCLA Anderson's Career Services have been in transition. Under a new director, Kathleen Van Ness, positive changes are occurring. Career Management services have always been above average at Anderson. Counseling, workshops, employer briefings and an active campus recruitment program assist students. The Center provides multiple ways for employers to build their image with MBA students, including advertising in the MBA weekly newspaper, *The Exchange*. Expect big things from this Center as the new director and staff get their initiatives in gear.

DISTINGUISHED PROGRAM/RESOURCES

Day-on-the-Job Program encourages employers to provide students with a day experience to see first-hand what job content and work environments are really like.

CAREER SERVICES

CAREER MANAGEMENT		RECRUITMENT	
Career Planning Program for First-Year Students	Yes	Employers Interviewing at School	110
Career Presentations in the Curricula	No	Interviews Conducted at School	4797
Alumni Network	Yes	Marketing to Employers	Yes
Summer Jobs Program/ Internships	Yes	Resume Books	Yes
Employer Associates Program	Yes	Resume Database to Employers	No
Job Search Course	Yes	Resume Database/ Referal System	Yes
		Career Fairs	No

CAREER SERVICES STAFF

Professional	1	Graduate Assistants	0
Support	2	Peer Advisors	0

FIRST-JOB STATISTICS AND SALARY DATA

	1993	1992	1991
Mean no. of Job Offers/Graduate	N/A	N/A	N/A
STARTING SALARY	MEAN	MEAN	MEAN
Acct/Finance	$58,090	$53,500	
Marketing	54,640	52,400	
Operations/Services	60,000	49,000	
Management/Strategy	60,760	51,900	
Health Care	—	—	
Consulting	65,570	65,300	
Operations/Production	—	—	N/A
Tech/Info Systems	45,000	—	
HR/LR/O. Dev/	—	—	
Public Admin.	—	—	
Entrepreneur	55,000	—	
Small Business	—	—	
International	—	—	

TOP TEN EMPLOYERS BY HIRES

1. Deloitte & Touche
2. Merrill Lynch
3. ARCO
4. Goldman Sachs
5. Smith Barney
6. Nestle'
7. Arthur Andersen
8. Morgan Stanley
9. Procter & Gamble
10. Bankers Trust

STUDENT LIFE

Students can participate in a variety of intellectual, social, cultural and athletic activities. The Association of Students of Business and the Anderson Association of Students work together to build relationships between students and the business community. Other clubs and organizations provide services to the local community. Several clubs offer mentor programs that match first-and second-year students on a one-to-one basis. Beach, mountain and desert resorts are easily accessible by car. The mild Southern California climate makes outdoor sports such as tennis, skiing, biking, hiking and golf year-round activities.

UCLA's student body has a reputation for being friendly and enthusiastic. Thursday night beer busts, held on the school patio, are popular with students; so too, are activities that support charitable organizations. In 1992, students raised over $75,000 for the Special Olympics in the annual Challenge for Charity, a contest held with a number of other West Coast business schools. Students also enjoy visiting the numerous attractions in the Los Angeles area during their free time.

FACILITIES AND TECHNOLOGY

Currently set in the five-acre Franklin D. Murphy Sculpture Garden, the Anderson School expects to occupy a new management complex in 1995. The new academic village, located in the Stone Canyon Creek area, will consist of seven buildings, each focusing on a different aspect of graduate management education. One of the buildings has been named "Entrepreneur Hall," attesting to the focus on entrepreneurship at Anderson.

The Anderson School of Management Library holds over 145,000 volumes, and includes special collections such as the Goldsmith's Kress Library of Economic Literature and the Robert E. Gross Collection of Rare Books in Business and Economics.

The Anderson School has an HP9000 Unix-based mainframe system, two high-quality print centers, and a presentation/multimedia lab. The University's IBM ES/9000 is also available for high-powered modeling and research needs. Dial-in access to the school's network is provided.

SCHOLARSHIPS AND FINANCIAL ASSISTANCE

UCLA offers students various financial assistance programs, including need-based financial aid, student loans, research and teaching assistantships and fellowships. Federal Stafford Loans of up to $8,500 with deferred interest are available. Special fellowships are available to exceptional minority students.

COMMUNITY/CITY LIFE

Los Angeles Population: 3,000,000
Weather: Mild year round, with temperatures ranging from the high 50's in the winter months to the 80's in the summer.

Los Angeles, a major center for international trade, is home to numerous multi-billion dollar companies as well as thousands of start-up firms. One of the two great urban economies on the Pacific Rim, Los Angeles is a busy port city with an international population. It offers numerous and varied cultural events, a diversity of restaurants and clubs, and, of course, world-class entertainment. The UCLA campus is located in the California foothills, bordering Bel Air, an exclusive residential neighborhood. The school is a short drive from famous California beaches, and a nearby national forest provides opportunities for hiking and camping.

HOUSING AND LIVING COSTS

Affordable housing is difficult to find. Student dormitories for the academic year can average approximately $420 per month, which includes three meals a day. Apartments in neighboring areas start at $650 per month.A limited number of rent-stabilized apartments are available in nearby Santa Monica.

CARNEGIE MELLON UNIVERSITY

GRADUATE SCHOOL OF INDUSTRIAL ADMINISTRATION

5000 Forbes Avenue
Pittsburgh, PA 15213-3890
Tel: 412-268-2272
Fax: 412-268-8163

AT A GLANCE

First-Year Students:	211	Employer Ranking:	#6 of 61
Second-Year Students:	190	Student/Faculty Ratio:	6:1
Location:	Major City	Annual Tuition:	
No. of Employers		in-state:	$19,000
Recruiting on Campus:	110+	out-of-state:	$19,000

Strengths: Manufacturing/Production, Finance and Entrepreneurship. Ties to leading CMU engineering program; top research initiatives with practical links to business community.

Distinctions: World famous semester-long "Management Game"; Students have won several competitions; new building is exceptional.

Goals: Continued emphasis on integrated curriculum and creating a "global information highway" for business schools.

Words From the Dean: Robert S. Sullivan   Tenure: 3 years
"GSIA's goal is to remain the most significant defining influence on management education, research and practice in the world."

OVERVIEW

Already well known for quantitative analysis and manufacturing, Carnegie Mellon is working to broaden its image. It has one of the smallest (4-1) faculty-student ratios, thus allowing for personal, individualized and small-group skills development. Research is what motivates faculty and it's the criteria by which they are evaluated; cutting-edge knowledge across all management disciplines is never far from the classrooms. Both "moot corp" and The "Management Game" provide experiential lessons and are nationally known. The Game includes Pittsburgh executives and meetings are often held in their boardrooms. Pittsburgh (actually suburban Oakland), which includes Carnegie Mellon, the University of Pittsburgh, several museums, a library and the Carnegie Concert Hall, as well as numerous comfortable ethnic neighborhoods, provides an ideal academic environment.

ACADEMIC BRIEF

Carnegie Mellon offers a two-year, full-time program, an early graduation option and a three-year flex-time program leading to a Master of Science in Industrial Administration degree. The program is comprised of "mini-semesters," which are approximately half as long as a typical semester. As a result, there are four semesters per year. The first-year curriculum starts with a foundation in basic scientific disciplines such as economics, behavioral science and quantitative methods. During this time, students gain a general understanding of marketing, finance, production, accounting and strategy. During the second year, the curriculum allows students to apply what they have learned and explore their areas of interest through elective courses.

KEYS TO ADMISSIONS AND APPLICATION

1-minimal   2-somewhat   3-significant

CRITERIA	IMPORTANCE	OTHER CONSIDERATIONS
GPA	3	
GMAT Scores	3	
Quality of Undergraduate Inst.	2	
Quality of Undergrad. Major	2	N/A
Years Experience	3	
Recommendations	3	
Activities	2	
Essay	3	
Interview	3	

PROFILE OF ENROLLED STUDENTS

Number Applicants:	1232	Mean GPA Enrolled:	3.2
Number of Offers:	410	Mean GMAT Enrolled:	640
Number Enrolled:	211		

Percentile GPA ranking			Percentile ranking by GMAT		
N/A	%	N/A	90	%	700+
80	%	3.5+	70	%	670
50	%	3.2	50	%	640

DEMOGRAPHICS

First-Year Students	211	Women	84
Second-Year Students	190	Men	317
International Students	141	Minorities	35
		African American	9
Mean Age	26	Native American	0
Mean Class Size	63.4	Asian American	24
Mean Years Experience	3.8	Hispanic American	N/A

% UNDERGRADUATE MAJOR		% HOME REGIONS	
Arts/Humanities	3%	New England	7%
Business/Management	20%	Mid-Atlantic	26%
Natural/ Physical		Southeast	9.5%
Sciences	5%	Southwest	4%
Technical/Engineering,	48%	Mid West	9.0%
Computer Science		Rocky Mountain	N/A
Social Sciences	6%	Far West	10.5%

ACADEMIC STRENGTHS/FEATURES*

KEY	REPUTATION	RESOURCE COMMITMENT NEXT 2 YEARS	
	A-exceptionally well known; national reputation	+ increase = same - less	
	B-well respected	RELATIONSHIP TO CORE PROGRAM	
	C-building; targeted as key area	1=Required	4=Not offered
	D-standard program	2=Elective	5=Plan to offer
	E-not provided	3=Part of other courses	

BUSINESS FUNCTION	REPUTATION	RESOURCES COMMITTED
Consulting	A	=
Marketing	B	+
Management/Strategy	B	=
Operations-Service	B	+
Operations-Production	A	+
Finance/Accounting	A	=
HR/ILR/Organizational Behavior	B	+
Technology/Information Systems	A	=
Other		

SPECIAL INTERESTS	REPUTATION	RESOURCES COMMITTED	RELATIONSHIP TO CORE PROGRAM
International	B		2
Small Business	A		2
Entrepreneurial	A		2
Diversity	B		2
Communications	A		1
Manufacturing	A		1
Emerging Business	A	N/A	2
Family Business	E		4
Health Care	E		4
Public Administration	E		4
Ethics	A		2
Other	—		—

TEACHING METHODOLOGIES	PERCENTAGE OF ALL COURSES	SKILLS DEVELOPMENT	PERCENTAGE OF ALL COURSES
Case Study	20%	Quantitative/ Technical	40%
Lecture	20%	Managerial	40%
Experiential	10%	Communication	20%
Combination	40%	Other	—
Other	10%		

*Reported by Dean's Office

CAREER SERVICES

This is a time of transition for the Career Opportunities Center following the retirement of longtime dean and director, Ed Mosier. The Center is directed by acting head Leslie Bonner, who, with her small staff, delivers a range of traditional counseling and recruitment services. The recruitment sign-up/candidate tracking system has recently been computerized and the Center is in "state-of- the-art" facilities in its new building. The list of new companies recruiting on campus numbers over 20, which is impressive in this time of cutbacks on campus trips. CMU joins with prestigious neighbors Tuck (Dartmouth) and Darden (Virginia) in a special San Francisco recruitment forum.

DISTINGUISHED PROGRAM/RESOURCES

The Management Game—one of the first computer simulated learning exercises in the MBA market; includes meetings at top Pittsburgh companies. Required of all second year students.

CAREER SERVICES

CAREER MANAGEMENT		RECRUITMENT	
Career Planning Program for First-Year Students	Yes	Employers Interviewing at School	110
Career Presentations in the Curricula	Yes	Interviews Conducted at School	N/A
Alumni Network	Yes	Marketing to Employers	Yes
Summer Jobs Program/ Internships	Yes	Resume Books	Yes
Employer Associates Program	Yes	Resume Database to Employers	Yes
Job Search Course	No	Resume Database/ Referral System	Yes
		Career Fairs	No

CAREER SERVICES STAFF

Professional	2	Graduate Assistants	0
Support	4	Peer Advisors	13

FIRST-JOB STATISTICS AND SALARY DATA

	1993	1992	1991
Mean no. of Job Offers/Graduate	1.8	1.5	N/A
STARTING SALARY	MEAN	MEAN	MEAN
Acct/Finance	$54,926	$50,802	
Marketing	56,566	50,670	
Operations/Services	55,524	50,140	
Management/Strategy	52,400	56,525	
Health Care	—	—	
Consulting	66,777	58,988	
Operations/Production	—	—	N/A
Tech/Info Systems	54,000	55,801	
HR/LR/O. Dev.	—	—	
Public Admin.	—	—	
Other	55,418	55,000	
Small Business	—	—	
International	—	—	

TOP TEN EMPLOYERS BY HIRES

1. Coopers & Lybrand
2. Ford
3. Deloitte & Touche
4. MBA Enterprise Corporation
5. AT&T
6. Citibank
7. PRTM
8. Gemini Consulting
9. American Management Systems
10. Xerox

STUDENT LIFE

The serious workload at GSIA brings students together for a variety of social and supportive activities. The school has a reputation for students both working and playing hard. The student body is diverse and includes many international students. The GSIA Social Committee is active in organizing events and outings.

Laura, a second-year Marketing student, said she appreciated CMU's unique curriculum, which offers five different courses every seven weeks, and the opportunity to design her own program or follow one that covers all major business functions.

FACILITIES AND TECHNOLOGY

The new GSIA building, located right in the middle of the campus and central to everything, has received rave reviews. Total square footage is double that of the old facility. Technological facilities are first-rate, as you'd expect at technology-elite CMU. Classrooms and study-group areas all use high-tech teaching media and on-line services provide access to campus, community and world information.

SCHOLARSHIPS AND FINANCIAL ASSISTANCE

Financial assistance is usually met through a combination of fellowship aid, work-study employment and student loans. Because funds are limited, they are awarded on the basis of financial need. Fellowships are awarded to both first- and second-year students. Teaching Assistantships and Endowment Fellowships are awarded to second-year students only.

COMMUNITY/CITY LIFE

Pittsburgh Population: 423,000
Weather: Average January temperature—29°; average July temperature—72°

Pittsburgh is economically solid and rich with culture, sports and recreation. Actually, CMU is located in a unique part of the city, Oakland, which also includes the University of Pittsburgh, the Carnegie Center for Performing Arts and several museums. Also nearby are several ethnic communities with wonderful restaurants and Schenley Park, one of the largest urban parks.

HOUSING AND LIVING COSTS

All students live off campus in neighboring areas such as Oakland, Squirrel Hill and Shadyside, which offer a diverse selection of accommodations. The Admissions and Housing offices assist students in finding affordable housing. Approximate cost for room and board during the academic year is $6,220.

THE UNIVERSITY OF CHICAGO

GRADUATE SCHOOL OF BUSINESS

1101 East 58th Street
Chicago, IL 60637
Tel: 312-702-7128
Fax: 312-702-3730

AT A GLANCE

First-Year Students:	530	Employer Ranking:	#8 of 61
Second-Year Students:	613	Student/Faculty Ratio:	240
Location:	Major City	Annual Tuition:	
No. of Employers		in-state:	$20,000
Recruiting on Campus	240	out-of-state:	$20,000

Strengths: Finance and Economics, Marketing and International Business. New Downtown Center located in heart of Chicago's business community. Quantitative business. Quality of faculty.

Distinctions: Selected for grant from U.S. Education Department to establish Center for International Business Education and Research. Four Nobel Prize winners on economics faculty.

Goals: Establish international MBA program in Barcelona; increase use of new Downtown Center; expand international focus with new Center for International Business Education and Research.

Words From the Dean: Robert Hamada   Tenure: 2 years
"From the time of its founding in 1898, Chicago has been at the innovative frontier of teaching and research in business. Over the years, we have developed an educational strategy widely emulated...called, simply, the Chicago approach to business education."

OVERVIEW

From polished literature, formal discussions with employers and informal chats with students, people speak proudly of the "Chicago approach" to graduate management education. The approach embodies a concern for theory, analytical tools and the practical experiences to put learning into practice. International exchange for both faculty and students is commonplace; flexibility in curriculum includes taking courses in the Weekend/MBA program, which has the same faculty as the Campus/MBA. Being a part of a major research university like Chicago presents unique opportunities for students such as working with the entrepreneurship program at Argonne National Laboratory—developed to assist faculty with inventions and ideas for marketing. The city of Chicago is virtually unmatched for vibrant business and culture.

ACADEMIC BRIEF

Chicago is committed to preparing students for high-level careers in management. The courses are designed to "provide understanding of the components of managerial decision-making while furnishing perspective on the role of business as an economic, political, and social institution." Chicago offers both a full- and part-time program and a four-quarter-per-year class schedule that allows students flexibility in planning their courses. Conservative, quantitatively oriented and rich in tradition, the University of Chicago steps out of character by contracting with Chicago's Second City comedy group for the communications piece of their new leadership training/outward bound experience.

KEYS TO ADMISSIONS AND APPLICATION

1-minimal   2-somewhat   3-significant

CRITERIA	IMPORTANCE	OTHER CONSIDERATIONS
GPA	3	
GMAT Scores	3	
Quality of Undergraduate Inst.	3	
Quality of Undergrad. Major	3	
Years Experience	3	N/A
Recommendations	3	
Activities	3	
Essay	3	
Interview	3	

PROFILE OF ENROLLED STUDENTS

Number Applicants:	3000	Mean GPA Enrolled:	3.5
Number of Offers:	1087	Median GMAT Enrolled:	650
Number Enrolled:	496		

Percentile GPA ranking		Percentile ranking by GMAT	
13.7 %	<3.0	13.7 %	<500
49.8 %	3.0-3.49	49.8 %	500-599
36.5 %	3.5-4.0	36.5 %	600-699

DEMOGRAPHICS

First-Year Students	530	Women	255
Second-Year Students	613	Men	1030
International Students	278	Minorities	227
		African American	23
Mean Age	27	Native American	2
Mean Class Size	45	Asian American	177
Mean Years Experience	n/a	Hispanic American	25

% UNDERGRADUATE MAJOR		% HOME REGIONS	
Arts/Humanities	8.3%	New England	22.6 %
Business/Management	28.8%	Mid-Atlantic	N/A
Math	8.1%	Southeast	8.7%
Science	19.9%	Southwest	6.3%
Social Sciences	11.8%	Mid West	20.3%
Economics	22.8%	Plains	3.4%
		Far West	17.2%

ACADEMIC STRENGTHS/FEATURES*

KEY	REPUTATION	RESOURCE COMMITMENT NEXT 2 YEARS	
K E Y	A-exceptionally well known; national reputation B-well respected C-building; targeted as key area D-standard program E-not provided	+ increase = same - less	
		RELATIONSHIP TO CORE PROGRAM	
		1=Required 2=Elective 3=Part of other courses	4=Not offered 5=Plan to offer

BUSINESS FUNCTION	REPUTATION	RESOURCES COMMITTED
Consulting	A	=
Marketing	A	+
Management/Strategy	A	+
Operations-Service	A	=
Operations-Production	A	=
Finance/Accounting	A	=
HR/ILR/Organizational Behavior	A	=
Technology/Information Systems	B	=
Quality Management	A	+=

SPECIAL INTERESTS	REPUTATION	RESOURCES COMMITTED	RELATIONSHIP TO CORE PROGRAM
International	A	+	2
Small Business	A/C	+	2
Entrepreneurial	A/C	+	2
Diversity	A	=	3
Communications	A	=	2/3
Manufacturing	A	=	2
Emerging Business	A	=	3
Family Business	A	—	3
Health Care	A	=	2
Public Administration	A	=	2
Ethics	A	=	2/3
Other	—	—	—

TEACHING METHODOLOGIES	PERCENTAGE OF ALL COURSES	SKILLS DEVELOPMENT	PERCENTAGE OF ALL COURSES
Case Study	10%	Quantitative/ Technical	33.3%
Lecture	10%	Managerial	33.3%
Experiential	—	Communication	33.3%
Combination	80%	Other	—
Other	—		

*Reported by Dean's Office

CAREER SERVICES

The weaker economy influences even Chicago, which has traditionally relied on campus interviews as the mainstay of service to both students and employers. Career counseling, career management programs and hard marketing to diverse, smaller employers who don't visit campuses have been added to the repertoire. Employers have adjusted their recruiting visits to coincide with actual "hiring requirements" so Career Services is doing more. Financial Services is still the major industry recruiting Chicago graduates—49.1% of the graduates. New director Paula Delattles has a number of new services in development.

DISTINGUISHED PROGRAM/RESOURCES

Outstanding career-planning program for 500 first-year students; comprehensive interview training for first years.

CAREER SERVICES

CAREER MANAGEMENT		RECRUITMENT	
Career Planning Program for First-Year Students	Yes	Employers Interviewing at School	240
Career Presentations in the Curricula	No	Interviews Conducted at School	10,000
Alumni Network	Yes	Marketing to Employers	Yes
Summer Jobs Program/ Internships	Yes	Resume Books	Yes
Employer Associates Program	Yes	Resume Database to Employers	Yes
Job Search Course	Yes	Resume Database/ Referral System	Yes
		Career Fairs	—

CAREER SERVICES STAFF

Professional	5	Graduate Assistants	15
Support	8	Peer Advisors	36

FIRST-JOB STATISTICS AND SALARY DATA

	1993	1992	1991
Mean no. of Job Offers/Graduate	3.0	3.0	3.2
STARTING SALARY	MEAN	MEAN	MEAN
Acct/Finance	$62,000		
Marketing	57,000		
Operations/Services	56,900		
Management/Strategy	58,000		
Health Care	-		
Consulting	70,000		
Operations/Production	-	N/A	N/A
Tech/Info Systems	57,500		
HR/LR/O. Dev/	45,467		
Public Admin.	-		
General Mangement	57,500		
Project Management	56,000		
Small Business	-		
International	-		

TOP TEN EMPLOYERS BY HIRES

1. Coopers & Lybrand
2. Deloitte & Touche
3. Merrill Lynch & Co.
4. J.P. Morgan & Co. Inc.
5. McKinsey & Co.
6. Booz, Allen & Hamilton
7. A.T. Kearney
8. Citibank/ Citicorp
9. Procter & Gamble
10. Ernst & Young

STUDENT LIFE

The focal point for student life on campus is the Business School Association (BSA). The BSA coordinates meetings with speakers from business and industry, social gatherings and quality-improvement projects. Musically inclined GSB students can participate in or be entertained by the University Symphony Orchestra, the Concert Choir, the Chamber Orchestra and a variety of other music groups.

Students can compete in over 45 intramural sports and make use of athletic facilities such as the newly renovated Henry Crown Field House, Bartlett Gymnasium and Ida Noyes Hall.

Steve, second-year student in Behavior Science and Policy, praised the laboratory courses and said that the program's "rigor" pays dividends in skills and knowledge that can give graduates a decided edge in the market.

University of Chicago

FACILITIES AND TECHNOLOGY

The University of Chicago maintains over 175 buildings on a 172- acre campus near the Lake Michigan waterfront. The main campus is based on a quadrangular concept set by Henry I. Cobbs in 1890, and its ivy-covered gray limestone buildings, with their gargoyles and spires, impart a feeling of midwest Ivy League. The Joseph Regenstein Library, built in 1970, includes an extensive business and economics collection.

The Graduate School of Business fills a complex of 3 interconnected buildings in the heart of the main quadrangle, and is accessible by high-speed train. While the University itself is situated in a "safe area," students need to be cautious when going outside the University grounds.

GSB students must purchase a personal computer and related hardware/software. The Computing Services department within the GSB provides students with the computer accounts and passwords necessary for course work or other activities that require use of the GSB VAX mainframe.

SCHOLARSHIPS AND FINANCIAL ASSISTANCE

The Graduate School of Business awards scholarships on the basis of academic excellence, leadership qualities and financial need. Student loans are available based on financial need. The work-study program is federally funded and provides credit-based loans. Minority fellowships and financial assistance for foreign students are also available.

COMMUNITY/CITY LIFE

Chicago population: 3,000,000
Weather: Midwest climate, 25° in January and 75° in July.

Cosmopolitan Chicago offers students easy access to a great variety of cultural and recreational activities. With its strong ethnicity, the city provides many opportunities for diversity through eateries, night life and festivals. For culture buffs there is symphony, opera, theater, an art institute and many museums. Major league sports, including the three-time NBA champion Chicago Bulls, are available year-round, as are opportunities to participate in recreational sports, including an annual marathon. Much of the city's recreational activity centers around the lakefront area of Chicago.

HOUSING AND LIVING COSTS

The new Graduate Residence is the most modern on-campus residence. Common areas include weight rooms, a music room and community kitchens. This residence is open only to first-year business students. Rates for the 1992-93 academic year were $6,065 for a large single room, $5,005 for a single room and $3,840 per person for a double room. The International House is a "home away from home" for many of the University's foreign students. Private housing in neighboring areas is very difficult to find. The University does not have an off-campus housing office.

COLUMBIA UNIVERSITY

COLUMBIA BUSINESS SCHOOL

Uris Hall
New York, NY 10027
Tel: 212-854-6040
Fax: 212-854-3050

AT A GLANCE

First-Year Students:	650	Employer Ranking:	—
Second-Year Students:	650	Student/Faculty Ratio:	12:1
Location:	Major City	Annual Tuition:	
No. of Employers		in-state:	$19,000
Recruiting on Campus	250	out-of-state:	$19,000

Strengths: Finance, Organization Management and International Business. Distinguished alumni in high places.

Distinctions: Main building, Uris Hall, is state-of-the-art computer-equipped. Contact with over 500 NYC executives who are involved in programs and courses.

Goals: Enhance global awareness of faculty and students, improve quality of life for students—take steps toward constructing a new building.

Words From the Dean: Meyer Feldberg   Tenure: 6 years
"Every day, students work on field projects in corporate home offices and public sector centers located a short distance from the campus. What happens inside Columbia's classrooms reflects this dynamic: our curriculum is up to date and relevant to the constantly changing global economic environment."

OVERVIEW

Although Columbia University dates back to 1754, when King George of England chartered Kings College, the Business School was formally founded in 1916. A 1990 self-study emphasizes four key strengths—intellectual capacity, diversity of the Business School family, New York location and internationalism. Columbia Business School employs an "integrated curriculum" focusing on globalization, ethics, total quality and human resources management across all curricula.   What can you say about New York City? You love it or hate it. Most people at Columbia Business list "The City" as one of the reasons why they are there. They love it.

ACADEMIC BRIEF

Columbia offers the flexibility of a three-term program. Students must take eight core courses out of a total of 20 courses required for the MBA. Columbia offers 11 concentrations including Accounting, Finance, Business Economics and Public Policy.

Diego, class of '94, chose Columbia for its international focus and likes the idea of studying with a class that is 30% international. He was particularly excited about the Chazen Institute, developed to increase the relationship with the School of International and Public Affairs and to further international contacts.

71

KEYS TO ADMISSIONS AND APPLICATION

1-minimal   2-somewhat   3-significant

CRITERIA	IMPORTANCE	OTHER CONSIDERATIONS
GPA	2	
GMAT Scores	2	
Quality of Undergraduate Inst.	2	
Quality of Undergrad. Major	2	
Years Experience	2	N/A
Recommendations	2	
Activities	2	
Essay	3	
Interview	2	

PROFILE OF ENROLLED STUDENTS

Number Applicants:	2802	Mean GPA Enrolled:	N/A
Number of Offers:	795	Mean GMAT Enrolled:	N/A
Number Enrolled:	457		

Percentile GPA ranking		Percentile ranking by GMAT	
N/A % N/A		N/A % N/A	
N/A % N/A		N/A % N/A	
N/A % N/A		N/A % N/A	

DEMOGRAPHICS

First-Year Students	650	Women	390
Second-Year Students	650	Men	901
International Students	340	Minorities	
		African American	35
Mean Age	26	Native American	4
Mean Class Size	25/53	Asian American	76
Mean Years Experience	4-6	Hispanic American	32

% UNDERGRADUATE MAJOR		% HOME REGIONS	
Arts/Humanities	19%	New England	6%
Business/Management	24%	Mid-Atlantic	52%
Natural/ Physical		Southeast	3%
Sciences	5%	Southwest	2%
Technical/Engineering,		Mid West	4%
Computer Science	13%	Rocky Mountain	2%
Social Sciences	14%	Far West	7%

ACADEMIC STRENGTHS/FEATURES*

REPUTATION	RESOURCE COMMITMENT NEXT 2 YEARS
A-exceptionally well known; national reputation	+ increase = same - less
B-well respected	**RELATIONSHIP TO CORE PROGRAM**
C-building; targeted as key area	1=Required 4=Not offered
D-standard program	2=Elective 5=Plan to
E-not provided	3=Part of offer
	other courses

BUSINESS FUNCTION	REPUTATION	RESOURCES COMMITTED
Consulting	A	+
Marketing	A	+
Management/Strategy	A	+
Operations-Service	A	+
Operations-Production	A	=
Finance/Accounting	A	+
HR/ILR/Organizational Behavior	A	=
Technology/Information Systems	B	=
Accounting	A	+

SPECIAL INTERESTS	REPUTATION	RESOURCES COMMITTED	RELATIONSHIP TO CORE PROGRAM
International	A	+	1/3
Small Business	A	+	2
Entrepreneurial	A	+	2/3
Diversity	A	+	1
Communications	A	+	1
Manufacturing	A	=	1
Emerging Business	A	+	2
Family Business	B	+	2
Health Care	A	=	2
Public Administration	A	+	2
Ethics	A	+	1/3
Quality	A	+	1/3

TEACHING METHODOLOGIES	PERCENTAGE OF ALL COURSES	SKILLS DEVELOPMENT	PERCENTAGE OF ALL COURSES
Case Study	5%	Quantitative/	
Lecture	5%	Technical	40%
Experiential	5%	Managerial	30%
Combination	85%	Communication	20%
Other	—	Computer	10%
		Other	—

*Reported by Dean's Office

CAREER SERVICES

As a "key school" for most MBA employers, Columbia Business School has enjoyed "good years and high numbers" for campus interviews through its office of MBA Career Services. Additionally, the staff has taken on an ambitious schedule of workshops and shows significant innovation by developing case studies for a workshop on negotiations. The Office is run in a business-like manner, conducting it's own customer-satisfaction survey. Switching to a Fall recruiting cycle for its May and October graduates was one of the changes made to better meet student needs.

DISTINGUISHED PROGRAM/RESOURCES

Programs and services that connect students to smaller, emerging businesses including workshops, consulting and specialized marketing.

CAREER SERVICES

CAREER MANAGEMENT		RECRUITMENT	
Career Planning Program for First Year Students	Yes	Employers Interviewing at School	250
Career Presentations in the Curricula	No	Interviews Conducted at School	10,000
Alumni Network	Yes	Marketing to Employers	Yes
Summer Jobs Program/ Internships	Yes	Resume Books	Yes
Employer Associates Program	Yes	Resume Database to Employers	Yes
Job Search Course	No	Resume Database/ Referral System	Yes
		Career Fairs	No

CAREER SERVICES STAFF

Professional	5	Graduate Assistants	2
Support	N/A	Peer Advisors	10

The Best Graduate Business Schools

FIRST-JOB STATISTICS AND SALARY DATA

	1993	1992	1991
Mean no. of Job Offers/Graduate	2	2	2
STARTING SALARY	MEDIAN	MEDIAN	MEDIAN
Acct/Finance	$64,500	52,000	
Marketing	62,000	63,500	
Operations/Services	—		
Management/Strategy	58,000	55,250	
Health Care	40,000		
Consulting	89,000	82,000	
Operations/Production	63,500	66,000	N/A
Tech/Info Systems	60,000	57,000	
HR/LR/O. Dev/	49,000	56,000	
Public Admin.	39,500	37,500	
Tax Consulting	60,000		
Law	89,000		
Small Business	—		
International	—		

TOP TEN EMPLOYERS BY HIRES

1. Citicorp/Citibank
2. Coopers & Lybrand
3. Merrill Lynch
4. Chemical Bank
5. J.P. Morgan
6. Booz, Allen & Hamilton, Inc.
7. Bank of New York
8. Prudential Securities
9. Morgan Stanley & Co. Inc.
10. Goldman, Sachs & Co.

STUDENT LIFE

The Columbia Business School attracts a diverse and international student body. Among the 65 student organizations are MBAs for Greener Business, Australasia Club, Hispanic Business Students Association and the Jewish Business Student Association. The Graduate Business Association (GBA) represents the entire student body on all academic and campus issues. The GBA sponsors weekly Thursday Happy Hours (there are no Friday classes), as well as periodic barbecues throughout the year. Twice a year, students write and produce a "roasting" of the school, the dean, and the faculty. The major social event of the year is the annual spring ball, a glitzy black-tie event. News of other social events and activities can be found in *The Bottom Line*, a weekly student-run newspaper.

Student volunteerism is on the rise at the Columbia Business School. The Young Entrepreneurs Program matches MBA students with local high school students. Business students tutor Harlem teens in a joint program with the Law School, as well as participate in the University-wide Community Impact organization, which provides a variety of community services to the Columbia area.

FACILITIES AND TECHNOLOGY

Located on the Morningside campus, the Business School is in Uris Hall, an eight-story gray concrete building. Students have commented for many years that the building is not adequate for the school, and Dean Feldberg is listening. The Dean initiated a "Fix-It" Committee, which receives $100,000 each year for improvements the student committee members deem most important. While the Committee and its actions have been popular, there is a realization that a new building is needed to overcome major problems such as the heating and air conditioning systems and a lack of meeting space.

The Thomas J. Watson Library of Business and Economics, the second largest business library in the U.S., is housed in Uris Hall. Students also have access to 25 other libraries on the Columbia campus.

All MBA students are required to have a 386 notebook computer. Students will soon be able to access outside database systems from their dorms, their homes and the library. Over 100 personal computers, both IBM-compatible and Macintosh, are located at the Dohr Computer Center on the second floor of Uris Hall. The PCs are connected to a local area network and have access to a variety of software.

SCHOLARSHIPS AND FINANCIAL ASSISTANCE

Approximately 66% of all students receive some sort of financial assistance. The school offers need-based scholarships and merit-based fellowships.

COMMUNITY/CITY LIFE

New York City Population: 8,000,000
Weather: Moderate; 33° average January temperature; 74° in July.

The New York City metro area, the largest such area in the country, provides an abundance of educational, recreational and social opportunities for Columbia students. Since many Fortune 500 companies have their headquarters in the area, and the heart of the financial community, Wall Street, is only minutes away, many students are able to experience the business world first-hand. Students are also able to enjoy such cultural experiences as Broadway plays, world-class museums and galleries, and diverse ethnic restaurants. Professional sports of every type are available, as well as opportunities to participate in recreational sports.

HOUSING AND LIVING COSTS

Approximately half of the students live in school-owned housing, which is very economical. On-campus housing is available, but students have reported great difficulty in getting housing. The most cost-effective living accommodation for a single student is in a residence hall, which averages $4,252 for the academic year.

CORNELL UNIVERSITY

JOHNSON GRADUATE SCHOOL OF MANAGEMENT

Malott Hall
Ithaca, NY 14853-4210
Tel: 607-255-4888
Fax: 607-255-4522

AT A GLANCE

First-Year Students:	261	Employer Ranking:	#7 of 61
Second-Year Students:	260	Student/Faculty Ratio:	9:1
Location:	Small Town	Annual Tuition:	
No. of Employers		in-state:	$18,500
Recruiting on Campus:	101	out-of-state:	$18,500

Strengths: Finance, Accounting, Marketing, Manufacturing; involving students with regional business.

Distinctions: Close connections to all of Cornell University including, a large number of Academic Centers; sense of collegiality and support among students.

Words From the Dean: Alan G. Merten
"At the Johnson School, there are no reduced teaching loads for the research stars. We expect all our faculty members to both develop and disseminate knowledge."

OVERVIEW

"Ithaca is Gorges" reads the bumper sticker referring to the regional topography and surrounding Finger Lakes. Johnson is serious in its approach to MBA education, especially in areas of diversity and international connections—33% of the students are international; it is common to have membership in study groups assigned to assure a good mix of backgrounds and perspectives. Johnson offers a variety of exchange programs with schools abroad—opportunities in Japan are noteworthy. The links between Johnson and Cornell University are strong. Cooperation exists through Centers for Manufacturing Enterprise, Engineering and Behavior Economics and Decision Science, which are national leaders. Students are involved in running their own businesses; Student Agencies, Inc. is the oldest independent, student-run company in the country with $4.8 million in real estate.

ACADEMIC BRIEF

During the first year, students take core courses in such areas as financial accounting, marketing management and organization behavior. First-year students are also offered individual counseling and group programs on letter and resume writing. During the second year, students can design their own program of study. They can choose to focus on traditional areas like accounting, economics, finance and marketing or they

77
Cornell University

can plan a broader area of study. The Johnson School also offers programs in international study. It co-sponsors two programs on Japanese business and participates in nine international student exchange programs.

KEYS TO ADMISSIONS AND APPLICATION

1-minimal   2-somewhat   3-significant

CRITERIA	IMPORTANCE	OTHER CONSIDERATIONS
GPA GMAT Scores Quality of Undergraduate Inst. Quality of Undergrad. Major Years Experience Recommendations Activities Essay Interview	N/A	N/A

PROFILE OF ENROLLED STUDENTS

Number Applicants:	N/A	Mean GPA Enrolled:	3.09
Number of Offers:	N/A	Mean GMAT Enrolled:	640
Number Enrolled:	521		

Percentile GPA ranking			Percentile ranking by GMAT		
N/A	%	N/A	N/A	%	N/A
N/A	%	N/A	N/A	%	N/A
N/A	%	N/A	N/A	%	N/A

DEMOGRAPHICS

First-Year Students	250	Women	27%
Second-Year Students	250	Men	73%
International Students	171	Minorities	6%
		African American	N/A
Mean Age	27	Native American	N/A
Mean Class Size	40	Asian American	N/A
Mean Years Experience	4	Hispanic American	N/A

% UNDERGRADUATE MAJOR		% HOME REGIONS	
Arts/Humanities	13%	New England	8%
Business/Management	28%	Mid-Atlantic	37%
Natural/ Physical		Southeast	7%
Sciences	9%	Southwest and	
Technical/Engineering,		Rocky Mountain	6%
Computer Science	16%	Far West	9%
Social Sciences	30%	International	33%

ACADEMIC STRENGTHS/FEATURES*

K E Y	REPUTATION A-exceptionally well known; national reputation B-well respected C-building; targeted as key area D-standard program E-not provided	RESOURCE COMMITMENT NEXT 2 YEARS + increase = same - less **RELATIONSHIP TO CORE PROGRAM** 1=Required 4=Not offered 2=Elective 5=Plan to 3=Part of offer other courses

BUSINESS FUNCTION	REPUTATION	RESOURCES COMMITTED
Consulting	B	=
Marketing	A	=
Management/Strategy	A	+
Operations-Service	D	=
Operations-Production	A	=
Finance/Accounting	A	=
HR/ILR/Organizational Behavior	A	+
Technology/Information Systems	B	=
Management Decision Making	A	N/A

SPECIAL INTERESTS	REPUTATION	RESOURCES COMMITTED	RELATIONSHIP TO CORE PROGRAM
International	A	+	1
Small Business	A	=	3
Entrepreneurial	A	=	2
Diversity	E	=	3
Communications	A	=	2
Manufacturing	A	=	1
Emerging Business	A	=	2
Family Business	E	=	4
Health Care	E	=	4
Public Administration	E	=	2
Ethics	A	=	2
Other	—	—	2

TEACHING METHODOLOGIES	PERCENTAGE OF ALL COURSES	SKILLS DEVELOPMENT	PERCENTAGE OF ALL COURSES
Case Study	—	Quantitative/ Technical	60%
Lecture	—	Managerial	30%
Experiential	—	Communication	10%
Combination	100%	Other	—
Other	—		

*Reported by Dean's Office

Cornell University

CAREER SERVICES

Career Services at Johnson have come a long way. Director Steve Johansson has built a program where campus recruiting is strong in the midst of a host of other creative and technological resources for students. Partnerships are taken seriously; there are many productive relationships with outside employer databases as well as resume referral and alumni services. The result is a quality and quantity of career resources for students that appear unmatched in any other top business school. The office also enjoys a productive relationship with Mobil Corporation whereby an extensive interview preparation program has been given to Johnson Career Services. Brian, a career changer from government to manufacturing, praised the office for its responsiveness to student input. When students expressed the need for assistance with job offer negotiations, a seminar was offered within the month.

DISTINGUISHED PROGRAM/RESOURCES

Number and quality of relationships with both service companies and recruiting corporations resulting in "top drawer" job search resources for students.

CAREER SERVICES

CAREER MANAGEMENT		RECRUITMENT	
Career Planning Program for First Year Students	Yes	Employers Interviewing at School	Yes
Career Presentations in the Curricula	No	Interviews Conducted at School	Yes
Alumni Network	Yes	Marketing to Employers	Yes
Summer Jobs Program/ Internships	Yes	Resume Books	Yes
Employer Associates Program	Yes	Resume Database to Employers	Yes
Job Search Course	No	Resume Database/ Referral System	Yes
		Career Fairs	Yes

CAREER SERVICES STAFF

Professional	3	Graduate Assistants	—
Support	3.5	Peer Advisors	—

FIRST-JOB STATISTICS AND SALARY DATA

	1993	1992	1991
Mean no. of Job Offers/Graduate	1.4	1.7	1.4
STARTING SALARY	MEAN	MEAN	MEAN
Acct/Finance	$52,000		
Marketing	60,000		
Operations/Services	63,500		
Management/Strategy	56,000		
Health Care	—		
Consulting	59,000		
Operations/Production	52,000	N/A	N/A
Tech/Info Systems	38,000		
HR/LR/O. Dev/	53,000		
Public Admin.	—		
Real Estate	54,500		
General Mangement	59,500		
Small Business	—		
International	—		

TOP TEN EMPLOYERS BY HIRES

1. Procter & Gamble
2. Deloitte & Touche
3. Andersen Consulting
4. Mobil
5. First Empire
6. Chase Manhattan
7. Hewlett-Packard
8. IBM
9. McKinsey
10. Price Waterhouse

STUDENT LIFE

New students participate in Community Weekend, a weekend of team and community-building exercises held at a camp on Lake Cayuga. Students commend the Finger Lakes Consulting company that provides consulting services throughout the area. Johnson Volunteers is a student organization dedicated to improving the community. The university offers a variety of theatrical performances, film festivals and live concerts as well as 18 men's and 14 women's intercollegiate sports.

Students have a knack for finding creative opportunities; for example, they did a study on solving "growing pains" problems for a San Francisco company called From Start to Finish Biking Shops. Johnson and Cornell resources and innovation are a difficult combination to match anywhere in the very competitive top group of MBA programs.

FACILITIES AND TECHNOLOGY

The Johnson School is located in the center of the Cornell University campus. The campus overlooks Cayuga Lake and is lined with oak and maple trees, well-tended gardens and an apple orchard. Within the Johnson School are the Andre and Bella Meyer computing laboratories. The Andre Meyer lab has Digital Equipment Corporation's personal computers containing MS-DOS. The Bella Meyer lab has Apple Macintosh computers. Both labs are networked to application-software servers and to the Johnson School's VAX system and world-wide resources via the Internet. VAX offers electronic mail, bulletin boards, course registration and job search information.

SCHOLARSHIPS AND FINANCIAL ASSISTANCE

Financial assistance is divided into two categories: merit-based scholarship funds and need-based loans and work-study funds. Every student is automatically considered for a scholarship. Cornell also offers low-interest loans, grants and fellowships.

COMMUNITY/CITY LIFE

Ithaca population: 28,000
Weather: Winters are in the 20°range—sometimes colder; summers in the 70's.

The Johnson School is located in Ithaca in upstate New York's Finger Lakes region. The entire area is known for its rolling hills, various lakes, state parks and wide-open countryside. Upstate New York attracts visitors from around the world who participate in sailing, skiing and swimming. There are also many flourishing wineries in the area.

HOUSING AND LIVING COSTS

Single students can find housing in residence halls and university-owned apartments. The most cost-effective living accommodation for a single student is in a residence hall, which averages $4,352 for the academic year. The residences all contain kitchen, laundry and recreation facilities. Cornell has three apartment complexes available for married students and their families; all are within one mile of the campus. Students can also rent rooms or efficiency apartments nearby. Approximate cost to rent a single room is $200-300 per month; a small efficiency costs $375-600; apartments with 3-5 bedrooms cost more than $650 per month.

DARTMOUTH COLLEGE

THE AMOS TUCK SCHOOL OF BUSINESS ADMINISTRATION

100 Tuck Hall
Hanover, NH 03755-9030
Tel: 603-646-3162
Fax: 603-646-1308

Strengths: Strategy, Management Communications, Managerial Economics. Long known as "the small group school." Emphasized teamwork and communications long before AACSB required it for accreditation.

Distinctions: Outstanding faculty in both research and teaching, with a flow back and forth that benefits the student. No academic departments at Tuck, which had an integrated curriculum and cross-functional business emphasis before these became watchwords.

Goals: Continue to bring the latest research back to the classroom. Maintain the highest teaching standards of any business school in the world.

Words From the Dean: Edward A. Fox   Tenure: 4.5 years
"With a strong financial base, the world's best teaching-oriented research faculty, first- class facilities, magnificent location and strong ties to the U.S. and international business communities, the Tuck School will end its first century of operation healthier than ever."

OVERVIEW

"Tuck at Dartmouth" draws upon its rich history as the world's first graduate business school based on the charge from William Tucker, then President of Dartmouth College, that the country needs "training commensurate with the larger meaning of business." Tuck has always been known for its small classes and emphasis on a "generalist" approach to management. Consistent with its founder's view of business, Tuck has built numerous "international, integrative and interactive" elements into its program. A good example is the first-year required consulting exercise where students are involved in all aspects of a business. Once a bastion of formality, Tuck is now known for its pervasive sense of team spirit. Hanover is rich in New England charm.

ACADEMIC BRIEF

During the first year, all students take 13 required courses which focus on basic principles of economics, behavioral science and quantitative sciences. The second-year curriculum allows students to choose from 50 electives without requiring a definite major.

83

KEYS TO ADMISSIONS AND APPLICATION

1-minimal   2-somewhat   3-significant

CRITERIA	IMPORTANCE	OTHER CONSIDERATIONS
GPA	2,3	
GMAT Scores	2,3	
Quality of Undergraduate Inst.	2,3	
Quality of Undergrad. Major	2,3	
Years Experience	2	N/A
Recommendations	3	
Activities	2	
Essay	3	
Interview	2,3	

PROFILE OF ENROLLED STUDENTS

Number Applicants:	2077	Mean GPA Enrolled:	3.39
Number of Offers:	402	Mean GMAT Enrolled:	658
Number Enrolled:	183		

Percentile GPA ranking		Percentile ranking by GMAT	
N/A % N/A		N/A % N/A	
N/A % N/A		N/A % N/A	
N/A % N/A		N/A % N/A	

DEMOGRAPHICS

First-Year Students	180	Women	99
Second-Year Students	180	Men	241
International Students	76	Minorities	40
		African American	8
Mean Age	26.6	Native American	0
Mean Class Size	N/A	Asian American	21
Mean Years Experience	4-6	Hispanic American	11

% UNDERGRADUATE MAJOR		% HOME REGIONS	
Arts/Humanities	13%	New England	27.5 %
Business/Management	14.5%	Mid-Atlantic	31.5%
Natural/ Physical		Southeast and	
Sciences	5%	Southwest	10%
Technical/Engineering,		Mid West	11.5%
Computer Science	20%	Rocky Mountain and	19.3%
Social Sciences	14.5%	Far West	

ACADEMIC STRENGTHS/FEATURES*

KEY	REPUTATION	RESOURCE COMMITMENT NEXT 2 YEARS	
	A-exceptionally well known; national reputation	+ increase = same - less	
	B-well respected	RELATIONSHIP TO CORE PROGRAM	
	C-building; targeted as key area	1=Required	4=Not offered
	D-standard program	2=Elective	5=Plan to
	E-not provided	3=Part of other courses	offer

BUSINESS FUNCTION	REPUTATION	RESOURCES COMMITTED
Consulting	A	=
Marketing	B	=
Management/Strategy	A	=
Operations-Service	C	+
Operations-Production	B	=
Finance/Accounting	A	=
HR/ILR/Organizational Behavior	B+	=
Technology/Information Systems	C	+
Corporate Communication	A	=

SPECIAL INTERESTS	REPUTATION	RESOURCES COMMITTED	RELATIONSHIP TO CORE PROGRAM
International	A	+	1
Small Business	E	-	4
Entrepreneurial	B	=	2
Diversity	B	+	1
Communications	A	-	1
Manufacturing	B	=	1
Emerging Business	—	-	—
Family Business	E	-	4
Health Care	D	-	2
Public Administration	E	=	2
Ethics	C	+	1
Other	—	—	—

TEACHING METHODOLOGIES	PERCENTAGE OF ALL COURSES	SKILLS DEVELOPMENT	PERCENTAGE OF ALL COURSES
Case Study	40%	Quantitative/ Technical	30%
Lecture	40%	Managerial	30%
Experiential	10%	Communication	30%
Combination	-	Other	10%
Other	10%		

*Reported by Dean's Office

CAREER SERVICES

On a first-name basis as evidenced by the Office of Career Planning and Placement staff photo directory in their Recruiting Handbook, services are solid and personalized. The "esprit" Tuck is famous for is evident here, too. Employers are encouraged to participate in career panels and classes along with their traditional recruiting role. Tuck students have hardly noticed the downsizing of corporations and accompanying decrease in campus recruitment. An active career office and an alumni network second to none in loyalty make a difference. The high quality of graduates may have a lot to do with it as well.

DISTINGUISHED PROGRAM/RESOURCES

Every first-year student at Tuck is required to do a "real world" consulting project, in which groups of students are assigned to help solve business problems in nearby communities.

CAREER SERVICES

CAREER MANAGEMENT		RECRUITMENT	
Career Planning Program for First-Year Students	Yes	Employers Interviewing at School	111
Career Presentations in the Curricula	No	Interviews Conducted at School	N/A
Alumni Network	Yes	Marketing to Employers	No
Summer Jobs Program/ Internships	Yes	Resume Books	Yes
Employer Associates Program	Yes	Resume Database to Employers	No
Job Search Course	Yes	Resume Database/ Referral System	No
		Career Fairs	Yes

CAREER SERVICES STAFF

Professional	3	Graduate Assistants	10
Support	3	Peer Advisors	0

	1993	1992	1991
Mean no. of Job Offers/Graduate	N/A	N/A	N/A
STARTING SALARY	MEDIAN	MEDIAN	MEDIAN
Acct/Finance	$58,000		
Marketing	57,000		
Operations/Services	—		
Management/Strategy	60,000		
Health Care	—		
Consulting	75,000		
Operations/Production	—	N/A	N/A
Tech/Info Systems	—		
HR/LR/O. Dev/	—		
Public Admin.	—		
Other	—		
Small Business	—		
International	—		

TOP TEN EMPLOYERS BY HIRES

1. Coopers & Lybrand
2. J.P. Morgan & Co. Inc.
3. McKinsey & Company, Inc.
4. Andersen Consulting
5. Braxton Associates

6. General Mills
7. Goldman Sachs & Co.
8. Merrill Lynch & Co.
9. Booz, Allen & Hamilton Inc.
10. Citicorp/Citibank

STUDENT LIFE

Given the small size of the MBA program at Tuck, and the fact that most first-year students live in campus dorms, students comment that they can really get to know their classmates. There are regular student-faculty games and inter-business-school competitions, as well as low-cost golf and ski lessons. Students are further encouraged to get to know their peers and faculty better through such events as the monthly "Tuck 'Tails," a casual wine and cheese gathering held in the recently renovated Stell Hall. Tuck sponsors an annual Winter Carnival (downhill skiing) and Hockey Tournament that draw business-school teams nationwide.

A variety of student clubs exist, including Women in Management, Marketing Club, Tuck Volunteers, and Quality of Life Committee (social and community activities). Social events include the Winter Formal Dance, the International Dinner and the Tuck Charity Ball. Many student activities are sponsored by the Student Board, Tuck's student-governing body.

Dartmouth College

FACILITIES AND TECHNOLOGY

Dartmouth, the ninth oldest college in the nation and a member of the Ivy League, is located on a 200-acre campus set on the banks of the Connecticut River. Tuck, the oldest graduate business school in the nation, is located on 13 acres at the western edge of the Dartmouth campus, and consists of seven Georgian-style interconnected buildings. Included in the complex are the Feldberg Business Library, career library and placement offices, a computer lab, modern classrooms in the new Byrne Hall, group study facilities and a new student commons area. All buildings at Dartmouth, including the dorms, are connected via underground tunnels for the students' protection and convenience.

Tuck has approximately 200 personal computers that have access to Dartmouth mainframes and to worldwide networks.

SCHOLARSHIPS AND FINANCIAL ASSISTANCE

Tuck offers assistance to residents of the United States and Canada based on financial need. The financial aid program includes various deferred-payment loans, low interest loans and approximately 50 scholarships and fellowships. A work/study program, where students are awarded grants, is also available. Several part-time jobs in the school's dining room, mail room or computer room are available based on financial need and experience.

COMMUNITY/CITY LIFE

Hanover Population: 10,000
Weather: New England winters. Average temperatures: 28° in winter, 71° in summer.

Hanover, New Hampshire, a small New England college town, boasts charming brick-facade shops, cozy Main Street restaurants and lovely colonial homes. Outdoor activities are popular in Hanover, with skating and skiing the winners in the winter months, and canoeing, hiking and bicycling in the warmer months. Hanover is within a two-hour drive of Boston, a five-hour drive of New York, and a three-hour drive of Montreal.

HOUSING AND LIVING COSTS

The three on-campus dormitories are Chase, Woodbury and Buchanan Residence Hall. Approximate costs for a dorm room during the 1993-94 academic year averaged $3,900.

DUKE UNIVERSITY

THE FUQUA SCHOOL OF BUSINESS

Science Drive
Durham, NC 27708-0112
Tel: 919-660-7705
Fax: 919-681-8025

OVERVIEW

Fuqua and Duke don't easily come together in common speech, but in academia and business, they represent a formidable combination. The unique name—Fuqua—comes from philanthropist J.B. Fuqua, chairman of Fuqua companies in Atlanta. Duke needs no explanation—its reputation is global. Few people, however, know it's named after James B. Duke, industrialist and tobacco millionaire, who tried to start the university in New Jersey.   Like its rivals in Chapel Hill and Raleigh, Duke/Fuqua enjoys the rich resources of the "Research Triangle" with all its companies, culture and recreation.

ACADEMIC BRIEF

Each semester begins with a week long Integrative Learning Experience followed by two seven-week terms. The Integrative Learning Experience is a series of exercises, role playing and simulations in four areas: team building and leadership development, managing quality and diversity, competitive strategy, and complex management problems. First-year students take core courses and a year-long Individual Effectiveness course, which sharpens speaking, writing and computing skills. During the second year, students take a minimum of 10 elective courses.

KEYS TO ADMISSIONS AND APPLICATION

1-minimal   2-somewhat   3-significant

CRITERIA	IMPORTANCE	OTHER CONSIDERATIONS	
GPA	3	Leadership	3
GMAT Scores	3		
Quality of Undergraduate Inst.	2	Community Serice	3
Quality of Undergrad. Major	3		
Years Experience	2	Language Skills	2
Recommendations	3		
Activities	2	International Living	2
Essay	3		
Interview	3	Working Expereience	2

PROFILE OF ENROLLED STUDENTS

Number Applicants:	1932	Mean GPA Enrolled:	3.28
Number of Offers:	666	Median GMAT Enrolled:	625
Number Enrolled:	329		

Percentile GPA ranking			Percentile ranking by GMAT		
%				%	
80	%	2.8-3.8	80	%	550-710
50	%	3.0-3.6	50	%	580-680

DEMOGRAPHICS

First-Year Students	329	Women	172
Second-Year Students	330	Men	487
International Students	97	Minorities	79
		African American	48
Mean Age	26	Native American	2
Mean Class Size	N/A	Asian American	17
Mean Years Experience	3-4	Hispanic American	12

% UNDERGRADUATE MAJOR		% HOME REGIONS	
Arts/Humanities	13%	New England	34%
Business/Management	32%	Mid-Atlantic	N/A
Natural/ Physical Sciences	4%	Southeast	26%
Technical/Engineering Sciences	21%	Southwest	3%
Social Sciences	6%	Mid West	12%
Economics	21%	Rocky Mountain	N/A
Other	3%	Far West	10%

The Best Graduate Business Schools

ACADEMIC STRENGTHS/FEATURES*

KEY	REPUTATION	RESOURCE COMMITMENT NEXT 2 YEARS
	A-exceptionally well known; national reputation	+ increase = same - less
	B-well respected	**RELATIONSHIP TO CORE PROGRAM**
	C-building; targeted as key area	1=Required 4=Not offered
	D-standard program	2=Elective 5=Plan to offer
	E-not provided	3=Part of other courses

BUSINESS FUNCTION	REPUTATION	RESOURCES COMMITTED
Consulting	A	=
Marketing	A	=
Management/Strategy	B	+
Operations-Service	B	+
Operations-Production	B	+
Finance/Accounting	A	=
HR/ILR/Organizational Behavior	B	=
Technology/Information Systems	B	+
Other		

SPECIAL INTERESTS	REPUTATION	RESOURCES COMMITTED	RELATIONSHIP TO CORE PROGRAM
International	A	+	1
Small Business	B	=	2
Entrepreneurial	B	=	2
Diversity	A	=	1
Communications	A	=	1
Manufacturing	B	+	1
Emerging Business	A	+	2
Family Business	E	—	4
Health Care	A	+	2
Public Administration	E	—	4
Ethics	C	+	2
Other	—	—	—

TEACHING METHODOLOGIES	PERCENTAGE OF ALL COURSES	SKILLS DEVELOPMENT	PERCENTAGE OF ALL COURSES
Case Study	—	Quantitative/	
Lecture	—	Technical	25%
Experiential	—	Managerial	50%
Combination	100%	Communication	15%
Other	—	Teamwork	10%
		Other	—

*Reported by Dean's Office

Duke University

CAREER SERVICES

Dan Nagy, Career Services Director for the Fuqua School of Business, has outstanding credentials for this key post. He has held leadership positions in corporate recruiting, centralized university placement, MBA placement, executive education and corporate consulting. Students expect and receive some major innovations and excellence in services. There is a required career planning program for first-year students, and career management is being integrated into several academic courses. The international resume book is first-rate.

DISTINGUISHED PROGRAM/RESOURCES

Number and variety of career workshops including an outstanding negotiations seminar.

CAREER SERVICES

CAREER MANAGEMENT

Career Planning Program for First-Year Students	Yes
Career Presentations in the Curricula	Yes
Alumni Network	Yes
Summer Jobs Program/ Internships	Yes
Employer Associates Program	Yes
Job Search Course	No

RECRUITMENT

Employers Interviewing at School	198
Interviews Conducted at School	5,171
Marketing to Employers	Yes
Resume Books	Yes
Resume Database to Employers	No
Resume Database/ Referral System	Yes
Career Fairs	Yes

CAREER SERVICES STAFF

Professional	3	Graduate Assistants	4
Support	4	Peer Advisors	20

FIRST-JOB STATISTICS AND SALARY DATA

	1993	1992	1991
Mean no. of Job Offers/Graduate	2.1	1.8	1.6
STARTING SALARY	MEAN	MEAN	MEAN
Acct/Finance	$54,000	$53,500	
Marketing	55,000	53,000	
Operations/Services	57,000	55,000	
Management/Strategy	—	—	
Health Care	—	—	
Consulting	64,000	55,000	
Operations/Production	—	—	N/A
Tech/Info Systems	—	—	
HR/LR/O. Dev/	46,500	44,000	
Public Admin.	—	—	
General Mangement	57,000	55,000	
Investment Banking	53,000	55,000	
Small Business	—	—	
International	—	—	

TOP TEN EMPLOYERS BY HIRES

1. Merrill Lynch & Co.
2. DeLoitte & Touche
3. American Airlines
4. General Motors Corp.
5. Compaq Computers Corp.
6. Chase Manhattan Bank, N.A.
7. Ford Motor Company
8. Goldman, Sachs & Co.
9. Coopers & Lybrand
10. Procter & Gamble

STUDENT LIFE

Utilizing their entrepreneurial skills, Fuqua students help finance activities of the MBA Association through such ventures as the "The Kiosk," a student-run food service and sportswear business. Teamwork and student activism are encouraged by the school's administration, and, as one student put it, "...this sense of ownership is so exhilarating you really want to get involved." One example of such activism is the Fuqua-MBA Games, a gathering of MBA students from many of the nation's leading business schools for two days of competition, including such events as "Recruiting Obstacle Course" and the "Briefcase Toss," to raise money for the North Carolina Special Olympics. Other groups, such as the Community Involvement Club, Success Through Entrepreneurial Projects, the Black MBA Organization and the Christian Business Fellowship also sponsor activities supporting the local community. Many MBA students also take an active role on committees that affect the School's policies and practices.

Students typically gather at the business school each Friday for beer and socializing. MBA students also sponsor an annual open-pit pig roast on the first Saturday in April for the entire university.

FACILITIES AND TECHNOLOGY

Situated on Duke's West Campus, Fuqua consists of three interconnected modern concrete and glass buildings. MBA classes take place primarily in the east wing, with six amphitheater-style teaching classrooms, an auditorium, seminar rooms and breakout rooms for team work. Also in the east wing are the Fuqua Library, computer labs, the student lounge and the student-operated snack bar.

Recognizing the importance of strong oral and written communication skills, Fuqua has created the Management Communication Center (MCC). The MCC provides classes, programs and individual instruction to enhance students' communication effectiveness.

Fuqua's Computer Center manages all instructional, research and administrative computing in the school. Two labs are equipped with 60 NCR 486 Personal Computers. Twenty-four additional PCs are located in the various team rooms. Most PCs are networked together and have access to laser printers and a wide variety of software. The Center also maintains an IBM mainframe computer. Each classroom and auditorium is equipped with a PC connected to a large-screen projector.

SCHOLARSHIPS AND FINANCIAL ASSISTANCE

Fuqua awards several dozen scholarships each year, based on academic and leadership abilities. Private and corporate-sponsored scholarships are also available.

COMMUNITY/CITY LIFE

Durham, North Carolina Population: 101,000
Weather: Hot, humid summers. Mild winters. Spring and fall are long and warm.

Durham, located in the northeast corner of North Carolina's Central Piedmont or foothills region, is part of the "Research Triangle," which has the highest per capita population of Ph.D. scientists and engineers in the world. With a low crime rate and a mild year-round climate, Durham regularly appears on many of the "best of" lists that rank U.S. cities for quality of life. Outdoor activities are popular, with numerous golf courses and jogging trails, as well as a minor league baseball franchise-- the Durham Bulls. Durham is the permanent home to the American Dance Festival, and also supports other cultural activities such as its own arts council, symphony, choral society and theater groups.

HOUSING AND LIVING COSTS

The most cost-effective living accommodation is a shared house/apartment or on-campus housing. Each will cost approximately $2,835 for the academic year. A one-bedroom apartment costs approximately $3,870 for the academic year.

GEORGETOWN UNIVERSITY

SCHOOL OF BUSINESS

Old North
Washington DC 20057-1008
Tel: 202-687-4200
Fax: 202-687-7809

AT A GLANCE

First-Year Students:	208	Employer Ranking:	#10 of 61
Second-Year Students:	182	Student/Faculty Ratio:	1:11
Location:	Major City	Annual Tuition:	
No. of Employers		in-state:	$18,000
Recruiting on Campus:	56	out-of-state:	$18,000

Strengths: International Business Ethics, Business-Government Relations; relationships with Washington D.C. international community; opportunities for students to get involved in local business/government.

Distinctions: Center for International Business Education and Research; centrally located in a modern facility on a 200-year-old campus; Group and communications work.

Goals: Increase student and faculty international exchanges; increase international student enrollment.

Words From the Dean: Robert Parker   Tenure: 8 years
"Fundamental to the school's mission are the interconnected themes that distinguish the School: global business education, linking global business conduct to an understanding of political and regulatory environments; use of values and ethical criteria in decisions and effective communications in an intercultural environment."

OVERVIEW

It's no accident that Georgetown, with its Jesuit school background, "down M Street" access to major government agencies and cross-campus relationship with the top foreign service school in the world, offers strong programs in ethics, public administration and internationalism. A large percentage of students are from other countries and a majority of students are bilingual. Although relatively young, the Georgetown School of Business is making its mark on a number of fronts. As one recruiter said, "It's no longer just a fine small business school in charming surroundings—it competes with any top program."

ACADEMIC BRIEF

Georgetown's business program is dedicated to training students as future business leaders capable of competing in a global environment. The curriculum focuses on business-government relations, ethics and management communication. The program incorporates a 200-year-old traditional liberal arts and business management education. It offers general management training along with a strong base in practical areas of business. The curriculum's required courses cover various functional areas of business such as financial management, accounting, ethics, marketing, statistics and the global environment of business.

Joint Programs: JD/MBA

KEYS TO ADMISSIONS AND APPLICATION

1-minimal   2-somewhat   3-significant

CRITERIA	IMPORTANCE	OTHER CONSIDERATIONS
GPA	3	Non-native language
GMAT Scores	3	proficiency - 2
Quality of Undergraduate Inst.	2	
Quality of Undergrad. Major	2	
Years Experience	2	
Recommendations	2	
Activities	2	
Essay	3	
Interview	2	Recommended

PROFILE OF ENROLLED STUDENTS

Number Applicants:	1062	Mean GPA Enrolled:	3.16
Number of Offers:	509	Mean GMAT Enrolled:	602
Number Enrolled:	208		

Percentile GPA ranking		Percentile ranking by GMAT		
1062	% 3.70-3.97	1062	%	690-760
509	% 3.39-3.68	509	%	630-690
208	% 3.15-.3.39	208	%	600-630

DEMOGRAPHICS

First-Year Students	208	Women	141
Second-Year Students	182	Men	249
International Students	106	Minorities	44
		African American	10
Mean Age	27	Native American	1
Mean Class Size	39	Asian American	19
Mean Years Experience	3-4	Hispanic American	14

% UNDERGRADUATE MAJOR		% HOME REGIONS	
Arts/Humanities	16%	New England	16%
Business/Management	19%	Mid-Atlantic	26%
Natural/ Physical		Southeast	9%
Sciences	19%	Southwest	3%
Technical/Engineering,		Mid West	6%
Computer Science	N/A%	Rocky Mountain	N/A
Social Sciences	50%	Far West	13%

ACADEMIC STRENGTHS/FEATURES*

KEY	REPUTATION	RESOURCE COMMITMENT NEXT 2 YEARS
	A-exceptionally well known; national reputation	+ increase = same - less
	B-well respected	**RELATIONSHIP TO CORE PROGRAM**
	C-building; targeted as key area	1=Required 4=Not offered
	D-standard program	2=Elective 5=Plan to
	E-not provided	3=Part of offer
		other courses

BUSINESS FUNCTION	REPUTATION	RESOURCES COMMITTED
Consulting	B	=
Marketing	B	=
Management/Strategy	B	+
Operations-Service	C	+
Operations-Production	C	+
Finance/Accounting	B	=
HR/ILR/Organizational Behavior	B	=
Technology/Information Systems	D	=
Other		

SPECIAL INTERESTS	REPUTATION	RESOURCES COMMITTED	RELATIONSHIP TO CORE PROGRAM
International	A	+	1
Small Business	E	=	4
Entrepreneurial	B	+	2
Diversity	D	+	3
Communications	A	+	1
Manufacturing	D	+	1
Emerging Business	D	=	2
Family Business	E	=	4
Health Care	E	=	4
Public Administration	B	=	2
Ethics	A	+	1
General Management	A	=	1

TEACHING METHODOLOGIES	PERCENTAGE OF ALL COURSES	SKILLS DEVELOPMENT	PERCENTAGE OF ALL COURSES
Case Study	50%	Quantitative/ Technical	20%
Lecture	10%	Managerial	50%
Experiential	20%	Communication	20%
Combination	—	Analytical	10%
Discussion	20%	Other	—
Other	—		

*Reported by Dean's Office

CAREER SERVICES

The MBA Career Management Center has instituted a student-oriented, yet business-like approach to career services. The staff (formerly headed by Dr. Christopher Shinkman) is top-drawer and the number of companies recruiting on campus is up 10%. Several students commented on the office's development. "Last Spring MBACM conducted a brainstorming session with MBA students in which ten issues were identified. When we returned in the fall, Career Management had taken action on each of these issues. The office is much more focused on marketing the program to potential employers than it had been in previous years," stated John, a second-year student.

Besides undertaking an ambitious schedule of new programs under the title of "Manager Development Workshops" and an informative newsletter, Career Management also works with student and alumni groups to bring big-name speakers on campus such as Ben Cohen, co-founder of Ben and Jerry's.

DISTINGUISHED PROGRAM/RESOURCES

Emphasis on student feedback (customer satisfaction), incorporating results into programs and publications.

Manager Development Workshops and Georgetown's new award winning *Career Guide* use business terminology in its comprehensive approach to career development.

CAREER SERVICES

CAREER MANAGEMENT

Career Planning Program for First-Year Students	Yes		
Career Presentations in the Curricula	No		
Alumni Network	Yes		
Summer Jobs Program/ Internships	Yes		
Employer Associates Program	No		
Job Search Course	No		

RECRUITMENT

Employers Interviewing at School	56
Interviews Conducted at School	578
Marketing to Employers	Yes
Resume Books	Yes
Resume Database to Employers	No
Resume Database/ Referral System	Yes
Career Fairs	No

CAREER SERVICES STAFF

Professional	3	Graduate Assistants	2
Support	1	Peer Advisors	0

FIRST-JOB STATISTICS AND SALARY DATA

	1993	1992	1991
Mean no. of Job Offers/Graduate	N/A	N/A	N/A
STARTING SALARY	MEAN	MEAN	MEAN
Acct/Finance	$44,405		
Marketing	51,271		
Operations/Services	—		
Management/Strategy	—		
Health Care	—		
Consulting	53,716		
Operations/Production	—	N/A	N/A
Tech/Info Systems	50,000		
HR/LR/O. Dev/	—		
Public Admin.	—		
Corporate Planning	66,786		
General Management	40,000		
Research Analysts	48,500		
Other	43,000		

TOP TEN EMPLOYERS BY HIRES

1. Andersen Consulting
2. Ernst & Young
3. American Management Systems, Inc.
4. Coopers & Lybrand
5. OPIC
6. Bell Atlantic
7. MCI Telecommunications
8. Procter & Gamble
9. —
10. —

STUDENT LIFE

By pledging to the "Shared Value Statement," adopted in the Spring of 1992, Georgetown students agree to "...uphold our common obligations to fairness, accuracy, integrity, honesty and mutual respect in an effort to foster a cooperative environment." This commitment to a fair and ethical environment flows into the student-initiated MBA Volunteer Organization. With over half of the MBA student population participating, the group is involved with the Joshua House, a transitional employment program for previously homeless men; the I Have A Dream Foundation; Aids Education; the Zacchaeus Free Clinic, and Bread for the City. The group also sponsors the "Ultimate Four Basketball Tournament" with other top Business Schools, to raise money for the I Have A Dream Foundation.

Georgetown student organizations reflect the diverse population and the global focus of the school. Groups such as Women in Business, Students for Eastern European Development, International Business Forum and the Alliance for Cultural Awareness help students gain a greater awareness of issues by sponsoring speakers, internships and field trips.

FACILITIES AND TECHNOLOGY

Located in the relatively safe area of Georgetown, the School of Business is in Old North Hall, built in 1795 and renovated several years ago. The building now has case-style classrooms, a state-of-the-art computer lab and an MBA lounge. Six campus libraries are available to students, including the Lauinger Library, which houses the business collection. Lauinger also provides access to on-line resources such as ABI/Inform and the National Trade Databank. Students also make use of the rich range of research facilities in the Washington area.

The School of Business maintains its own Technology Center with two personal computer classroom/labs containing both IBM- compatible and Macintosh systems. All PC's are connected to a local area network from which students can use a variety of software and printers. The LAN is connected to the main university network, so business students can utilize mainframe systems as well as access other networks and services. A computer workshop is held the week prior to the beginning of classes, offering students introductory instruction on software packages.

SCHOLARSHIPS AND FINANCIAL ASSISTANCE

Georgetown offers students a variety of full and partial tuition scholarships and financial aid options. Every student who is offered admission is considered for scholarship awards. Some of the funds offered include: Federal Stafford Student Loans, Federal Perkins Loans and the Federal Work-Study Program.

COMMUNITY/CITY LIFE

Population: Washington D.C. 630,000
Weather: Moderate winters. Hot humid summers with an average temperature of 78°.

The campus is located in the center of the historic Georgetown area of Washington, D.C. near the Potomac River. A cosmopolitan city, Washington D.C. provides a variety of educational, cultural and recreational activities at places like the Smithsonian Institution and the Kennedy Center for the Performing Arts.

The business community includes such national and international corporations as the World Bank, Mobil Oil, Marriott Corporation, Martin Marietta and MCI. The downtown area is comprised of many trendy restaurants, night clubs, art galleries and shops.

HOUSING AND LIVING COSTS

Georgetown offers small and slightly restrictive on-campus housing in an expensive area for graduate students. Students live off-campus in shared apartments and townhouses. Rent for an apartment can average well over $1,000 per month. More affordable apartments can be found in Arlington, Alexandria and neighboring areas. A shared apartment for the academic year is approximately $2,835; a shared house for the academic year costs approximately $3,307.

HARVARD UNIVERSITY

GRADUATE SCHOOL OF BUSINESS ADMINISTRATION

Soldiers Field Road   Boston, MA   02163
Tel: 617-495-6127   Fax: 617-496-9272

AT A GLANCE

First-Year Students:	816	Employer Ranking:	#5 of 61
Second-Year Students:	815	Student/Faculty Ratio:	N/A
Location:	Major City	Annual Tuition:	
No. of Employers		in-state:	$19,750
Recruiting on Campus:	300	out-of-state:	$19,750

Strengths: Outstanding faculty and breadth of excellence. Size and quality of alumni network.

Distinctions: Considered in top five in most business functional areas—consulting and finance are premier areas. Largest number of recruiters on campus of top 10 schools.

Words From the Dean: John H. McArtur, Dean of the Faculty
"We hope you'll agree that the Harvard MBA Program has much to offer its participants. We welcome applications from highly competent, responsible and morally sensitive women and men who hope to serve as tomorrow's leaders."

OVERVIEW

HBS, as it's often known around campus and around the world, has impressive public relations materials like other outstanding business programs. The lead sentence, however, best summarizes the difference—"The HBS is an intellectual community with strong traditions and unparalleled resources." It is these three qualities that make the strongest case for Harvard's supremacy.

The Harvard-case study method is the first (and most imitated) method of study. The practice of dividing classes into "Sections" of 88 students who take all their first-year classes together fosters a unique balance of competition and support. The HBS campus— 61 beautiful acres and 27 buildings adjacent to the Charles River—provides a highly efficient and idyllic environment. Despite recent criticism from corporations and business publications for not being in touch with business, Harvard is and always will be Harvard. The quality of faculty and students is superb—and leaders are always under fire.

ACADEMIC BRIEF

One of the unique characteristics of the Harvard Business School is the "Section" concept. Each fall, the incoming class is divided into nine sections of approximately 88 students each. The students in each group take all of their first-year classes together. Eventually, the group becomes an integral part of each student's academic experience and social activities. The case method of the Harvard Business School differs from that of other schools. In most programs, "case method" refers to the use

101

of a written description of a business problem and outcome. At Harvard, students are presented with the description of a problem, along with limited information, and they must decide what action to take. Currently, Harvard is undergoing a major self-study and change is expected, specifically an increased emphasis on teamwork, an increase in women faculty and scrutiny of the hallowed regulation that 10% of students in every class must receive a "low pass" grade.

KEYS TO ADMISSIONS AND APPLICATION

1-minimal   2-somewhat   3-significant

CRITERIA	IMPORTANCE	OTHER CONSIDERATIONS
GPA	N/A	
GMAT Scores	not required	
Quality of Undergraduate Inst.	N/A	
Quality of Undergrad. Major	N/A	
Years Experience	N/A	N/A
Recommendations	N/A	
Activities	N/A	
Essay	N/A	
Interview	N/A	

PROFILE OF ENROLLED STUDENTS

Number Applicants:	5,933	Mean GPA Enrolled:	3.4
Number of Offers:	N/A	Mean GMAT Enrolled:	Not required
Number Enrolled:	807		

Percentile GPA ranking			Percentile ranking by GMAT		
N/A	%	N/A	N/A	%	N/A
N/A	%	N/A	N/A	%	N/A
N/A	%	N/A	N/A	%	N/A

DEMOGRAPHICS

First-Year Students	816	Women	472
Second-Year Students	815	Men	1159
International Students	25%	Minorities	15%
		African American	N/A
Mean Age	26	Native American	N/A
Mean Class Size	N/A	Asian American	N/A
Mean Years Experience	4	Hispanic American	N/A

% UNDERGRADUATE MAJOR		% HOME REGIONS	
Arts/Humanities	50%	New England	N/A
Business/Management	19%	Mid-Atlantic	N/A
Natural/ Physical		Southeast	N/A
Sciences	5%	Southwest	N/A
Technical/Engineering,		Mid West	N/A
Computer Science	25%	Rocky Mountain	N/A
Social Sciences	N/A	Far West	N/A

The Best Graduate Business Schools

ACADEMIC STRENGTHS/FEATURES*

KEY	REPUTATION	RESOURCE COMMITMENT NEXT 2 YEARS	
	A-exceptionally well known; national reputation	+ increase　　= same　　- less	
	B-well respected	RELATIONSHIP TO CORE PROGRAM	
	C-building; targeted as key area	1=Required	4=Not offered
	D-standard program	2=Elective	5=Plan to
	E-not provided	3=Part of other courses	offer

BUSINESS FUNCTION	REPUTATION	RESOURCES COMMITTED
Consulting Marketing Management/Strategy Operations-Service Operations-Production Finance/Accounting HR/ILR/Organizational Behavior Technology/Information Systems Other	N/A	N/A

SPECIAL INTERESTS	REPUTATION	RESOURCES COMMITTED	RELATIONSHIP TO CORE PROGRAM
International Small Business Entrepreneurial Diversity Communications Manufacturing Emerging Business Family Business Health Care Public Administration Ethics Other	N/A	N/A	N/A

TEACHING METHODOLOGIES	PERCENTAGE OF ALL COURSES	SKILLS DEVELOPMENT	PERCENTAGE OF ALL COURSES
Case Study	100%	Quantitative/ Technical	
Lecture	—	Managerial	N/A
Experiential	—	Communication	
Combination	—	Other	
Other	—		

*Reported by Dean's Office

Harvard University

CAREER SERVICES

Although probably better known for its innovations in recruitment, campus interviewing and the first "resume database system" to supplement the traditional resume book, the Office of Career Development also has impressive educational programs. The workshops, seminars and publications assist students in all phases of career management, including assessment and goal setting. And, of course, the Alumni Network is second to none. The placement statistic that 67% of the graduates accept a position with an organization that comes to Harvard to recruit is unrivaled and speaks volumes.

DISTINGUISHED PROGRAM/RESOURCES

Summer Recruiting Program provides multiple opportunities for first-year students; their annual report is packed with useful data and information summaries.

CAREER SERVICES

CAREER MANAGEMENT		RECRUITMENT	
Career Planning Program for First-Year Students	N/A	Employers Interviewing at School	300
Career Presentations in the Curricula	N/A	Interviews Conducted at School	10,000
Alumni Network	Yes	Marketing to Employers	Yes
Summer Jobs Program/ Internships	Yes	Resume Books	Yes
Employer Associates Program	N/A	Resume Database to Employers	Yes
Job Search Course	Yes	Resume Database/ Referral System	Yes
		Career Fairs	Yes

CAREER SERVICES STAFF

Professional	9	Graduate Assistants	N/A
Support	7	Peer Advisors	N/A

FIRST-JOB STATISTICS AND SALARY DATA

	1993	1992	1991
Mean no. of Job Offers/Graduate	2	N/A	N/A
STARTING SALARY	MEDIAN	MEDIAN	MEDIAN
Acct/Finance	$65,000		
Marketing	62,000		
Operations/Services	-		
Management/Strategy	65,000		
Health Care	55,000		
Consulting	75,000		
Operations/Production	60,000	N/A	N/A
Tech/Info Systems	-		
HR/LR/O. Dev/	-		
Public Admin.	-		
General Management	65,000		
Mergers/Acquisitions	69,500		
Small Business	-		
International	-		

TOP TEN EMPLOYERS BY HIRES

1.		6.	
2.		7.	
3.	N/A	8.	N/A
4.		9.	
5.		10.	

STUDENT LIFE

When asked what they remember most about the Harvard Business School program, students most frequently respond with "my classmates." Student interaction is key to the Business School, and many deep friendships are developed in the small study groups that are encouraged by the school. The school is also very supportive of partners who come to Boston with their significant others. The Partner's Club organizes a wide variety of social and educational activities and an advising network that helps spouses and partners find jobs in the area.

A well-organized intramural sports program provides a welcome change of pace for many students. Regular events, services and activities promote wellness and fitness. Shad Hall, a new facility featuring a jogging track, exercise classes and a variety of courts, is well used by students.

Over 75% of Business School students participate in some degree of community service, including the HBS Volunteers and Project Outreach.

FACILITIES AND TECHNOLOGY

The Harvard Business School is located on a beautiful 61-acre campus across the Charles River from Cambridge and Harvard Square, and just 15 minutes from downtown Boston. The setting is pure Ivy League, with red brick, neo-Georgian buildings. The interiors of the buildings are modern, tiered classrooms with state-of-the-art facilities. The campus, completely separated from the rest of the University, has four restaurants, a post office, a barber shop, a chapel and the multi-million-dollar Shad Hall.

The Harvard Business School boasts the world's largest business library, with over 500,000 volumes and 6,500 periodicals that cover the entire spectrum of management subjects.

SCHOLARSHIPS AND FINANCIAL ASSISTANCE

Financial assistance consists of fellowships and loans. Fellowships are awarded during the second year of study to those students who demonstrate the highest level of financial need. Loans are available through various sources, including the Stafford Loan, Supplemental Loans and the Perkins Loan. International students can apply for private or bank loans.

COMMUNITY/CITY LIFE

Boston Population: 578,000
Weather: New England winters and summer temperatures in the 70s.

Rich in history, culture, and intellectual opportunities, Boston is home to the Harvard Business School and over 60 other colleges and universities. Students enjoy getting to know Boston better during their free time, and comment that the cafes and shops of Harvard Square, along with the sporting events and cultural offerings in Boston, make achieving a good balance between studies and personal time easier. Business School students can take advantage of boating activities, as well as just relaxing along the banks of the Charles River. Beautiful New England beaches are within driving distance, as are the White and Green Mountains of New England.

HOUSING AND LIVING COSTS

The Harvard Business School residence halls are all located on campus. Approximately half of the first- and second-year students live in the dorms. Dorm room rates for the academic year average $3,250 to $5,310. HBS also offers housing for married students and students with domestic partners in apartments such as Peabody Terrace and Soldiers Field Park, which are located close to campus.

THE UNIVERSITY OF ILLINOIS AT URBANA-CHAMPAIGN

COLLEGE OF COMMERCE AND BUSINESS ADMINISTRATION

350 Commerce West
Urbana, Il   61820
Tel: 217-333-4555/322-6469

AT A GLANCE

First-Year Students:	252	Employer Ranking:	—
Second-Year Students:	313	Student/Faculty Ratio:	1:4
Location:	Large Town	Annual Tuition:	
No. of Employers		in-state:	$4,000
Recruiting on Campus:	72	out-of-state:	$9,600

Strengths: Accounting, Finance, International Business. Experiential learning with cases and simulations integrated with curriculum.

Distinctions: Alma Mater of more partners of "big 6" accounting firms than any other school. Extensive connections to Chicago business and emerging companies around Champaign-Urbana. Allerton Capstone, a retreat focusing on business issues, available to second-year students.

Goals: Curriculum innovation with emphasis on globalization and interdisciplinary studies.

Words From the Dean: Howard Thomas   Tenure: 2.5 years
"Now, as never before, the College of Commerce and Business Administration at the University of Illinois is truly poised to fulfill the mission of a land grant university... and to help lead American business through the uncertain competitive business environment of the 21st century."

OVERVIEW

The University of Illinois continues to hold a lofty position among national and world universities. Illini graduates occupy 22 CEO positions among *Fortune* 500 companies. Additionally, more partners in the former "big six" public accounting firms come from Illinois than from any other business school. Accounting is the top program in the MBA curriculum within The College of Commerce and Business Administration. The Office for Information Managment is an innovative resource serving students and faculty in research, support and training functions. The Executive in Residence, CFO Lecture Series and Career Line, where alumni can call with questions are also exemplary. Champaign-Urbana has a high quality of life and is in the middle of a region where small business thrives.

ACADEMIC BRIEF

The programs of the College of Commerce and Business Administration concentrate on three basic components: administrative foundations, managerial functions and professional concentrations. During the first year, students must take required core courses. During the second year, students still take core courses, but they must also integrate six elective courses into their programs.

Jeanette, a first-year student in Human Resources and Hospital Administration and a mother of four who knows the importance of time management, complimented the faculty for their helpfulness outside the classroom.

KEYS TO ADMISSIONS AND APPLICATION

1-minimal   2-somewhat   3-significant

CRITERIA	IMPORTANCE	OTHER CONSIDERATIONS
GPA	3	
GMAT Scores	3	
Quality of Undergraduate Inst.	3	
Quality of Undergrad. Major	3	
Years Experience	3	N/A
Recommendations	2	
Activities	1	
Essay	2	
Interview	N/A	

PROFILE OF ENROLLED STUDENTS

Number Applicants:	832	Mean GPA Enrolled:	3.4
Number of Offers:	534	Median GMAT Enrolled:	600
Number Enrolled:	252		

Percentile GPA ranking			Percentile ranking by GMAT		
90	%	4.0-3.85	90	%	780-660
70	%	3.8-3.56	70	%	660-620
50	%	3.56-3.3	50	%	620-590

DEMOGRAPHICS

First-Year Students	252	Women	167
Second-Year Students	313	Men	403
International Students	200	Minorities	66
		African American	30
Mean Age	24	Native American	0
Mean Class Size	45	Asian American	28
Mean Years Experience	1-3	Hispanic American	8

% UNDERGRADUATE MAJOR		% HOME REGIONS	
Arts/Humanities	9%	New England	1%
Business/Management	48%	Mid-Atlantic	4%
Natural/ Physical		Southeast	3%
Sciences	10%	Southwest	2%
Technical/Engineering,		Mid West	49%
Computer Science	21%	Rocky Mountain	2%
Social Sciences	8%	Far West	4%

The Best Graduate Business Schools

ACADEMIC STRENGTHS/FEATURES*

K E Y	REPUTATION A-exceptionally well known; national reputation B-well respected C-building; targeted as key area D-standard program E- not provided	RESOURCE COMMITMENT NEXT 2 YEARS + increase = same - less RELATIONSHIP TO CORE PROGRAM 1=Required 4=Not offered 2=Elective 5=Plan to 3=Part of offer other courses

BUSINESS FUNCTION	REPUTATION	RESOURCES COMMITTED
Consulting	B	=
Marketing	A	=
Management/Strategy	A	+
Operations-Service	B	=
Operations-Production	B	+
Finance/Accounting	A	=
HR/ILR/Organizational Behavior	A	+
Technology/Information Systems	A	+
Accounting	A+	

SPECIAL INTERESTS	REPUTATION	RESOURCES COMMITTED	RELATIONSHIP TO CORE PROGRAM
International	A	+	2
Small Business	B	=	2
Entrepreneurial	B	+	2
Diversity	C	+	1
Communications	C	+	2
Manufacturing	B	=	1
Emerging Business	D	=	2
Family Business	D	=	3
Health Care	A	=	2
Public Administration	E	=	4
Ethics	C	+	2
Other	A	—	—

TEACHING METHODOLOGIES	PERCENTAGE OF ALL COURSES	SKILLS DEVELOPMENT	PERCENTAGE OF ALL COURSES
Case Study	25%	Quantitative/ Technical	50%
Lecture	30%	Managerial	40%
Experiential	15%	Communication	10%
Combination	5%	Other	—
Group Projects	25%		
Other	—		

*Reported by Dean's Office

The University of Illinois

CAREER SERVICES

The Commerce Placement Office (CPO) serves both undergraduate and graduate students. Its recruiting program operates on a "by invitation only" policy, which means recruiting companies select students with whom they want to interview. The office provides a full range of services including a Job Search Guide containing useful articles written by alumni for students.

DISTINGUISHED PROGRAM/RESOURCES

Illinois MBA Career Focus: This one-day event brings speakers together from a variety of business functions and includes keynote addresses by distinguished alumni and a consultant addressing the topic, "Is Corporate America Kicking the MBA Habit?"

CAREER SERVICES

CAREER MANAGEMENT		RECRUITMENT	
Career Planning Program for First-Year Students	Yes	Employers Interviewing at School	72
Career Presentations in the Curricula	No	Interviews Conducted at School	556
Alumni Network	Yes	Marketing to Employers	Yes
Summer Jobs Program/ Internships	Yes	Resume Books	Yes
Employer Associates Program	No	Resume Database to Employers	No
Job Search Course	No	Resume Database/ Referral System	No
		Career Fairs	Yes

CAREER SERVICES STAFF			
Professional	3	Graduate Assistants	1
Support	2	Peer Advisors	—

FIRST-JOB STATISTICS AND SALARY DATA

	1993	1992	1991
Mean no. of Job Offers/Graduate	1.3	1.1	N/A
STARTING SALARY	MEAN	MEAN	MEAN
Acct/Finance	$39,657	$41,000	
Marketing	44,357	33,000	
Operations/Services	40,000	42,700	
Management/Strategy	—	—	
Health Care	—	—	
Consulting	39,900	39,500	
Operations/Production	—	—	N/A
Tech/Info Systems	42,000	40,666	
HR/LR/O. Dev/	36,250	35,000	
Public Admin.	—	—	
General Mangement	31,000	45,000	
Teaching	36,000	30,700	
Small Business	—	—	
International	—	—	

TOP TEN EMPLOYERS BY HIRES

1. Ford Motor Company
2. Arthur Andersen
3. Andersen Consulting
4. NBD Bank
5. Baxter Healthcare
6. Procter & Gamble
7. Citibank
8. Continental Bank
9. Ernst & Young
10. Michelin Tire Corporation

STUDENT LIFE

Many students of the MBA Program are involved in the sports activities of the Urbana-Champaign area. The MBA Association sponsors intramural sports, along with other events, such as career forums, an annual spring banquet and tailgate barbecues on football weekends. An MBA newsletter is produced to keep students abreast of career-oriented events. Students can also participate in other organizations, such as the Investment Forum.

Known as one of the best performing arts facilities in the nation, the Krannert Center for the Performing Arts attracts many of the world's greatest performers to the campus. More than 300 performances of theatre, music, ballet and opera are held each year. Also on campus, the Assembly Hall is host to athletic events, Broadway-style shows and concerts.

FACILITIES AND TECHNOLOGY

The University of Illinois at Urbana-Champaign has over 250 buildings on a 700-acre campus. Set along tree-lined walks are many buildings of note, including the Krannert Center for the Performing Arts, the outstanding University of Illinois Library and the Commerce Library, which is of great interest to MBA students.

Using space in both Commerce West and David Kinley Hall, the Business School has a number of tiered classrooms with state-of-the-art technology for MBAs. Students are encouraged to mix with faculty during scheduled daily coffee breaks.

The MBA Program offers a unique, non-credit semester-long "Computer Competency Sequence" designed to enable its first-year students to become proficient in the use of microcomputers. All students are provided with hands-on training in such areas as spreadsheets, electronic mail and database management.

SCHOLARSHIPS AND FINANCIAL ASSISTANCE

There are various forms of financial assistance available, including scholarships, loans, work-study programs and assistantships. There are a limited number of merit-based loans available to incoming students. Second-year students can receive aid in the form of assistantships. Here, students are involved in teaching an undergraduate course or in administration.

COMMUNITY/CITY LIFE

Urbana-Champaign Population: 100,000
Weather: Average temperatures range from the mid 20's in the winter to the low 70's in the summer.

The twin cities of Urbana and Champaign, located on the "Grand Prairie," provide a vibrant university community for this midwestern business school. The community is very sports-minded, with Illinois State High School Tournaments in the spring, Olympic-style competition during the Prairie State Games in the summer and college "Fighting Illini" football games in the fall. Orchards abound for a "Pick Your Own" experience, and dining fare runs the gamut from fast food to elegant.

HOUSING AND LIVING COSTS

The most cost-effective living accommodation is in an on-campus dormitory, which averages $1,795 for the academic year. The University has graduate residence facilities for approximately 1,000 single students. There are also approximately 1,000 apartments available for students with families. Students may also find living accommodations in private apartments, rooms and houses in the neighboring community. An off-campus apartment can average $270 per month for one bedroom and $300 per month for two bedrooms.

INDIANA UNIVERSITY

GRADUATE SCHOOL OF BUSINESS

Tenth and Fee Lane
Bloomington, IN   47405-1701
Tel: 812-855-8006
Fax: 812-855-9039

AT A GLANCE

First-Year Students:	293	Employer Ranking:	#4 of 61
Second-Year Students:	236	Student/Faculty Ratio:	N/A
Location:	Large Town	Annual Tuition:	
No. of Employers		in-state:	$6,000
Recruiting on Campus:	235	out-of-state:	$12,000

Strengths: Finance, Marketing, Human Resources Management. Size and quality of placement services, a $2 million operation.

Distinctions: First-year curriculum is fully integrated. Offers students and faculty a "home buying day" where real estate leaders are brought in. MBA Advantage Series focuses on life and employment decisions.

Goals: Continued development of the integrated curriculum and creative ways to apply MBA to business environment.

Words From the Dean: John Rau   Tenure: 1 year
"At Indiana, we believe in the power of both teamwork and cross-functional integration; the days of the 'lone ranger' are over and one of our key objectives is to give our students every opportunity to learn the importance of multi-functional teams."

OVERVIEW

Indiana University touts itself as a "top ten" Business School. Considering its new European Center for Continuing Education, its young and highly credentialed dean, placement services that take a backseat to none, and its newly formed alliance to assist minorities in business, this boast may be difficult to dispute.

Bloomington is a lively, very livable college town; small business is doing well and connecting to IU business resources. In winter, basketball has always been and will always be king.

ACADEMIC BRIEF

Indiana University's "new" business program has gained the backing of key Fortune 500 CEOs. The program has eliminated the standard traditional MBA courses and focuses instead on "next century management thinking." The program enables students to gain insights from faculty, peers and executives from major corporations. Indiana University offers a two-week course called the Executive Management Program that is open to individuals who are "high potential managers" and who have a minimum of ten years of business experience and "cross-functional" management responsibilities.

KEYS TO ADMISSIONS AND APPLICATION

1-minimal   2-somewhat   3-significant

CRITERIA	IMPORTANCE	OTHER CONSIDERATIONS
GPA	3	
GMAT Scores	3	
Quality of Undergraduate Inst.	2	
Quality of Undergrad. Major	2	
Years Experience	3	N/A
Recommendations	2	
Activities	3	
Essay	3	
Interview	3	

PROFILE OF ENROLLED STUDENTS

Number Applicants:	1565	Mean GPA Enrolled:	3.2
Number of Offers:	799	Median GMAT Enrolled:	600
Number Enrolled:	296		

Percentile GPA ranking			Percentile ranking by GMAT		
N/A	%	N/A	N/A	%	N/A
N/A	%	N/A	N/A	%	N/A
N/A	%	N/A	N/A	%	N/A

DEMOGRAPHICS

First-Year Students	293	Women	129
Second-Year Students	236	Men	400
International Students	72	Minorities	66
		African American	30
Mean Age	27	Native American	2
Mean Class Size	N/A	Asian American	12
Mean Years Experience	4-6	Hispanic American	N/A

% UNDERGRADUATE MAJOR		% HOME REGIONS	
Arts/Humanities	4%	New England	9 %
Business/Management	44%	Mid-Atlantic	9%
Natural/ Physical		Southeast	6%
Sciences	N/A	Southwest	3%
Technical/Engineering,		Mid West	44%
Computer Science	27%	Rocky Mountain	4%
Social Sciences	23%	Far West	10%

ACADEMIC STRENGTHS/FEATURES*

KEY	REPUTATION	RESOURCE COMMITMENT NEXT 2 YEARS
K E Y	A-exceptionally well known; national reputation B-well respected C-building; targeted as key area D-standard program E- not provided	+ increase = same - less RELATIONSHIP TO CORE PROGRAM 1=Required 4=Not offered 2=Elective 5=Plan to 3=Part of offer other courses

BUSINESS FUNCTION	REPUTATION	RESOURCES COMMITTED
Consulting	B	=
Marketing	A	+
Management/Strategy	B	+
Operations-Service	B	=
Operations-Production	B	=
Finance/Accounting	A	+
HR/ILR/Organizational Behavior	A	+
Technology/Information Systems	B	=
Other		

SPECIAL INTERESTS	REPUTATION	RESOURCES COMMITTED	RELATIONSHIP TO CORE PROGRAM
International	A	+	1
Small Business	B	+	2
Entrepreneurial	A	+	2
Diversity	A	+	1
Communications	B	+	1
Manufacturing	B	=	2
Emerging Business	B	=	3
Family Business	C	=	3
Health Care	E	=	4
Public Administration	E	=	4
Ethics	N/A	=	1
Other	N/A	—	—

TEACHING METHODOLOGIES	PERCENTAGE OF ALL COURSES	SKILLS DEVELOPMENT	PERCENTAGE OF ALL COURSES
Case Study	20%	Quantitative/ Technical	30%
Lecture	20%	Managerial	60%
Experiential	10%	Communication	10%
Combination	50%	Other	—
Other	—		

*Reported by Dean's Office

CAREER SERVICES

Director of Career Services Dr. Randy Powell is the author of a respected career planning resource, *Career Planning and Placement Today,* which is used as the text for the required course for all non-business undergraduate students registering with the office. MBA FOCUS, the educational program required for MBAs, develops career awareness and career search skills. As evidenced by the size and quality of its Career Service Office Staff, IU clearly attaches great importance to career and placement services. The office is strong in technology, offering employers electronic access to resumes as well as tracking all phases of recruiter activity on and off campus.

DISTINGUISHED PROGRAM/RESOURCES

MBA FOCUS—a comprehensive career development program introducing students to career opportunities and specific employers, and developing job search skills. Required for all first-year MBA's.

Publications—the Placement Office provides students with a professional placement handbook, called the *Career Street Journal* of job opportunities. This first-rate annual report is packed with inside information and all the facts job hunters need to know.

CAREER SERVICES

CAREER MANAGEMENT

Career Planning Program for First-Year Students	Yes
Career Presentations in the Curricula	No
Alumni Network	Yes
Summer Jobs Program/ Internships	Yes
Employer Associates Program	No
Job Search Course	Yes

RECRUITMENT

Employers Interviewing at School	235
Interviews Conducted at School	3450
Marketing to Employers	Yes
Resume Books	Yes
Resume Database to Employers	Yes
Resume Database/ Referral System	Yes
Career Fairs	Yes

CAREER SERVICES STAFF

Professional	9	Graduate Assistants	15
Support	7	Peer Advisors	—

FIRST-JOB STATISTICS AND SALARY DATA

	1993	1992	1991
Mean no. of Job Offers/Graduate	N/A	N/A	N/A
STARTING SALARY	MEAN	MEAN	MEAN
Acct/Finance	$49,090	$48,890	
Marketing	51,050	47,050	
Operations/Services	51,360	37,670	
Management/Strategy	—	—	
Health Care			
Consulting	56,330	53,000	
Operations/Production	—	—	N/A
Tech/Info Systems	48,870	46,600	
HR/LR/O. Dev/	49,170	46,500	
Public Admin.	—	—	
General Management	46,350	51,000	
Other	—	—	
Small Business	—	—	
International	—	—	

TOP TEN EMPLOYERS BY HIRES

1. Ford Motor Corporation
2. NBD Bank, N.A.
3. NCR Corporation
4. Procter & Gamble
5. Deloitte & Touche
6. Eli Lilly & Company
7. Cummins Engine Co.
8. Andersen Consulting
9. Avery Dennison Corporation
10. Kimberly Clark

STUDENT LIFE

The MBA Association enjoys almost 100% participation by students. Because the school is located in a small town, MBAA activities are frequent and popular. Clubs produce the MBA newsletter, coordinate social events and help students network by bringing in guest speakers from industry, and planning and conducting field trips in the club's particular area of interests, such as investments .

Both a popular means of transportation and a passionate hobby for many students, cycling at the University was immortalized by the Little 500 bicycle race in the movie *Breaking Away*, which was filmed on campus. Big Ten basketball and football, as well as 16 other varsity team sports, are also popular pastimes.

FACILITIES AND TECHNOLOGY

The Graduate School of Business is located on Indiana University's 2,000-acre campus. Many of the buildings on campus are constructed of Indiana limestone and harmonized architecturally, making the heavily wooded campus one of the most beautiful in the nation.

The School of Business occupies two modern buildings in the center of the main campus. Included in these buildings are a business library, an MBA lounge and eight computer-equipped labs and classrooms.

All MBA students are required to have a personal computer. All students and faculty are also connected by an E-mail system, with access to the Dow Jones News/Retrieval Service, and connections to other mainframe systems worldwide through Bitnet. B-School students are also able to use the 3 VAX 8600 computers, which provide user assistance.

SCHOLARSHIPS AND FINANCIAL ASSISTANCE

Indiana University offers more than $150,000 each year in scholarships. Thirty-eight percent of students receive some form of financial assistance. Financial assistance is awarded on the basis of academic merit, leadership abilities, work experience and career interest. Money is awarded regardless of financial need.

COMMUNITY/CITY LIFE

Bloomington Population: 60,000
Weather: Temperatures average from the high 20's in the winter to the mid 70's in the summer.

While thoughts of Indiana might bring flat plains to mind, Bloomington is set among rolling green hills. Safe and affordable, Bloomington offers 15 museums and galleries, and is something of an artists' community. Opera is a popular attraction at Indiana's School of Music, and there's a winery just outside of town. Restaurants run the gamut from Cajun to Tibetan, and if you can't find what you want here, Indianapolis is just 45 minutes away.

HOUSING AND LIVING COSTS

Unlike many other B-Schools, Indiana's Graduate School of Business offers off-campus housing that is both affordable and available. More than 70% of students live off campus, with rents ranging from $400 a month for a one-bedroom apartment to $800 a month for a three-bedroom apartment.

MASSACHUSETTS INSTITUTE OF TECHNOLOGY (MIT)

SLOAN SCHOOL OF MANAGEMENT

50 Memorial Drive
M.I.T.
Cambridge, MA 02142-1347
Tel: 617-253-3730
Fax: 617-253-6405

AT A GLANCE

First-Year Students:	226	Employer Ranking:	#4 of 61
Second-Year Students:	240	Student/Faculty Ratio:	1:5
Location:	Major City	Annual Tuition:	
No. of Employers		in-state:	$20,000
Recruiting on Campus:	160	out-of-state:	$20,000

Strengths: Operations/Manufacturing, Finance, Information Technologies. Boston location and connections. Scientific inquiry applied to management.

Distinctions: Tradition as a department growing from the engineering program in 1914. Two-week international trips for students. 600 Massachusetts companies were founded by MIT graduates.

Goals: Completion of new academic/student-life building; enhancement of new master's curriculum.

Words From the Dean: Glen Urban   Tenure: 2 years
"...Sloan is essentially engaged in a single mission: using the innovative techniques and creative thinking that come naturally to engineers and scientists to give managers the competitive edge. But you don't have to be a techie to thrive at Sloan...."

OVERVIEW

Although sometimes lost in the shadow of its Harvard neighbor on the Charles or even in its own "family" by the renowned Engineering School, M.I.T. Sloan can stand on its own merits. Exemplary offerings include a unique Master of Science degree (not an MBA) featuring rich involvement with university research centers and a combined offering with the engineering school.

The annual Study Tour to Eastern Europe provides students with an outstanding experience in educational, personal and career development. And closer to home, Boston has everything for an aspiring executive who desires to study, work and play with the best.

ACADEMIC BRIEF

Sloan's program begins with a special organizational development workshop, which students say is important because of the heavy workload and high expectations of the program.

TEAM is the name for a project that teaches students group and team-building skills. One group is building a "Sloan Disney Roller Coaster" from legos, and team members are learning to get consensus on design and actual building tasks.

KEYS TO ADMISSIONS AND APPLICATION

1-minimal   2-somewhat   3-significant

CRITERIA	IMPORTANCE	OTHER CONSIDERATIONS
GPA	2	
GMAT Scores	2	
Quality of Undergraduate Inst.	2	
Quality of Undergrad. Major	2	Interpersonal skills, leader-
Years Experience	2	ship potential and a sense of
Recommendations	3	purpose are very important.
Activities	2	
Essay	3	
Interview	2	

PROFILE OF ENROLLED STUDENTS

Number Applicants:	1,635	Mean GPA Enrolled:	3.4-4.0
Number of Offers:	337	Median GMAT Enrolled:	650
Number Enrolled:	226		

Percentile GPA ranking			Percentile ranking by GMAT		
N/A	%	N/A	N/A	%	N/A
N/A	%	N/A	N/A	%	N/A
N/A	%	N/A	N/A	%	N/A

DEMOGRAPHICS

First-Year Students	226	Women	122
Second-Year Students	240	Men	345
International Students	N/A	Minorities	60
		African American	N/A
Mean Age	28	Native American	N/A
Mean Class Size	N/A	Asian American	N/A
Mean Years Experience	3-5	Hispanic American	N/A

% UNDERGRADUATE MAJOR		% HOME REGIONS	
Arts/Humanities	N/A	New England	40%
Business/Management	12%	Mid-Atlantic	23%
Natural/ Physical		Southeast	11%
Sciences	11%	Southwest	N/A
Technical/Engineering,		Mid West	11%
Computer Science	48%	Rocky Mountain	N/A
Social Sciences/Humanities	29%	Far West	15%

ACADEMIC STRENGTHS/FEATURES*

KEY	REPUTATION	RESOURCE COMMITMENT NEXT 2 YEARS	
	A-exceptionally well known; national reputation	+ increase = same - less	
	B-well respected	RELATIONSHIP TO CORE PROGRAM	
	C-building; targeted as key area	1=Required	4=Not offered
	D-standard program	2=Elective	5=Plan to offer
	E-not provided	3=Part of other courses	

BUSINESS FUNCTION	REPUTATION	RESOURCES COMMITTED
Consulting	A	+
Marketing	A	+
Management/Strategy	A	+
Operations-Service	A	+
Operations-Production	A	+
Finance/Accounting	A	+
HR/ILR/Organizational Behavior	A	=
Technology/Information Systems	A	+
System Dynamics	A	—

SPECIAL INTERESTS	REPUTATION	RESOURCES COMMITTED	RELATIONSHIP TO CORE PROGRAM
International	A	+	2
Small Business	B	+	2
Entrepreneurial	B	+	2
Diversity	C	+	1
Communications	D	=	1
Manufacturing	A	=	2
Emerging Business	D	=	2
Family Business	D	=	4
Health Care	D	=	2
Public Administration	E	=	3
Ethics	D	=	2
Organizational Learning	A	—	—

TEACHING METHODOLOGIES	PERCENTAGE OF ALL COURSES	SKILLS DEVELOPMENT	PERCENTAGE OF ALL COURSES
Case Study	20%	Quantitative/ Technical	40%
Lecture	20%	Managerial	40%
Experiential	20%	Communication	20%
Combination	40%	Other	—
Other	—		

*Reported by Dean's Office

Massachusetts Institute of Technology

CAREER SERVICES

With a bare bones staff of two professionals and two assistants, the Career Development Office delivers significant career help for Sloan students. The comprehensive career development program follows thoughtful and orderly lines as delineated in their publication, *Career Management Guide*. The Guide is not glossy or slick like most, but its editorial content is second to none.

DISTINGUISHED PROGRAM/RESOURCES

The Sloan Alumni Network is not a passive file box or printout, but an active program that students use.

CAREER SERVICES

CAREER MANAGEMENT

Career Planning Program for First-Year Students	No
Career Presentations in the Curricula	No
Alumni Network	Yes
Summer Jobs Program/ Internships	Yes
Employer Associates Program	No
Job Search Course	No

RECRUITMENT

Employers Interviewing at School	160
Interviews Conducted at School	3800
Marketing to Employers	Yes
Resume Books	Yes
Resume Database to Employers	Yes
Resume Database/ Referral System	Yes
Career Fairs	Yes

CAREER SERVICES STAFF

Professional	2	Graduate Assistants	—
Support	2	Peer Advisors	—

FIRST-JOB STATISTICS AND SALARY DATA

	1993	1992	1991
Mean no. of Job Offers/Graduate	3	3	3
STARTING SALARY	MEDIAN	MEDIAN	MEDIAN
Acct/Finance	$55,800	$55,000	
Marketing	59,500	59,000	
Operations/Services	64,800	62,500	
Management/Strategy	60,000	60,000	
Health Care	—	—	
Consulting	75,000	70,000	
Operations/Production	—	—	N/A
Tech/Info Systems	70,000	55,000	
HR/LR/O. Dev/	—	—	
Public Admin.	—	—	
General Management	60,000	60,000	
Other	—	58,000	
Small Business	—	—	
International	—	—	

TOP TEN EMPLOYERS BY HIRES

1. McKinsey & Co.
2. Booz, Allen & Hamilton
3. Citicorp/Citibank
4. Coopers & Lybrand
5. A.T. Kearney
6. Hewlett Packard
7. United Technologies Corporation
8. Bain & Co.
9. Chrysler Corporation
10. CSC/Index, Inc.

STUDENT LIFE

About one-third of Sloan students are from foreign countries, and the school's social events reflect this diversity. Several times each semester, students from the more than 40 countries hold events that focus on the food, drink and music of their native lands. In addition, the Graduate Management Society (GMS) sponsors intramural sports, barbecues, ski trips, holiday parties, weekly Consumption Functions, the annual Sloan Follies and an end-of-the-year dinner dance. Clubs, ranging from the Asian Business Club to the Homebrewers Club (which tours local breweries and contributes home-brewed beer for the Consumption Function), are supported by students. Sloan students can also contribute to the *MIT Management Review*, one of the largest management journals in the United States.

Sloan students can take courses at several of Harvard's graduate schools, and they can enroll in double-degree programs at MIT and other universities. These options are plentiful with over 60 colleges and universities located in the Boston area.

FACILITIES AND TECHNOLOGY

In keeping with the strong mathematical/scientific focus of MIT, most buildings are numbered, not named. The Sloan School of Management is located in four buildings on MIT's East Campus, along with the departments of economics and political science. The Sloan Building houses offices, seminar rooms, a cafeteria, a student lounge and the East Campus computer facility. Additional offices and seminar rooms, as well as the Dewey Library of Management and Social Sciences, are located in the Hermann Building. Classrooms, lecture halls and another student lounge are located at Seventy Memorial Drive, with the major research centers located at One Amherst Street. While a number of the buildings have gone through some renovations, students and faculty agree that the facilities of the school are less than ideal, with small classrooms and not enough blackboard space.

SCHOLARSHIPS AND FINANCIAL ASSISTANCE

Various financial assistance programs are available. MIT has a bursary payment plan that allows students to pay tuition and fees in installments over time during their period of study. Several merit scholarships and loan programs are offered, and a few work-study jobs are also available.

COMMUNITY/CITY LIFE

Cambridge Population: 95,000
Weather: Average temperatures range from the low 30's in the winter to the mid 70's in the summer.

Just across the Charles River from Boston, Cambridge is MIT's home. The Sloan buildings have a beautiful view of the river and the city of Boston. Students from Europe comment that Boston's Beacon Hill, Back Bay and financial district remind them of home. Students also enjoy the ease with which they can get around the city on the "T" subway, and the closeness of other attractions such as Cape Cod and the White and Green Mountains of New England.

HOUSING AND LIVING COSTS

The most cost-effective living accommodation is a shared apartment, which averages $4,725 for the academic year. Students say housing for single students is hard to come by. Married students have a better chance of obtaining on-campus housing, which averages $5,670.

UNIVERSITY OF MICHIGAN

MICHIGAN BUSINESS SCHOOL
701 Tappan St.
Ann Arbor, MI 48109-1234
Tel: 313-763-5484
Fax: 313-763-5688

AT A GLANCE

First-Year Students:	426	Employer Ranking:	#3 of 61
Second-Year Students:	427	Student/Faculty Ratio:	1:19
Location:	—	Annual Tuition:	
No. of Employers		in-state:	$12,000
Recruiting on Campus:	300	out-of-state:	$18,500

Strengths: Unique MAP program in which students engage in full-time field projects inside corporations; Corporate Strategy, Marketing. Across-the-board excellence in communications, international connections, faculty and leading business practices.

Distinctions: Joint manufacturing initiative with Engineering. Diversity—25% of students represent minorities; new Michigan MBA program in Hong Kong.

Goals: Continue leadership on MBA market with emphasis on customer satisfaction, globalization and partnering with business.

Words From the Dean: B. Joseph White   Tenure: 4 years
"The Michigan MBA is leading the world in innovations by giving students the knowledge and experience that it takes to solve real business problems. We use our vast experience in executive education, in corporate partnering and in scholarship to create a unique learning environment."

OVERVIEW

There's no grass growing under the feet of this Business School, despite its pastoral Ann Arbor campus. Everyone's talking "curriculum development," but Michigan may have actually started it. Its shorter terms and courses also allow the school to respond to the needs of business in a more expedient way. The school's MAP (Multi-disciplinary Action Program) places students in live case-study situations with managers in a variety of industries. The MBA Executive Skills program allows MBA students to tap into the top-ranked Executive Education Program. And the "M-Track" Database promotes students' planning and monitoring of their own professional development. Ann Arbor's winter weather may be uninviting, but its small-town charm and big-time resources seem to make up for it.

ACADEMIC BRIEF

Each entering class is divided into "Cohort Groups" of approximately 40 students. These groups help build team skills because the students in a group are required to take specific courses together and to work together on group assignments. The full-time, two-year program consists of courses in the following areas: core courses, required subjects, field of concentration and electives. Students are also encouraged to participate in paid or unpaid internships between their first and second year of study.

KEYS TO ADMISSIONS AND APPLICATION

1-minimal   2-somewhat   3-significant

CRITERIA	IMPORTANCE	OTHER CONSIDERATIONS
GPA	—	
GMAT Scores	—	
Quality of Undergraduate Inst.	—	All of these criteria are im-
Quality of Undergrad. Major	—	portant. Every application is
Years Experience	—	evaluated in its individual
Recommendations	—	merits.
Activities	—	
Essay	—	
Interview	—	

PROFILE OF ENROLLED STUDENTS

Number Applicants:	2700	Mean GPA Enrolled:	3.25
Number of Offers:	1023	Mean GMAT Enrolled:	621
Number Enrolled:	426		

Percentile GPA ranking			Percentile ranking by GMAT		
Top	90 %	3.60-4.0	Top	90 %	680-780
Top	45 %	3.30-4.0	Top	50 %	630-780

DEMOGRAPHICS

First-Year Students	426	Women	229
Second-Year Students	427	Men	624
International Students	127	Minorities	235
		African American	122
Mean Age	26	Native American	3
Mean Class Size 60: core/40: electives		Asian American	122
Mean Years Experience	—	Hispanic American	61

% UNDERGRADUATE MAJOR		% HOME REGIONS	
Arts/Humanities	7%	New England	17%
Business/Management	27%	Mid-Atlantic	6%
Natural/ Physical		Southeast	5%
Sciences	6%	Southwest	N/A
Technical/Engineering,		Mid West	35%
Computer Science	27%	Rocky Mountain	5%
Social Sciences	11%	Far West	12%

The Best Graduate Business Schools

ACADEMIC STRENGTHS/FEATURES*

K E Y	REPUTATION A-exceptionally well known; national reputation B-well respected C-building; targeted as key area D-standard program E-not provided	RESOURCE COMMITMENT NEXT 2 YEARS + increase = same - less RELATIONSHIP TO CORE PROGRAM 1=Required 4=Not offered 2=Elective 5=Plan to 3=Part of offer other courses

BUSINESS FUNCTION	REPUTATION	RESOURCES COMMITTED
Consulting	A	+
Marketing	A	=
Management/Strategy	A+	+
Operations-Service	N/A	=
Operations-Production	A	+
Finance/Accounting	A	=
HR/ILR/Organizational Behavior	A+	=
Technology/Information Systems	A	=
Field Projects	A+	+

SPECIAL INTERESTS	REPUTATION	RESOURCES COMMITTED	RELATIONSHIP TO CORE PROGRAM
International	A+	+	1,3
Small Business	A	+	2
Entrepreneurial	A+	+	2
Diversity	A+	+	2,3
Communications	A	+	1.2
Manufacturing	A	+	1,2
Emerging Business	—	+	2
Family Business	—	—	—
Health Care	A	—	—
Public Administration	A	—	—
Ethics	—	=	1
Executive skills	A+	—	2

TEACHING METHODOLOGIES	PERCENTAGE OF ALL COURSES	SKILLS DEVELOPMENT	PERCENTAGE OF ALL COURSES
Case Study	40%	Quantitative/ Technical	30%
Lecture	30%	Managerial	40%
Experiential	20%	Communication	20%
Combination	N/A	Other	10%
Interactive TV	10%		
Other	—		

*Reported by Dean's Office

CAREER SERVICES

As expected from an elite program, the Office of Career Development reports record job offers and salaries over previous years. The Office also reaches out to employers by implementing innovative events like a New York City recruiting forum called Executive Recruiter Forum, which brings search firms from every region of the country, and a special five-day career program on "Selling Yourself in a Competitive Job Market."

DISTINGUISHED PROGRAM/RESOURCES

Use of employer and alumni advisory boards; M-track—innovative database and electronic tool for career planning.

CAREER SERVICES

CAREER MANAGEMENT		RECRUITMENT	
Career Planning Program for First-Year Students	Yes	Employers Interviewing at School	300
Career Presentations in the Curricula	No	Interviews Conducted at School	8400
Alumni Network	Yes	Marketing to Employers	Yes
Summer Jobs Program/ Internships	Yes	Resume Books	Yes
Employer Associates Program	Yes	Resume Database to Employers	No
Job Search Course	No	Resume Database/ Referal System	Yes
		Career Fairs	No

CAREER SERVICES STAFF

Professional	3	Graduate Assistants	—
Support	4	Peer Advisors	11

FIRST-JOB STATISTICS AND SALARY DATA

	1993	1992	1991
Mean no. of Job Offers/Graduate	2.5	2.5	2.7
STARTING SALARY	MEAN	MEAN	MEAN
Acct/Finance	$61,100	$53,400	
Marketing	57,350	54,400	
Operations/Services	—	—	
Management/Strategy	65,325	—	
Health Care	—	—	
Consulting	74,600	72,000	
Operations/Production	59,750	56,300	N/A
Tech/Info Systems	55,000	57,250	
HR/LR/O. Dev/	—	—	
Public Admin.	—	—	
Product Management	65,000-	58,800	
Other	—	—	
Small Business	—	—	
International	—	—	

TOP TEN EMPLOYERS BY HIRES

1. Ford Motor Company
2. General Motors
3. Deloitte & Touche
4. Proctor & Gamble
5. Coopers & Lybrand
6. Allied Signal
7. Intel Corporation
8. Chemical Bank
9. Kraft General Foods
10. IBM Corporation

STUDENT LIFE

A student governing body, elected by the student body, is the primary organization that coordinates the clubs and social activities at the University of Michigan Business School, including the spring term "Business Follies," a campus spoof. With over two dozen clubs and professional associations, Business School students are able to indulge their interests in such areas as Human Resources, Entrepreneurship, Marketing and Real Estate. Michigan also has a reputation for attracting key speakers from industries, such as Steven Jobs from Apple Computer, Inc. and John S. Reed, Chairman and CEO of Citibank/Citicorp.

Athletics are a mainstay for many of the Business School students. Following the football Wolverines is somethingt of an obsession, but there are also year-round Top Ten sports teams in baseball, basketball and swimming.

FACILITIES AND TECHNOLOGY

Officially established in 1924, the University of Michigan Business School has undergone a number of significant physical changes over the last several years. A record-breaking $15 million capital campaign has allowed the school to triple the size of the original facility. A key addition to the school is the Kresge Business Administration Library, one of the nation's largest business libraries. With over 210,000 volumes, and numerous on-line and CD-ROM database services, the Kresge Business Library supports the research and instructional activities of faculty, students and staff.

Another significant addition is the Computer/Executive Education Center, perhaps the finest facility found in a business school. This facility houses the School's Computing Center and the Cognitive Science and Machine Intelligence Laboratory, a research and support group funded by outside grants. In the Student Computing Labs, over 140 networked personal computers with associated business software and peripherals are available seven days a week to business school students.

SCHOLARSHIPS AND FINANCIAL ASSISTANCE

There are various types of fellowships, scholarships and financial assistance available. Up to five newly admitted students can receive Eli Broad Scholarships based on academic excellence. There are also general fellowships and scholarships available based on achievement, need and leadership potential.

In addition, there are a limited number of assistantships available that require ten to 20 hours of work per week. These provide a monthly stipend and carry a fee waiver for out-of-state tuition for six credits per semester. Minority graduate fellowships and assistantships are also available.

COMMUNITY/CITY LIFE

Ann Arbor Population: 100,000
Weather: Average temperatures range from the mid 20's in the winter to the low 70's in the summer.

Once a quiet college town, Ann Arbor has developed into an attractive and vital city, with many of its students opting to stay in this area after graduation. Cited as being one of the best places in the country to start a new business, Ann Arbor has much to offer its residents—from four-star restaurants to high-tech industrial parks, and from Victorian homes to the University of Michigan Wolverine football team. Being only one hour from Detroit, Ann Arbor has an international population and a cosmopolitan character, with off-Broadway theater productions, concerts and sporting events.

HOUSING AND LIVING COSTS

On-campus housing is available for both single and married students. A single room in the campus dorm averages approximately $1,676 per semester. A double room is approximately $1,440 (which includes a $280 board credit). A one-bedroom apartment is approximately $384 per month. Married students can rent a one-bedroom apartment for approximately $355 per month or a two-bedroom for $391 per month.

130

UNIVERSITY OF MINNESOTA

CARLSON SCHOOL OF MANAGEMENT

271 19th Avenue South
Minneapolis, MN 55455
Tel: 612-625-0027
Fax: 612-624-6375

AT A GLANCE

First-Year Students:	148	Employer Ranking:	—
Second-Year Students:	102	Student/Faculty Ratio:	N/A
Location:	Major City	Annual Tuition:	
No. of Employers		in-state:	$7,000
Recruiting on Campus:	122	out-of-state:	$11,200

Strengths: Human Resources/Organizational Behavior/Strategic Management; MIS and Marketing. Positive business environment of the Twin Cities.

Distinctions: Executive mentor program for all students in teams of 2—3. Board of Overseers includes 45 CEOs from the area. New building being developed. Field projects include consulting, technology or entrepreneurship tracks.

Goals: Global MBA and increased international partnerships. Expansion of career networking opportunities.

Words From the Dean: David S. Kidwell   Tenure: 4 years
"Our vision is to create a unique professional learning community that takes full advantage of our many strengths as we become one of the top five public business schools in the U.S. We are now implementing...a cutting edge MBA program, stronger community links, more student services, renewed commitment to teaching excellence, increased international activities, a more diverse student body and reaffirmed dedication to research."

OVERVIEW

In the world of public graduate business schools, Carlson is "seizing the day," having renovated its curricula, doubled its faculty size and taken advantage of the prosperous Minneapolis/St. Paul business community. Carlson appears on the rolls of most surveys and rankings as a solid program with an exceptional program in MIS. Its location is a big plus from both economic and quality-of-life perspectives.

ACADEMIC BRIEF

First-year students take core courses in areas such as behavioral sciences, financial accounting, accounting, marketing, finance and business ethics.

Second-year students concentrate on team-based consulting projects, management perspectives and elective courses. They are able to select a course of study that will fit their individual career plans.

KEYS TO ADMISSIONS AND APPLICATION

1-minimal   2-somewhat   3-significant

CRITERIA	IMPORTANCE	OTHER CONSIDERATIONS
GPA	3	
GMAT Scores	3	
Quality of Undergraduate Inst.	2	
Quality of Undergrad. Major	2	
Years Experience	3	N/A
Recommendations	2	
Activities	1	
Essay	3	
Interview	2	

PROFILE OF ENROLLED STUDENTS

Number Applicants:	645	Mean GPA Enrolled:	3.23
Number of Offers:	370	Mean GMAT Enrolled:	596
Number Enrolled:	148		

Percentile GPA ranking			Percentile ranking by GMAT		
90	%	3.80	90	%	750
70	%	3.62	70	%	675
50	%	3.25	50	%	605

DEMOGRAPHICS

First-Year Students	148	Women	68
Second-Year Students	102	Men	182
International Students	48	Minorities	31
		African American	9
Mean Age	27.1	Native American	5
Mean Class Size	25-30	Asian American	14
Mean Years Experience	1-3	Hispanic American	3

% UNDERGRADUATE MAJOR		% HOME REGIONS	
Arts/Humanities	10%	New England	4%
Business/Management	35%	Mid-Atlantic	10%
Natural/ Physical		Southeast	1%
Sciences	10%	Southwest	5%
Technical/Engineering,		Mid West	50%
Computer Science	20%	Rocky Mountain	2%
Social Sciences	25%	Far West	10%

ACADEMIC STRENGTHS/FEATURES*

KEY	REPUTATION	RESOURCE COMMITMENT NEXT 2 YEARS	
	A-exceptionally well known; national reputation	+ increase = same - less	
	B-well respected	RELATIONSHIP TO CORE PROGRAM	
	C-building; targeted as key area	1=Required	4=Not offered
	D-standard program	2=Elective	5=Plan to
	E-not provided	3=Part of other courses	offer

BUSINESS FUNCTION	REPUTATION	RESOURCES COMMITTED
Consulting	D	+
Marketing	A	=
Management/Strategy	A	=
Operations-Service	C	+
Operations-Production	B	=
Finance/Accounting	B	=
HR/ILR/Organizational Behavior	A	=
Technology/Information Systems	A	+
Accounting	A	—

SPECIAL INTERESTS	REPUTATION	RESOURCES COMMITTED	RELATIONSHIP TO CORE PROGRAM
International	A	+	1
Small Business	C	=	2
Entrepreneurial	B	+	2
Diversity	D	+	3
Communications	B, C	+	1
Manufacturing	B	=	3
Emerging Business	A	=	3
Family Business	E	=	3
Health Care	E	=	3
Public Administration	E	=	3
Ethics	A	=	1
Quality	—	—	1

TEACHING METHODOLOGIES	PERCENTAGE OF ALL COURSES	SKILLS DEVELOPMENT	PERCENTAGE OF ALL COURSES
Case Study	40%	Quantitative/ Technical	25%
Lecture	10%	Managerial	60%
Experiential	10%	Communication	10%
Combination	40%	Other	—
Other	—		

*Reported by Dean's Office

CAREER SERVICES

As it is at other business schools, on-campus recruiting by major companies has fallen off at Carlson. But Jan Windemeir and her staff have found other creative approaches to linking students and employers. The office takes a proactive approach with the job market through aggressive mailings to alumni resulting in job leads as well as telemarketing to local, medium-size companies. Several students complimented the office on its helpful, knowledgeable staff.

DISTINGUISHED PROGRAM/RESOURCES

Tight Market Tactics—an innovative program of aggressively marketing Carlson students to alumni, local and medium-size employers.

CAREER SERVICES

CAREER MANAGEMENT		RECRUITMENT	
Career Planning Program for First-Year Students	Yes	Employers Interviewing at School	122
Career Presentations in the Curricula	No	Interviews Conducted at School	3310
Alumni Network	Yes	Marketing to Employers	Yes
Summer Jobs Program/ Internships	Yes	Resume Books	Yes
Employer Associates Program	No	Resume Database to Employers	No
Job Search Course	No	Resume Database/ Referal System	Yes
		Career Fairs	Yes

CAREER SERVICES STAFF

Professional	3	Graduate Assistants	4
Support	6	Peer Advisors	—

FIRST-JOB STATISTICS AND SALARY DATA

	1993	1992	1991
Mean no. of Job Offers/Graduate	N/A	N/A	N/A
STARTING SALARY	MEAN	MEAN	MEAN
Acct/Finance	$42,013	$41,943	
Marketing	43,653	44,980	
Operations/Services	39,855	37,800	
Management/Strategy	54,725	40,410	
Health Care	—	—	
Consulting	—	—	
Operations/Production	—	—	N/A
Tech/Info Systems	39,331	35,281	
HR/LR/O. Dev.	38,425	39,672	
Public Admin.	—	—	
Other	—	—	
Small Business	—	—	
International	—	—	

TOP TEN EMPLOYERS BY HIRES

1. Kimberly-Clark
2. 3M
3. Andersen Consulting
4. Pillsbury
5. First Bank System
6. Colgate-Palmolive Company
7. General Mills, Inc.
8. Norwest Corporation
9. Philip Morris, USA
10. A.C. Nielsen

STUDENT LIFE

Minneapolis/St. Paul ranks fifth in the country as the home of Fortune 500 company headquarters, and Carlson students benefit from this through visiting lecturers, executive forums, an executive mentor program, internships and consulting projects. Students enjoy taking part in the Andersen Consulting-sponsored MBA Big-Ten Case Competition, as well as the Deloitte & Touche "Consulting Challenge" each year.

Participating in community service is important to many Carlson students. Organizations and individuals volunteer in projects such as Junior Achievement, Toys for Tots, a senior citizens' assistance program and various other nonprofit groups. Student organizations also sponsor a number of social activities and seminars.

FACILITIES AND TECHNOLOGY

The University of Minnesota is located close to the downtown areas of both Minneapolis and St. Paul, with the Mississippi River dividing the grounds into east and west banks. Classes at the School of Management are typically held in the Management and Economics Building and the Humphrey Building on the west bank. The university's commitment to enhancing the business school is evidenced by the recent initiation of a capital campaign to raise funds for a new building.

The Carlson School has computer lab facilities for the exclusive use of MBA students. These labs contain both IBM-compatible and Macintosh systems, with a variety of software packages. Students may also access the university's IBM and DEC mainframe computing facilities, and other university personal computer labs. All computers are networked to Internet for E-mail and information services, with the ability to dial in to the network from home or other off-campus locations.

SCHOLARSHIPS AND FINANCIAL ASSISTANCE

Several forms of financial assistance are available, including graduate assistantships, work-study funds and need and no-need loan programs. Fellowships are available on the basis of academic merit. Graduate school minority and disadvantaged fellowships are also available.

COMMUNITY/CITY LIFE

Minneapolis Population: 370,000
Weather: Cold winters with temperatures in the teens; summer temperatures in the 70s. Short spring and fall seasons.

Minneapolis, the largest city in Minnesota, is located about 10 minutes from the state capital, St. Paul. Together these cities form a metropolitan area of more than 2 million people, and provide numerous cultural and social opportunities, including 90 theaters, 136 art galleries and 15 museums. Professional football, baseball and basketball are available, as well as the world-famous Mall of America, a 96-acre shopping and amusement park site. Residents enjoy the winter snow at 25 ski areas and on 400 miles of cross-country trails. Also within easy access of the city are over 900 lakes, 40 marinas, three major rivers and six regional parks. Minneapolis/St. Paul boasts a low crime rate, affordable housing and clean air.

HOUSING AND LIVING COSTS

The most cost-effective living accommodation is a shared house or apartment, which averages $2,835 per person for the academic year. On-campus housing costs approximately $3,360 for the academic year. A one-bedroom apartment in the surrounding community costs approximately $4,202 for the academic year.

NEW YORK UNIVERSITY

THE LEONARD N. STERN SCHOOL OF BUSINESS

Management Education Center
44 West 4th Street
New York NY   10012
Tel: 212- 998-0600
Fax: 212-995-4224

AT A GLANCE

First-Year Students:	365	Employer Ranking:	—
Second-Year Students:	462	Student/Faculty Ratio:	N/A
Location:	Major City	Annual Tuition:	
No. of Employers		in-state:	$17,500
Recruiting on Campus	155	out-of-state:	$17,500

Strengths: Finance, International Business, Management Communication. Close links with New York business. Several awards for international business; top faculty publications in finance and marketing.

Distinctions: 1/3 of students are from outside of the U.S. The International Exchange Program is the largest in the world, hooking up to 24 programs at 20 universities worldwide. Consulting opportunities.

Words From the Dean: George G. Daly   Tenure: 2 years
"In an increasingly competitive marketplace, a Stern MBA on a resume stands for quality. It is in this spirit of increasing competitiveness—in your workplace, in the global marketplace and in the world of MBA education—that the Stern School has launched its new curriculum, invested in new technology and facilities and variously bolstered our many world-class programs."

OVERVIEW

Stern Business used to be considered the outstanding management program for part-time students. With curriculum innovation and emphasis on the "Whole Manager" (integration of communications and teamwork into classes) and the new 68-million dollar Management Education Center, you can scratch the "part-time" from that definition. Stern offers an outstanding management program for any student. Its faculty includes international stars as impressive as those of any Ivy League school and the finance program has always been top ranked. New York City—arguably the world's city for business—and Stern have a number of creative ways of working together. Washington Square with its numerous fine eating and drinking places, makes an inviting setting for first-class Stern. The Standard and Poor's survey ranked Stern second to Harvard as the source for top executives of major corporations.

ACADEMIC BRIEF

Stern's new curriculum features a 33% increase in class time and classes that meet two times a week. It contains a strong core concentration with required courses in financial and managerial accounting, macroeconomics and microeconomics.

Students can supplement coursework with experiential opportunities and electives to develop management expertise.

KEYS TO ADMISSIONS AND APPLICATION

1-minimal 2-somewhat 3-significant

CRITERIA	IMPORTANCE	OTHER CONSIDERATIONS
GPA	N/A	
GMAT Scores	N/A	
Quality of Undergraduate Inst.	N/A	
Quality of Undergrad. Major	N/A	
Years Experience	N/A	N/A
Recommendations	N/A	
Activities	N/A	
Essay	N/A	
Interview	N/A	

PROFILE OF ENROLLED STUDENTS

Number Applicants:	N/A	Mean GPA Enrolled:	3.17
Number of Offers:	N/A	Mean GMAT Enrolled:	608
Number Enrolled:	365		

Percentile GPA ranking			Percentile ranking by GMAT		
N/A	%	N/A	8	%	520-690
N/A	%	N/A	N/A	%	N/A
N/A	%	N/A	N/A	%	N/A

DEMOGRAPHICS

First-Year Students	365	Women	25%
Second-Year Students	462	Men	75%
International Students	35%	Minorities	15.25%
		African American	5%
Mean Age	27	Native American	.25%
Mean Class Size	40	Asian American	8%
Mean Years Experience	4	Hispanic American	2%

% UNDERGRADUATE MAJOR		% HOME REGIONS	
Arts/Humanities	10%	New England	N/A
Business/Management	29%	Mid-Atlantic	N/A
Natural/ Physical		Southeast	N/A
Sciences and		Southwest	N/A
Technical/Engineering,		Mid West	N/A
Computer Science	23%	Rocky Mountain	N/A
Social Sciences	38%	Far West	N/A

The Best Graduate Business Schools

ACADEMIC STRENGTHS/FEATURES*

<table>
<tr><td rowspan="6">K E Y</td><td colspan="2">REPUTATION</td></tr>
<tr><td colspan="2">A-exceptionally well known; national reputation</td></tr>
<tr><td>B-well respected</td><td rowspan="4"></td></tr>
</table>

K E Y	**REPUTATION**	**RESOURCE COMMITMENT NEXT 2 YEARS**
	A-exceptionally well known; national reputation	+ increase = same - less
	B-well respected	**RELATIONSHIP TO CORE PROGRAM**
	C-building; targeted as key area	1=Required 4=Not offered
	D-standard program	2=Elective 5=Plan to
	E- not provided	3=Part of other courses

BUSINESS FUNCTION	REPUTATION	RESOURCES COMMITTED
Consulting	B	+
Marketing	B	+
Management/Strategy	B	+
Operations-Service	C	+
Operations-Production	C	+
Finance/Accounting	A	+
HR/ILR/Organizational Behavior	B	+
Technology/Information Systems	A	=
Tax	A	—

SPECIAL INTERESTS	REPUTATION	RESOURCES COMMITTED	RELATIONSHIP TO CORE PROGRAM
International	A	+	1,2,3
Small Business	B	+	2
Entrepreneurial	B	+	2
Diversity	C	+	1,2,3
Communications	A	+	1,2,3
Manufacturing	C	+	1,3
Emerging Business	B	+	2,3
Family Business	C	+	3
Health Care	D	+	3
Public Administration	A	=	3
Ethics	B	+	1,3
Accounting	A	—	—

TEACHING METHODOLOGIES	PERCENTAGE OF ALL COURSES	SKILLS DEVELOPMENT	PERCENTAGE OF ALL COURSES
Case Study	—	Quantitative/	—
Lecture	—	Technical	
Experiential	—	Managerial	—
Combination	100%	Communication	—
Other	—	Combination	100%
		Other	—

*Reported by Dean's Office

CAREER SERVICES

The Office of Career Development is headed by Assistant Dean Michael Dalton. The Dean title is one indication of Stern's commitment to career services; another indication is the first-rate Placement Report published by the office.

Services appear traditional and well-used with the major emphasis on campus recruitment. Their new Resume Database System package is sent to all employers, as are similiar packages from Harvard, Wharton, Stanford, Sloan, Chicago and Kellogg, among other top schools.

DISTINGUISHED PROGRAM/RESOURCES

Special initiatives with entrepreneurial placement and arts/media.

CAREER SERVICES

CAREER MANAGEMENT		RECRUITMENT	
Career Planning Program for First-Year Students	Yes	Employers Interviewing at School	155
Career Presentations in the Curricula	Yes	Interviews Conducted at School	5031
Alumni Network	Yes	Marketing to Employers	Yes
Summer Jobs Program/ Internships	Yes	Resume Books	Yes
Employer Associates Program	No	Resume Database to Employers	Yes
Job Search Course	No	Resume Database/ Referral System	Yes
		Career Fairs	Yes

CAREER SERVICES STAFF

Professional	9	Graduate Assistants	2
Support	7	Peer Advisors	100

FIRST JOB STATISTICS AND SALARY DATA

	1993	1992	1991
Mean no. of Job Offers/Graduate	N/A	N/A	N/A
STARTING SALARY	MEAN	MEAN	MEAN
Acct/Finance Marketing Operations/Services Management/Strategy Health Care Consulting Operations/Production Tech/Info Systems HR/LR/O. Dev. Public Admin. Other Small Business International	N/A	N/A	N/A

TOP TEN EMPLOYERS BY HIRES

1. Citibank
2. Coopers & Lybrand
3. Chemical Bank
4. AT&T
5. IBM
6. American Express
7. Merrill Lynch
8. Lehman Brothers
9. Chase Manhattan
10. Pfizer

STUDENT LIFE

Originally located in the Wall Street area of New York City and attracting after-work students, the Stern School has been known as a "commuter" school, with a large percentage of its student population being part-time. While this situation has the benefit of bringing real-life experiences into the classroom, Stern has been working to change this image by reducing the number of part-time students. Stern also has more student organizations than most other business schools, and with more full-time students, involvement in these organizations should grow. Social activities are organized by a number of the clubs. A weekly newsletter for MBA students, the *Stern School Update*, and a student-run newspaper, *Opportunity*, help keep students aware of what's going on at the school.

FACILITIES AND TECHNOLOGY

The Stern School has taken a giant leap by moving its main facilities from the Wall Street area to the heart of the NYU main campus in Greenwich Village. The move was facilitated by a donation from Hartz Group entrepreneur Leonard N. Stern, for whom the school was named. The new 11-story building, named the Management Education Center (MEC), is said to be the most expensive building in the history of management education and boasts state-of-the-art classrooms.

Stern students utilize the Elmer Holmes Bobst Library, one of the largest open-stack research libraries in the nation. A special reference center is available in the Bobst Library to serve the needs of Stern students. This center contains a comprehensive collection of business materials, including annual reports and 10-K reports for all companies traded on the New York and American Stock Exchanges.

The Academic Computing Center provides the computing resources for Stern students. Approximately 300 386-based personal computers with a variety of MS-DOS software are available. The transition to 486-based computers will occur over a period of time.

SCHOLARSHIPS AND FINANCIAL ASSISTANCE

Approximately 30% of all students receive financial assistance. Stern offers fellowships, scholarships, graduate assistantships and low-interest loans. Part-time work is available for students who show financial need. Several scholarships are available for minority and international students.

COMMUNITY/CITY LIFE

New York City Population: 8,000,000
Weather: Average January temperature is 33°F; 74° in July.

The New York-New Jersey-Connecticut area is the largest metropolitan area in the country, and offers an abundance of cultural, recreational and social opportunities. From the Metropolitan Museum of Art to the Museum of Natural History, from Broadway shows to comedy clubs, from professional sports of every type to every type of recreational sports, New York City has something for everyone. There are activities available 24 hours a day, and a wide variety of ethnic restaurants offering food for every palate. Hundreds of companies have their headquarters in the New York area, and Wall Street is the heart of the United States financial community.

HOUSING AND LIVING COSTS

University housing is available to graduate students. Most Stern students live together on specific floors in Alumni Hall, a residence hall on Third Avenue. Graduate housing is available in various other residence halls throughout the campus. Limited housing is available for married students with families. Approximate cost for a one-bedroom apartment for the academic year is $11,424.

142

UNIVERSITY OF NORTH CAROLINA
AT CHAPEL HILL

KENAN-FLAGLER BUSINESS SCHOOL

Campus Box 3490 Carroll Hall
Chapel Hill, NC 27599-3490
Tel: 919-962-3236
Fax: 919-962-1300

AT A GLANCE

First-Year Students:	193	Employer Ranking:	#12 of 61
Second-Year Students:	194	Student/Faculty Ratio:	7:1
Location:	Small Town	Annual Tuition:	
No. of Employers		in-state:	$2,200
Recruiting on Campus:	107	out-of-state:	$9,000

Strengths: Management/Strategy, Finance, Marketing/Operations. Case-study emphasis. Considered one of top public business schools.

Distinctions: Location in the #1 area for skilled workers, as defined by *Fortune Magazine*. New building under construction.

Goals: Increase emphasis on global management. Increase innovative executive education efforts as benefits for full-time MBAs.

Words From the Dean: Paul Fulton   Tenure: 1 year
"A third factor in my decision [to accept the Dean position] is the School's tradition of strong links to corporate leaders on local, state, national and international levels. These partnerships are essential to all our efforts."

OVERVIEW

With a new Dean from the corporate world of Sara Lee and a UNC alum, Kenan-Flagler appears ready to make additional moves to insure its status as an outstanding graduate business school. The school proudly announces its "A" grades for faculty and emphasizes themes of teamwork and diversity as hallmarks of its program. It's hard to beat Chapel Hill for lifestyle or climate and it's difficult to top the majesty of the UNC campus. All in all, Kenan-Flagler is the kind of school that makes "Harvard and company" slightly uncomfortable—and perhaps more innovative than they would otherwise be.

ACADEMIC BRIEF

NCAA basketball championships aren't the only sign of excellence in Chapel Hill in the 90s. The Kenan-Flagler School of Business has risen to the top tier in almost everybody's book through a combination of outstanding teachers, a Dean with vision and connections to the growing economy of the Research Triangle (Chapel Hill, Durham and Raleigh). As a state university with an out-of-state tuition of about $8,000 a year, it is the unchallenged "best buy" in MBA education.

Kenan-Flagler also offers a variety of innovative programs that get students producing in the work world. MBA Enterprises places students with startup companies in

143

Southeast Asia and in Eastern Europe. The school is also a leader in corporate partnerships that allow students to see, hear and experience business first hand from top executives. This corporate approach carries over to the mandatory small group-study teams that are formed during the first year. In fact, "teamwork in problem-solving" is a term used a lot at Kenan-Flagler and is viewed as a unifying hallmark of the curricula. It appears that basketball coach Dean Smith isn't the only leader at UNC who sees its value.

KEYS TO ADMISSIONS AND APPLICATION

1-minimal   2-somewhat   3-significant

CRITERIA	IMPORTANCE	OTHER CONSIDERATIONS
GPA	—	
GMAT Scores	—	
Quality of Undergraduate Inst.	—	
Quality of Undergrad. Major	—	
Years Experience	—	All factors weighed equally
Recommendations	—	
Activities	—	
Essay	—	
Interview	—	

PROFILE OF ENROLLED STUDENTS

Number Applicants:	1933	Mean GPA Enrolled:	3.2
Number of Offers:	387	Median GMAT Enrolled:	622
Number Enrolled:	177		

Percentile GPA ranking			Percentile ranking by GMAT		
N/A	%	N/A	N/A	%	N/A
N/A	%	N/A	N/A	%	N/A
N/A	%	N/A	N/A	%	N/A

DEMOGRAPHICS

First-Year Students	196	Women	94
Second-Year Students	194	Men	296
International Students	N/A	Minorities	49
		African American	21
Mean Age	27	Native American	1
Mean Class Size	N/A	Asian American	8
Mean Years Experience	2+	Hispanic American	16

% UNDERGRADUATE MAJOR		% HOME REGIONS	
Arts/Humanities	16%	New England	—
Business/Management	28%	Mid-Atlantic	36%
Natural/ Physical		Southeast	32%
Sciences	10%	Southwest	—
Technical/Engineering,		Mid West	11%
Computer Science	22%	Rocky Mountain	—
Social Sciences	34%	Far West	9%

ACADEMIC STRENGTHS/FEATURES*

<table>
<tr><td rowspan="2">K
E
Y</td><td>REPUTATION</td><td colspan="2">RESOURCE COMMITMENT
NEXT 2 YEARS</td></tr>
<tr><td rowspan="5">A-exceptionally well known;
   national reputation
B-well respected
C-building; targeted as
   key area
D-standard program
E-not provided</td><td colspan="2">+ increase   = same   - less</td></tr>
<tr><td colspan="2">RELATIONSHIP TO CORE PROGRAM</td></tr>
<tr><td>1=Required</td><td>4=Not offered</td></tr>
<tr><td>2=Elective</td><td>5=Plan to</td></tr>
<tr><td>3=Part of
   other courses</td><td>   offer</td></tr>
</table>

BUSINESS FUNCTION	REPUTATION	RESOURCES COMMITTED
Consulting	B	+
Marketing	A	+
Management/Strategy	A	+
Operations-Service	A	+
Operations-Production	A	+
Finance/Accounting	A	+
HR/ILR/Organizational Behavior	A	=
Technology/Information Systems	D	+
Accounting	B	

SPECIAL INTERESTS	REPUTATION	RESOURCES COMMITTED	RELATIONSHIP TO CORE PROGRAM
International	A	+	1,3
Small Business	E	=	4
Entrepreneurial	C	+	2
Diversity	A	+	2,3
Communications	B	+	1,2,3
Manufacturing	A	+	2,3
Emerging Business	B	+	3
Family Business	E	=	4
Health Care	E	=	4
Public Administration	E	=	4
Ethics	A	=	1
Other	—	—	—

TEACHING METHODOLOGIES	PERCENTAGE OF ALL COURSES	SKILLS DEVELOPMENT	PERCENTAGE OF ALL COURSES
Case Study	16%	Quantitative/ Technical	30%
Lecture	28%	Managerial	40%
Experiential	30%	Communication	30%
Combination	—	Other	—
Other	—		

*Reported by Dean's Office

University of North Carolina

CAREER SERVICES

Mike Ippolito, with 20-plus years of corporate college relations leadership, took the helm of Graduate Placement starting fall of 1993. His impact was immediately felt with a number of initiatives for students and employers including a Resume Database System that accompanies his resume books to all recruiting employers. Graduate Placement provides high-quality counseling, workshops and referral services to its students; and with its director's emphasis on productive employer relationships, there is every reason to believe that increased numbers and varieties of employers will be frequenting Kenan-Flagler's hallowed halls in the years ahead.

DISTINGUISHED PROGRAM/RESOURCES

High quality of personal relationships with employers and students; staff visits to employers in a variety of major cities.

CAREER SERVICES

CAREER MANAGEMENT		RECRUITMENT	
Career Planning Program for 1st-Year Students	Yes	Employers Interviewing at School	107
Career Presentations in the Curricula	No	Interviews Conducted at School	3083
Alumni Network	Yes	Marketing to Employers	Yes
Summer Jobs Program/ Internships	No	Resume Books	Yes
Employer Associates Program	Yes	Resume Database to Employers	Yes
Job Search Course	No	Resume Database/ Referral System	Yes
		Career Fairs	Yes

CAREER SERVICES STAFF

Professional	3	Graduate Assistants	5
Support	3	Peer Advisors	12

FIRST-JOB STATISTICS AND SALARY DATA

	1993	1992	1991
Mean no. of Job Offers/Graduate	2	2	N/A
STARTING SALARY	MEAN	MEAN	MEAN
Acct/Finance	$48,680	$52,827	
Marketing	57,216	52,884	
Operations/Services	56,180	49,331	
Management/Strategy	58,750	56,808	
Health Care	—	—	
Consulting	63,000	60,318	
Operations/Production	—	—	N/A
Tech/Info Systems	—	—	
HR/LR/O. Dev/	—	—	
Public Admin.	—	—	
Other	—	—	
Small Business	—	—	
International	—	—	

TOP TEN EMPLOYERS BY HIRES

1. Sara Lee Companies
2. Ford Motor Company
3. Mercer Management Consulting
4. Salomon Brothers
5. Eli Lilly
6. Northern Telecom
7. Coopers & Lybrand
8. Deloitte & Touche
9. Johnson & Johnson
10. —

STUDENT LIFE

The MBA Student Association (MBASA) serves as a liaison between students and faculty and sponsors groups and events for B-School students. Clubs, ranging from Consulting to Community Service, often sponsor guest speakers and job search trips to key cities. Examples of some of the group's activities include the Alliance of Minority Business Students which sponsors activities for Black History Month and Hispanic Heritage Month and the Community Service Committee which assists in the Special Olympics and the Senior Games.

Sports are also a big part of the social life at Kenan-Flagler. The U of NC basketball team has had several final four appearances and a national title. The MBASA-sponsored Sports Committee also encourages direct participation in athletic or intra-mural teams.

FACILITIES AND TECHNOLOGY

With its brick walkways and Greek revival architecture, the University of North Carolina at Chapel Hill is one of the most attractive universities in the nation. Kenan-Flagler students currently share facilities at Carroll Hall with undergraduate students. Through a $24 million campaign, Kenan-Flagler is building a new facility to accommodate both students and staff. Slated for completion in 1995, the new building is at the south end of the campus next to the Kenan Center, which houses the school's executive education programs.

An IBM mainframe computer is accessible to Kenan-Flagler students through terminals at the B-School. Students are able to communicate with their peers at universities world wide as well as with super computers, through a number of networks supported by the computer system. The B-School also has two microcomputing labs with IBM personal computers for use by students.

SCHOLARSHIPS AND FINANCIAL ASSISTANCE

Low-interest loans are available on the basis of need. Candidates who apply to the program by February 15th are considered for merit-based fellowships. The Consortium for Graduate Study in Management is a group of nine MBA programs who award fellowships to African-Americans, Hispanic-Americans and Native Americans.

COMMUNITY/CITY LIFE

Chapel Hill/Raleigh/Durham Population: 400,000
Weather: Mild year-round climate, with lows in the 40's during the winter, and highs averaging in the 70's in the summer.

Home to three major universities, Chapel Hill is often referred to as the "Southern Part of Heaven" and the "Perfect College Town." The mild climate and low crime rate have earned Chapel Hill a rating as one of the five healthiest places to live in the nation. From its location in the Research Triangle area of North Carolina, Chapel Hill affords easy access to the state's mountains and coast, and it's only minutes away from the large city offerings of Raleigh and Durham.

HOUSING AND LIVING COSTS

On-campus housing is not guaranteed, and only 2% of the students live in university-owned housing. The most cost-effective living accommodation for a single student is a shared two-bedroom apartment in Chapel Hill, which costs approximately $2,363 for the academic year. The University Married Housing is available for married students with and without children.

NORTHWESTERN UNIVERSITY

J. L. KELLOGG SCHOOL OF MANAGEMENT

2001 Sheridan Road
Evanston, IL 60208
Tel: 708-491-2829
Fax: 708-491-5071

AT A GLANCE

First-Year Students:	582	Employer Ranking:	#1 of 61
Second-Year Students:	596	Student/Faculty Ratio:	10-1
Location:	Small City	Annual Tuition:	
No. of Employers		in-state:	$19,000
Recruiting on Campus	276	out-of-state:	$19,000

Strengths: Consulting, Marketing, Finance. Breadth of excellence crossing curriculum, faculty, research, globalism, teaching and business partnership lines.

Distinctions: Proximity to Chicago creates wealth of opportunities. Negotiations class is nationally recognized.

Goals: Continue to select a diverse class of students and to equip them with the tools they and their employers need.

Words From the Dean: Donald Jacobs   Tenure: 19 years
"...In fact, we are emphasizing teaching quality like never before. For example, all new faculty are video-taped and their teaching style is critiqued...and if business schools are to be agents of change, their faculties must be heavily oriented towards research...and the resulting insights must be funneled right back to the classroom."

OVERVIEW

Dean Donald Jacobs deserves a lot of the credit for Kellogg's long-standing reputation for excellence in MBA education. As Dean for 19 years, he maintains that the core curriculum at Kellogg is in no need of overhaul—contrary to the words and deeds of most of his competitors. Kellogg has always emphasized teamwork and communication skills along with the "hard" knowledge and skills required for a top-notch graduate education. And Kellogg has remained at or near the top in most rankings of business schools over the years. Evanston is an affluent suburb of Chicago and students in the Management School look out over Lake Michigan as well as over meadows and woods.

ACADEMIC BRIEF

From its historical position as one of the founding schools of the American Assembly of Collegiate Schools of Business to its up-to-the-minute multi-lingual explanation of "What is a Manager" in its admissions booklet, Kellogg has always been committed to first-rate management education. Faculty are encouraged to do research and, more importantly, to get results into the hands of practicing managers.

Kellogg is known for its practical MM (Master in Management) degree, which can be

149

completed in one calendar year. Most students opt for the six-quarter, two-year MBA program. Kellogg provides a number of degree options besides the MBA and MM, including Health Services, Public and Nonprofit, Real Estate and Manufacturing.

KEYS TO ADMISSIONS AND APPLICATION

1-minimal   2-somewhat   3-significant

CRITERIA	IMPORTANCE	OTHER CONSIDERATIONS
GPA	2	
GMAT Scores	2	
Quality of Undergraduate Inst.	2	
Quality of Undergrad. Major	2	Global View - 3
Years Experience	2	Leadership - 3
Recommendations	2	
Activities	3	
Essay	3	
Interview	3	

PROFILE OF ENROLLED STUDENTS

Number Applicants:	4328	Mean GPA Enrolled:	3.3
Number of Offers:	1000	Median GMAT Enrolled:	635
Number Enrolled:	582		

Percentile GPA ranking			Percentile ranking by GMAT		
N/A	%	N/A	50	%	590-680
N/A	%	N/A	N/A	%	N/A
N/A	%	N/A	N/A	%	N/A

DEMOGRAPHICS

First-Year Students	582	Women	347
Second-Year Students	596	Men	831
International Students	295	Minorities	143
		African American	58
Mean Age	28	Native American	1
Mean Class Size	50	Asian American	53
Mean Years Experience	4.7	Hispanic American	31

% UNDERGRADUATE MAJOR		% HOME REGIONS	
Arts/Humanities	—	New England	21%
Business/Management	23%	Mid-Atlantic	9%
Natural/ Physical Sciences	—	Southeast	7%
Technical/Engineering,		Southwest	5%
Computer Science	24%	Mid West	19%
Social Sciences	32%	Rocky Mountain	—
Economics	21%	Far West	14%

ACADEMIC STRENGTHS/FEATURES*

KEY	REPUTATION	RESOURCE COMMITMENT NEXT 2 YEARS
	A-exceptionally well known; national reputation	+ increase = same - less
	B-well respected	**RELATIONSHIP TO CORE PROGRAM**
	C-building; targeted as key area	1=Required 4=Not offered
	D-standard program	2=Elective 5=Plan to
	E- not provided	3=Part of offer other courses

BUSINESS FUNCTION	REPUTATION	RESOURCES COMMITTED
Consulting	A	=
Marketing	A	=
Management/Strategy	A	=
Operations-Service	A	+
Operations-Production	A	+
Finance/Accounting	A	=
HR/ILR/Organizational Behavior	A	=
Technology/Information Systems	B	=
Transportation	A	—

SPECIAL INTERESTS	REPUTATION	RESOURCES COMMITTED	RELATIONSHIP TO CORE PROGRAM
International	A	+	2,3
Small Business	A	=	2
Entrepreneurial	A	+	2
Diversity	A	=	3
Communications	A	=	2
Manufacturing	A	=	2,3
Emerging Business	A	=	3
Family Business	A	=	2,3
Health Care	A	+	2
Public Administration	A	=	2,3
Ethics	A	+	N/A
Game Theory	A	—	—

TEACHING METHODOLOGIES	PERCENTAGE OF ALL COURSES	SKILLS DEVELOPMENT	PERCENTAGE OF ALL COURSES
Case Study	20%	Quantitative/	
Lecture	60%	Technical	60%
Experiential	10%	Managerial	30%
Combination	10%	Communication	10%
Other	—	Other	—

*Reported by Dean's Office

CAREER SERVICES

Companies like the combination of "hard and soft skills" stressed at Kellogg and the Office of Career Development and Placement remains active in educating students about the value of that balance. Roger Muller, former Director at Tuck, brings an Ivy League perspective to career services delivery. Kellogg's annual report shows off salary levels and job offers comparable to those at any Ivy League school. The office also provides advanced technical resources through a PC-run Resume Database System delivered to all employers and a valuable on-line system, KelloggExek, which allows alumni to access job descriptions via modem.

DISTINGUISHED PROGRAM/RESOURCES

Recruiter Day is an impressive day-long event for recruiting organizations, combining student panels and coverage of issues pertinent to Kellogg with national MBA recruitment. The approach is casual and representatives are asked to wear a company hat or shirt.

CAREER SERVICES

CAREER MANAGEMENT		RECRUITMENT	
Career Planning Program for First-Year Students	Yes	Employers Interviewing at School	276
Career Presentations in the Curricula	No	Interviews Conducted at School	12,045
Alumni Network	Yes	Marketing to Employers	Yes
Summer Jobs Program/ Internships	Yes	Resume Books	Yes
Employer Associates Program	Yes	Resume Database to Employers	Yes
Job Search Course	No	Resume Database/ Referral System	Yes
		Career Fairs	No

CAREER SERVICES STAFF

Professional	6	Graduate Assistants	—
Support	5.5	Peer Advisors	—

FIRST-JOB STATISTICS AND SALARY DATA

	1993	1992	1991
Mean no. of Job Offers/Graduate	N/A	N/A	N/A
STARTING SALARY	MEAN	MEAN	MEAN
Acct/Finance	$60,000	$55,000	
Marketing	57,000	55,750	
Operations/Services	56,000	55,200	
Management/Strategy	—	—	
Health Care	—	—	
Consulting	75,000	70,000	
Operations/Production	—	—	N/A
Tech/Info Systems	—	—	
HR/LR/O. Dev/	—	—	
Public Admin.	—	—	
General Management	60,000	55,000	
Investment Management	60,000	50,000	
Small Business	—	—	
International	—	—	

TOP TEN EMPLOYERS BY HIRES

1. McKinsey
2. Coopers & Lybrand
3. Boston Consulting Group
4. Deloitte & Touche
5. Goldman Sachs
6. Booz, Allen & Hamilton
7. CSC/Index
8. Hewlett Packard
9. Procter &Gamble
10. General Motors

STUDENT LIFE

Students comment that the team-oriented environment, along with over 40 diverse clubs and a multitude of extracurricular activities at Kellogg, makes for a unique and fulfilling student life. Coordinating most of these clubs and activities is the Graduate Management Association (GMA), which also conducts and compiles quarterly teacher and course evaluations, as well as a faculty honor roll. The GMA produces a monthly newspaper called *The Merger* and supports Business With A Heart (BWAH), a student service organization that raises close to $100,000 each year for local charities.

Greg, a second-year student concentrating in Marketing and Finance, said that his most rewarding experience was helping to plan and run a major business conference for African-American professionals that addressed the issue of diversity in the workplace.

Wednesdays are "free days," with no formal classes being held. The GMA sponsors TGIF parties each week for students, faculty and administration at Leverone Hall, the main Kellogg School building.

FACILITIES AND TECHNOLOGY

Situated in the center of Northwestern's beautiful 230-acre Evanston campus, Leverone Hall is the headquarters of the Kellogg School. Leverone contains classrooms, a student lounge, study rooms and computer labs. The facility may be cramped at present, but an extensive $26 million renovation is underway, and should be completed soon. Students also have limited access to one of the nation's largest and most modern executive education centers, the James L. Allen Center, located on the shores of Lake Michigan.

Discount pricing for computers is available to students. There are a number of computer labs on the campus, with a variety of Hewlett-Packard, IBM-compatible and Macintosh systems.

SCHOLARSHIPS AND FINANCIAL ASSISTANCE

Approximately 68% of the students receive some sort of financial assistance. The school awards more than $2 million in institutional and corporate-sponsored scholarship assistance and low-interest loans.

The Austin Scholarship, awarded to 18 students in each class, is granted on merit. Corporate-sponsored Minority Fellowships are awarded to those who have a demonstrated leadership ability and who meet other corporate-specific criteria. Procter and Gamble Company International Scholarships are awarded to foreign students.

COMMUNITY/CITY LIFE

Evanston Population: 74,000
Chicago Population : 2,900,000
Weather: Cold, windy winters with temperatures in the teens, 20s and 30s. Summers can be hot but also pleasant.

Kellogg is located in Evanston, Illinois, which adjoins Chicago along the shore of Lake Michigan. While Evanston provides a residential and college-town atmosphere, Chicago, only minutes away, offers all of the attractions of a large city, including the world-renowned Chicago Symphony and five professional sports teams.

With its tree-lined streets and its beautiful Victorian homes, Evanston also has much to offer Kellogg students. It is the sixth largest city in Illinois, and has a number of museums and theaters of its own, along with a diversity of restaurants.

HOUSING AND LIVING COSTS

Two main buildings on campus house single and married students. McManus Living/ Learning Center is a seven-story apartment complex with 208 units. It has two computer laboratories and a common area with a VCR and kitchen facilities. Engelhart Hall has one-and two-bedroom apartments and efficiencies. Off-campus housing can be found in the Evanston area. Most rental units are within walking distance of the school. Evanston's excellent public transportation systems allow students to live further away from the school.

UNIVERSITY OF PENNSYLVANIA

THE WHARTON SCHOOL
(GRADUATE DIVISION)

3733 Spruce Street 102 Vance Hall
Philadelphia, PA 19104-6361
Tel: 215-898-4853
Fax: 215-898-4449

AT A GLANCE

First-Year Students:	780	Employer Ranking:	#2 of 61
Second-Year Students:	760	Student/Faculty Ratio:	8:1
Location:	Major City	Annual Tuition:	
No. of Employers		in-state:	$21,050
Recruiting on Campus	280	out-of-state:	$21,050

Strengths: Finance, Consulting, International, Marketing. One of the preeminent schools of management in the world, Wharton continues to lead, most notably , in the development of global strategies, programs and policy with the total Wharton program.

Distinctions: Executive education programs have always set the standards. Joint program in technology with Penn's outstanding engineering school. Has 21 research centers. Comprehensive placement program.

Goals: The Wharton School MBA program provides cross-functional intergrative training in the context of a global perspective.

Words From the Dean: Thomas P. Gerrity   Tenure: 5 years
"As the world's first school of management, Wharton has a tradition of leadership and innovation in extending the frontiers of management education. Our MBA curriculum takes that leadership into the next century."

OVERVIEW

Founded in 1881 as the world's first collegiate school of management, Wharton refers to both undergraduate and graduate programs at Penn. Wharton was one of the early leaders in "globalizing" the business curriculum. Its new curriculum requires a foreign language proficiency. Wharton maintains regional offices in Europe and Asia and is by far the largest business school in the country. Pride in teaching and a healthy respect for the past are evidenced by the handsomely framed portraits of past Deans and Professors in the black marble lobby and the restored brass and oak Stock Exchange Post dating from the early 1900s.

ACADEMIC BRIEF

During the first year, students are divided into cohorts of 60, and take core courses together. Together they experience Wharton's "new" business core, which enhances fundamental skills, knowledge and perspectives. Semesters consist of four six-week quarters which expose students to many different subjects. Students are permitted to take two or more courses from a set of six mini-electives in such areas as geopolitics, risk and crisis management, and technology. Second-year students begin with integrative cases and a management simulation game that draws on skills developed in the first year. In their second year, students must choose one of two dozen majors. They are also permitted to choose electives from any business or graduate course in the university.

KEYS TO ADMISSIONS AND APPLICATION

1-minimal 2-somewhat 3-significant

CRITERIA	IMPORTANCE	OTHER CONSIDERATIONS
GPA	3	"All factors considered significant. Relative importance varies with each applicant, depending on background and experience."
GMAT Scores	3	
Quality of Undergraduate Inst.	3	
Quality of Undergrad. Major	3	
Years Experience	3	
Recommendations	3	
Activities	3	
Essay	3	
Interview	3	

PROFILE OF ENROLLED STUDENTS

Number Applicants:	4399	Mean GPA Enrolled:	3.4
Number of Offers:	1178	Median GMAT Enrolled:	642
Number Enrolled:	786		

Percentile GPA Ranking		Percentile ranking by GMAT	
	%		%
N/A	% N/A	N/A	% N/A
	%		%

DEMOGRAPHICS

First-Year Students	786	Women	26.1%
Second-Year Students	780	Men	73.9%
International Students	303	Minorities	14.6%
		African American	N/A
Mean Age	27.3	Native American	N/A
Mean Class Size	N/A	Asian American	N/A
Mean Years Experience	3-5	Hispanic American	N/A

% UNDERGRADUATE MAJOR		% HOME REGIONS	
Liberal Arts & Sciences	30.2%	Northeast	42.4%
Business Administration	24.9%	Mid Atlantic	16.5%
Economics	20.2%	West	14.6%
Engineering	16.8%	New England	14.3%
Other	7.9%	Midwest	8.1%
		South	4.1%

The Best Graduate Business Schools

ACADEMIC STRENGTHS/FEATURES*

BUSINESS FUNCTION	REPUTATION	
Consulting	A	
Marketing	A	
Management/Strategy	A	
Operations-Service	A	
Operations-Production	A	
Finance/Accounting	A	
HR/ILR/Organizational Behavior	A	
Technology/Information Systems	A	
Other	—	

SPECIAL INTERESTS	REPUTATION		RELATIONSHIP TO CORE PROGRAM
International	A		1
Small Business	A		2
Entrepreneurial	A		2
Diversity	A		1
Communications	A		1
Manufacturing	A		1
Emerging Business	A		2
Family Business	B		3
Health Care	A		2
Public Administration	A		2
Ethics	A		1
Other	—		-

TEACHING METHODOLOGIES	PERCENTAGE OF ALL COURSES	SKILLS DEVELOPMENT	PERCENTAGE OF ALL COURSES
Case Study	60%	Quantitative/	
Lecture	10%	Technical	50%
Experiential	30%	Managerial	40%
Combination	—	Communication	10%
Other	—	Other	—
Simulation	—		

*Reported by Dean's Office

CAREER SERVICES

The Wharton School has a separate suite of offices and facility for its MBA candidates. Undergraduate Wharton students use the centralized Career Services Office. The Graduate Division occupies a beautiful new suite of offices, with 40 recruiting/ interviewing rooms. Services and programs are numerous and as of Fall, 1994, Wharton is providing all its employers with a Resume Database System along with their "Resume Box," the standard bearer in resume delivery formats.

CAREER SERVICES

CAREER MANAGEMENT		RECRUITMENT	
Career Planning Program for First Year Students	Yes	Employers Interviewing at School	280
Career Presentations in the Curricula	Yes	Interviews Conducted at School	N/A
Alumni Network	Yes	Marketing to Employers	Yes
Summer Jobs Program/ Internships	Yes	Resume Books	Yes
Employer Associates Program	Yes	Resume Database to Employers	Yes
Job Search Course	Yes	Resume Database/ Referal System	Yes
		Career Fairs	Yes

CAREER SERVICES STAFF

Professional	8	Graduate Assistants	N/A
Support	N/A	Peer Advisors	N/A

FIRST JOB STATISTICS AND SALARY DATA

	1993	1992	1991
Mean no. of Job Offers/Graduate	N/A	N/A	N/A
STARTING SALARY	MEAN	MEAN	MEAN
Acct/Finance	$57,500		
Marketing	55,000		
Operations/Services	—		
Management/Strategy	58,230		
Health Care	70,000		
Consulting	75,000		
Operations/Production	77,500	N/A	N/A
Tech/Info Systems	—		
HR/LR/O. Dev/	—		
Public Admin.	—		
Other	—		
Small Business	—		
International	—		

TOP TEN EMPLOYERS BY HIRES

1. McKinsey & Co.
2. Coopers & Lybrand
3. Goldman, Sachs & Co.
4. Deloitte & Touche
5. Mercer Management Consulting
6. Boston Consulting Group
7. Booz, Allen & Hamilton
8. Citicorp/Citibank
9. Merrill Lynch
10. Procter & Gamble

STUDENT LIFE

With over 100 professional, social and academic affairs clubs and task forces to choose from, Wharton students can participate in any activity that meets their particular interests. More than 200 guest executive lecturers and speakers come to Wharton each year and eat with students during their stay. Students can be of service to the community through projects coordinated by the Wharton Community Outreach Program.

There's a black-tie ball each spring and an informal "Walnut Walk" after mid-terms. A happy hour is held each Thursday at the MBA pub. Students also write and produce the Wharton Follies, a humorous musical satirizing MBA life.

FACILITIES AND TECHNOLOGY

Wharton occupies its own "mini campus" within the 260-acre University of Pennsylvania campus. Wharton students enjoy the tree-lined walks of this Ivy League school, as well as its historical buildings and spacious lawns.

Vance Hall is the main Wharton building, housing offices, computing facilities and classrooms. Steinberg Hall-Dietrich Hall also provides personal computer labs, offices and research centers. The Steinberg Conference Center, which is home to Executive Education and the Executive MBA program, is also available to MBA students. Wharton's Lippincott Library contains nearly 200,000 volumes specific to business and management. The Corporation File is also available with annual reports and other information on over 5,000 domestic and international companies.

Wharton students have access to clusters of DEC VAX 6400 mainframe computers, as well as over 125 microcomputers. Training courses, documentation, and user assistance are available, with many of the computing labs open 24 hours a day.

SCHOLARSHIPS AND FINANCIAL ASSISTANCE

Approximately 65% of Wharton's students receive financial aid. Government loans, subsidized loans and Wharton grants are available. In addition, Wharton awards nearly $1.8 million in scholarships and fellowships each year to more than 50% of their entering students.

COMMUNITY/CITY LIFE

Philadelphia Population: 1,688,000
Weather: Average temperatures range from the mid 30's in the winter to the high 70's in the summer.

Wharton is based in Philadelphia, a city rich in both history and cultural diversity. Towering skyscrapers are found a block away from colonial buildings, and virtually every conceivable cuisine is available to be sampled. Philadelphia is home to numerous theaters and art galleries, and is situated within driving distance of New York City and Washington D.C., as well as Atlantic Ocean beaches and Pennsylvania mountain ranges. Wharton is located in what is called University City, which includes several colleges, business and government offices, and is the largest urban research park in the nation. Students caution that safety in some areas is questionable, especially at night.

HOUSING AND LIVING COSTS

On-campus high-rise apartments are available. Campus living facilities include furnished efficiencies and one- and two-bedroom apartments for married and single students. Students can live off campus in nearby apartments and Victorian houses. Room and board for the 1993-94 academic year averaged approximately $7,750.

PURDUE UNIVERSITY

KRANNERT GRADUATE SCHOOL OF MANAGEMENT

10 Krannert Building
West Lafayette, IN 47907-1310
Tel: 317-494-4370
Fax: 317-494-4360

AT A GLANCE

First-Year Students:	130	Employer Ranking:	—
Second-Year Students:	124	Student/Faculty Ratio:	1: 2.5
Location:	Mid-size Town	Annual Tuition:	
No. of Employers		in-state:	$3,000
Recruiting on Campus	58	out-of-state:	$8,000

Strengths: Manufacturing Management, Information Technology, International Management. Location in diverse industrial area connects well to manufacturing strengths and results in opportunities for students.

Distinctions: Awarded federal grant for Business Research Center. Winners of several case competitions. Each Friday devoted to experiential learning opportunities for students.

Goals: Leadership development in the student body. Use Total Quality Management approach to assessment and progress.

Words From the Dean: Dennis J. Weidenaar   Tenure: 5 years
"What do recruiters say about us? You're likely to hear this response: The Krannert School is a no-nonsense institution where the academic program is rigorous and the students reflect the kind of work ethic that we feel is important to our company."

OVERVIEW

Quantitative and analytical skills are what this program is about. Half of the students have technical undergraduate degrees. And Krannert has a reputation for heavy classroom workloads. The school is known for its education in "Operations" and "Manufacturing" but has recently added solid courses in Strategic Management, Operations for the Service Industry and Product Management Laboratories. West Lafayette is "midwestern friendly" but only hours from Chicago and Indianapolis. It offers the right environment for both study and local entertainment.

ACADEMIC BRIEF

Purdue offers an 11-month Master of Science in Industrial Administration and a two-year Master of Science in Management. The program's curriculum is quantitative and analytical. Students say the small size of the program is conducive to learning and teacher-student interaction.

KEYS TO ADMISSIONS AND APPLICATION

1-minimal   2-somewhat   3-significant

CRITERIA	IMPORTANCE	OTHER CONSIDERATIONS
GPA	3	—
GMAT Scores	3	—
Quality of Undergraduate Inst.	2	—
Quality of Undergrad. Major	2	—
Years Experience	3	—
Recommendations	2	—
Activities	2	—
Essay	2	—
Interview	3	Recommended

PROFILE OF ENROLLED STUDENTS

Number Applicants:	1030	Mean GPA Enrolled:	3.24
Number of Offers:	326	Median GMAT Enrolled:	607
Number Enrolled:	131		

Percentile GPA ranking			Percentile ranking by GMAT		
90	%	3.75-2.1	90	%	680-320
70	%	3.42-2.1	70	%	630-320
50	%	3.20-2.1	50	%	590-320

DEMOGRAPHICS

First-Year Students	130	Women	95
Second-Year Students	124	Men	159
International Students	40	Minorities	39
		African American	29
Mean Age	26	Native American	2
Mean Class Size	40	Asian American	5
Mean Years Experience	1-3	Hispanic American	3

% UNDERGRADUATE MAJOR		% HOME REGIONS	
Arts/Humanities	27%	New England	6%
Business/Management	23%	Mid-Atlantic	4%
Natural/ Physical		Southeast	4%
Sciences	13%	Southwest	4%
Technical/Engineering,		Mid West	51%
Computer Science	37%	Rocky Mountain	2%
Social Sciences	—	Far West	9%

ACADEMIC STRENGTHS/FEATURES*

KEY	REPUTATION	RESOURCE COMMITMENT NEXT 2 YEARS	
K E Y	A-exceptionally well known; national reputation B-well respected C-building; targeted as key area D-standard program E- not provided	+ increase = same - less	
		RELATIONSHIP TO CORE PROGRAM	
		1=Required 2=Elective 3=Part of other courses	4=Not offered 5=Plan to offer

BUSINESS FUNCTION	REPUTATION	RESOURCES COMMITTED
Consulting	E	=
Marketing	A	=
Management/Strategy	A	=
Operations-Service	D	=
Operations-Production	A	=
Finance/Accounting	A	=
HR/ILR/Organizational Behavior	A	=
Technology/Information Systems	A	+
Quantitative Methods	B	=

SPECIAL INTERESTS	REPUTATION	RESOURCES COMMITTED	RELATIONSHIP TO CORE PROGRAM
International	A	+	1,2
Small Business	A	=	2
Entrepreneurial	A	=	2
Diversity	C	+	1,2
Communications	B	=	1.2
Manufacturing	A	+	1.2
Emerging Business	A	+	2
Family Business	E	=	4
Health Care	E	=	4
Public Administration	E	=	4
Ethics	C	+	1,2
Leadership	B	+	1,2

TEACHING METHODOLOGIES	PERCENTAGE OF ALL COURSES	SKILLS DEVELOPMENT	PERCENTAGE OF ALL COURSES
Case Study	45%	Quantitative/ Technical	40%
Lecture	45%	Managerial	50%
Experiential	10%	Communication	10%
Combination	—	Other	—
Other	—		

*Reported by Dean's Office

CAREER SERVICES

The Management Placement Office takes a "no-nonsense, no-frills" approach to offering students solid, traditional job search services. Resume books, seminars, individual counseling, a helpful career resource library and a job fair scheduled the day before a Big Ten football game are some of the ways the office assists students and employers. The Director, Alan Ferrell, is very accessible to students and freely gives his telephone number to all takers.

DISTINGUISHED PROGRAM/RESOURCES

Student focus groups for conducting independent job searches; productive partnerships with top executive search and outplacement company for job search expertise.

CAREER SERVICES

CAREER MANAGEMENT		RECRUITMENT	
Career Planning Program for First-Year Students	No	Employers Interviewing at School	58
Career Presentations in the Curricula	Yes	Interviews Conducted at School	1159
Alumni Network	Yes	Marketing to Employers	Yes
Summer Jobs Program/ Internships	Yes	Resume Books	Yes
Employer Associates Program	Yes	Resume Database to Employers	No
Job Search Course	No	Resume Database/ Referral System	Yes
		Career Fairs	Yes

CAREER SERVICES STAFF			
Professional	1	Graduate Assistants	6
Support	1	Peer Advisors	—

The Best Graduate Business Schools

FIRST JOB STATISTICS AND SALARY DATA

	1993	1992	1991
Mean no. of Job Offers/Graduate	N/A	N/A	N/A
STARTING SALARY	MEAN	MEAN	MEAN
Acct/Finance	$50,100	$47,100	
Marketing	48,400	45,400	
Operations/Services	46,900	47,800	
Management/Strategy	54,300	56,900	
Health Care	—	—	
Consulting	—	—	
Operations/Production	—	—	N/A
Tech/Info Systems	44,900	—	
HR/LR/O. Dev/	42,800	41,400	
Public Admin.	—	—	
Other	—	—	
Other	—	—	
Small Business	—	—	
International	—	—	

TOP TEN EMPLOYERS BY HIRES

1. Ford	6. Merck
2. Intel	7. TRW
3. Hewlett-Packard	8. Owens-Illinois
4. IBM	9. Andersen Consulting
5. Allied Signal	10. Abbott Labs

STUDENT LIFE

With the demanding workload at Krannert, students comment that time for recreational pursuits is hard to come by. Students use the Recreational Gymnasium (also known as Co-Rec), which houses numerous athletic facilities, as well as the two university-maintained golf courses.

Even with snow on the ground, business school students sponsor an annual picnic and softball game on Groundhog Day. There is a potluck International Banquet to which students bring food from the countries of their ancestors. Big Ten basketball and football are popular pastimes, with pre- and post-game business school parties.

FACILITIES AND TECHNOLOGY

The Krannert Graduate School of Management is located in the seven-story, white concrete Krannert Building, on the southeast edge of Purdue's 1,565-acre campus. The Krannert Building has most of the facilities needed by business school students, including computer labs, a library, arena-style classrooms linked to the computer labs and a first floor "drawing room," where students enjoy morning coffee and receptions. The building is linked to a pair of graduate dorms and the Purdue Memorial Union via an underground tunnel.

Purdue University

Of particular note is the management and economics library, which maintains close to 158,000 volumes and is one of the top five such libraries in the nation. The library is home to the Corporate Records Collection, which contains corporate annual reports and related filings required by the SEC, as well as an 8,000 item rare book collection on the history of business and economic thought.

Krannert provides its own Computing Center (KCC), with over 150 personal computers and 12 laserwriter printers. The labs are open 18 hours on weekdays and 12 hours on weekends, and also provide user assistance for the over 100 applications that are available. To meet its goal of remaining on the cutting edge of instructional and research computing, Krannert has integrated computing analysis into its core courses. Krannert students also have access to the University's mainframe-based computing system (PUCC), which provides networking to numerous other systems.

SCHOLARSHIPS AND FINANCIAL ASSISTANCE

Fellowships range from $500 to $2,500 and are awarded to students with distinguished academic records. There are also a number of fellowships designated specifically for minority students. Federal Stafford Loans are also available.

COMMUNITY/CITY LIFE

West Lafayette Population: 70,000
Weather: Temperatures average from the high 20's in the winter to the mid 70's in the summer.

Located in the rolling hills of Indiana, the Lafayette/West Lafayette area is home to Krannert students, as well as the 36,000 other students at Purdue University. The area is an attractive university community with plenty of recreational activities. For more cosmopolitan pursuits students need travel only 120 miles to Chicago or 70 miles to Indianapolis. Lafayette offers a civic orchestra and theater, as well as a nationally accredited art musuem. The Lafayette/West Lafayette area enjoys a stable economic base, a low cost of living and a reputation for being a safe place to live.

HOUSING AND LIVING COSTS

The university's graduate houses provide reasonably priced accommodations for single students. Rents range from $254 to $432 for rooms with private baths. There are 1,330 apartments available for married students. Efficiencies and one- and two-bedroom apartments range from $270 to $392, depending on size and furnishings. There are a number of modern, privately owned apartment complexes available off campus. A one-bedroom apartment within walking distance of the campus averages $350-450 per month. A two-bedroom apartment averages $450-575 per month.

UNIVERSITY OF ROCHESTER

WILLIAM E. SIMON GRADUATE SCHOOL OF BUSINESS ADMINISTRATION

Dewey Hall
Rochester, NY 14627
Tel: 716-275-3736
Fax: 716-275-9331

AT A GLANCE

First-Year Students:	205	Employer Ranking:	—
Second-Year Students:	205	Student/Faculty Ratio:	6:1
Location:	Medium-size City	Annual Tuition:	
No. of Employers		in-state:	$17,000
Recruiting on Campus	92	out-of-state:	$17,000

Strengths: Finance, Accounting, Operations Management. Business innovation teams bringing new technology to industry.

Distinctions: Journals of Financial Economics, Accounting and Economics and Monetary Economics are high ranking. Research Centers for Policy Research and Manufacturing Operations.

Goals: Continue committment to interdisciplinary approach and team building. Enhance faculty-peer committee on teaching, executive seminars and customized programs.

Words From the Dean: Charles I. Plosser   Tenure: 1 year

OVERVIEW

Known for its quantitative analysis and research, Simon continues to climb higher in the MBA rankings. Access to Rochester's solid economy and to headquarters of *Fortune* 500 giants like Xerox and Bausch and Lomb are pluses. Simon does a good job in team building and communications; first-year students are required to join cohort groups. Winters are arduous but activities are numerous; students play hard when they aren't studying. The Executive MBA program is exemplary in connecting students with resources and experiences offered by its program in Europe. Technology is very much in place and students both study its management and use it in their program.

ACADEMIC BRIEF

During the first year, students are assigned study or cohort teams. These teams take all of the required courses together during the first three quarters of the program.

The first-year courses are devoted to the theoretical study of the market system and the development of analytical tools, providing a general business education that is the basis for advanced study.

KEYS TO ADMISSIONS AND APPLICATION

1-minimal   2-somewhat   3-significant

CRITERIA	IMPORTANCE	OTHER CONSIDERATIONS
GPA	3	Prefer breadth in the
GMAT Scores	3	transcript. Economics and
Quality of Undergraduate Inst.	2	calculus. Looking
Quality of Undergrad. Major	2	for evidence of
Years Experience	3	professional development.
Recommendations	3	Leadership potential.
Activities	2	
Essay	3	
Interview	3	

PROFILE OF ENROLLED STUDENTS

Number Applicants:	982	Mean GPA Enrolled:	3.20
Number of Offers:	402	Median GMAT Enrolled:	604
Number Enrolled:	150		

Percentile GPA ranking			Percentile ranking by GMAT		
90	%	3.70-4.0	90	%	700-760
70	%	3.44-3.56	70	%	650-670
50	%	3.23-3.32	50	%	620-630

DEMOGRAPHICS

First-Year Students	205	Women	24%
Second-Year Students	205	Men	76%
International Students	42%	Minorities	14%
		African American	N/A
Mean Age	28	Native American	N/A
Mean Class Size	38	Asian American	N/A
Mean Years Experience	4	Hispanic American	N/A

% UNDERGRADUATE MAJOR		% HOME REGIONS	
Arts/Humanities	10%	New England	7 %
Business/Management	24%	Mid-Atlantic	31%
Natural/ Physical		Southeast	9%
Sciences	4%	Southwest	2%
Technical/Engineering,		Mid West	5%
Computer Science	22%	Rocky Mountain	2%
Social Sciences	40%	Far West	2%

ACADEMIC STRENGTHS/FEATURES*

K E Y	REPUTATION A-exceptionally well known; national reputation B-well respected C-building; targeted as key area D-standard program E- not provided	RESOURCE COMMITMENT NEXT 2 YEARS + increase = same - less RELATIONSHIP TO CORE PROGRAM 1=Required 4=Not offered 2=Elective 5=Plan to offer 3=Part of other courses

BUSINESS FUNCTION	REPUTATION	RESOURCES COMMITTED
Consulting	E	=
Marketing	A	=
Management/Strategy	A	+
Operations-Service	A	+
Operations-Production	A	+
Finance/Accounting	A	=
HR/ILR/Organizational Behavior	E	=
Technology/Information Systems	A	+
Other		

SPECIAL INTERESTS	REPUTATION	RESOURCES COMMITTED	RELATIONSHIP TO CORE PROGRAM
International	A	+	2
Small Business	B	=	2
Entrepreneurial	A	=	2
Diversity	A	=	1
Communications	A	=	1
Manufacturing	A	+	1
Emerging Business	—	=	2
Family Business	—	=	4
Health Care	B	=	3
Public Administration	B	=	2
Ethics	D	=	1
Other	—	—	—

TEACHING METHODOLOGIES	PERCENTAGE OF ALL COURSES	SKILLS DEVELOPMENT	PERCENTAGE OF ALL COURSES
Case Study	25%	Quantitative/ Technical	20%
Lecture	10%	Managerial	70%
Experiential	5%	Communication	10%
Combination	60%	Other	—
Other	—		

*Reported by Dean's Office

CAREER SERVICES

Assistant Dean Lee Junkans, formerly Director of Career Services at Duke-Fuqua, took over leadership of Simon Career Services in the fall of 1993. Employment connections to small and major companies are achieved in a variety of creative ways. Campus recruitment is stable, despite Rochester's being a difficult place to get in and out of. Career Management has always been strong at Simon, with a Job Search Course for second-year students and Career Education course for first-year students.

DISTINGUISHED PROGRAM/RESOURCES

Effective use of expert corporate representatives for resume and interview preparation. Active participation in recruitment consortia.

CAREER SERVICES

CAREER MANAGEMENT		RECRUITMENT	
Career Planning Program for First-Year Students	Yes	Employers Interviewing at School	Yes
Career Presentations in the Curricula	Yes	Interviews Conducted at School	Yes
Alumni Network	Yes	Marketing to Employers	Yes
Summer Jobs Program/ Internships	Yes	Resume Books	Yes
Employer Associates Program	No	Resume Database to Employers	Yes
Job Search Course	Yes	Resume Database/ Referral System	Yes
		Career Fairs	Yes

CAREER SERVICES STAFF

Professional	4	Graduate Assistants	2
Support	2	Peer Advisors	0

FIRST JOB STATISTICS AND SALARY DATA

	1993	1992	1991
Mean no. of Job Offers/Graduate	N/A	N/A	N/A
STARTING SALARY	MEAN	MEAN	MEAN
Acct/Finance	$54,518		
Marketing	49,955		
Operations/Services	—		
Management/Strategy	—		
Health Care	—		
Consulting	52,282		
Operations/Production	44,609	N/A	N/A
Tech/Info Systems	47,000		
HR/LR/O. Dev/	—		
Public Admin.	—		
Investment Banking	62,571		
Small Business	—		
International	—		

TOP TEN EMPLOYERS BY HIRES

1. Xerox
2. Bausch & Lomb
3. Citicorp
4. Chemical Bank
5. First Empire
6. Wells Fargo
7. Deloitte & Touche
8. Arthur Andersen
9. Lehman Brothers
10. Johnson & Johnson

STUDENT LIFE

Students can participate in a variety of graduate business clubs, organizations and seminars. Students seem to like the bimonthly lunchtime presentations called "Broaden Your Horizons," at which foreign students make presentations about their country and its traditions. There are also numerous cultural and social events including a first-year formal dinner and the Winter Ball. Simon has an intramural sports program, a school-wide ski day and a student newspaper called *The World According to Simon.* The MBA student newspaper has a reputation for influencing issues around the business school. Michelle, class of '95, spoke about how being the editor enabled her to put a lot of theory into practice from her studies at Simon.

FACILITIES AND TECHNOLOGY

Opened in the fall of 1991, Schlegel Hall is home to the Simon School. Schlegel is a four-story classroom and student-services building, with nine case-style classrooms and 21 rooms for group study.

The Management Library is located on the third floor of the Rush Rhees Library, the central library of the university's river campus system. The Management Library provides over 2,000 reference volumes and computerized access to many data sources, including ABI/INFORM and the General Business File.

Over 40 IBM-compatible and 30 Macintosh microcomputers are available in the Simon School Computing Center, a 3,200 square-foot computing center, which is networked with the school's mainframe. Electronic mail services are available to all students free of charge, and printing services for in-house and laptop computers are provided in the Computing Center.

SCHOLARSHIPS AND FINANCIAL ASSISTANCE

The Simon School's financial aid program includes fellowships, assistantships, scholarships and a deferred-tuition loan program. Merit-based aid is available and emphasis is placed on academic excellence. Limited financial aid is available to foreign students.

COMMUNITY/CITY LIFE

Rochester Population: 241,000
Weather: Winters cold with temperatures in the teens. Summer temperatures in the 70s.

Situated on Lake Ontario, Rochester is the third largest urban area in New York State, and has been rated as the ninth best metropolitan area by the *Rand McNally Places Rated Almanac*. The world leader in the manufacture of photographic, optical, dental, check-protection, industrial-fluid-mixing and gear-cutting equipment, Rochester also ranks high in the manufacture of office copiers, communications and electronics equipment, automotive products, printing and lithography. The city offers numerous cultural and recreational activities, including the Rochester Philharmonic Orchestra and the University's Eastman School of Music. Minor-league baseball and hockey are popular, as is golf, with over 30 private, semiprivate and public golf courses.

HOUSING AND LIVING COSTS

Graduate students may be housed in apartments in a large building approximately two miles from the campus. The most cost-effective living accommodations are on campus in the Goler House or University Park for single students. Approximate cost for on-campus housing for the academic year is $2,625. A shared house or apartment will average $2,814.

UNIVERSITY OF SOUTHERN CALIFORNIA

GRADUATE SCHOOL OF BUSINESS ADMINISTRATION

Bridge Hall 101
Los Angeles, CA 90089-1421
Tel: 213-740-0156
Fax: 213-747-7263

AT A GLANCE

First-Year Students:	183	Employer Ranking:	—
Second-Year Students:	176	Student/Faculty Ratio:	N/A
Location:	56	Annual Tuition:	
No. of Employers		in-state:	$15,730
Recruiting on Campus	83	out-of-state:	$15,730

Strengths: Entrepreneurship, Finance, Management and Organizational Behavior. Access to L.A./Southern California Business and entry to Pacific Rim markets and opportunities.

Distinctions: International Business concentration is strong. Students have won or placed high in national case competitions. Building an entertainment management component.

Goals: Increase minority, women and international representation. Increase experiential opportunities for students.

Words From the Dean: Randolph Westerfield　　　　　　　　　　Tenure: 1 year
"To better prepare future business leaders to manage the world in a state of flux, USC School of Business Administration has established five management issues to focus its strategic mission—technology, individual and societal wealth, globalization, and leadership."

OVERVIEW

Strong in international business, entrepreneurship and organizational development, USC Graduate School of Business is also making strides on other fronts. As a small program in a large business school, MBA students have access to extensive faculty research and expertise covering a broad range of areas. A new building is in the planning stage and a new Career Services Director has been hired. First-year students follow a very structured program but it's open-ended after that. A Management Internship is required in the second year. Students seem content largely due to a strong faculty and possibly the combination of easy access to L.A. business, Santa Monica Beach and Big Bear Mountain with skiing in the winter.

ACADEMIC BRIEF

During the first year, students must take 13 required courses that will prepare them to move into selected areas of concentration. During the second year, students can tailor a program of study to their needs and career interests. The only required course is the Business Field Study. Here, students work in teams of three to five and address and resolve a business problem through oral and written presentations.

KEYS TO ADMISSIONS AND APPLICATION

1-minimal 2-somewhat 3-significant

CRITERIA	IMPORTANCE	OTHER CONSIDERATIONS
GPA	3	All criteria are equally
GMAT Scores	3	important in judging an
Quality of Undergraduate Inst.	3	applicant. Each applicant
Quality of Undergrad. Major	3	is carefully considered on
Years Experience	3	an individual basis and
Recommendations	3	the admissions committee
Activities	3	reviews the entire
Essay	3	applicant profile.
Interview	3	

PROFILE OF ENROLLED STUDENTS

Number Applicants:	1268	Mean GPA Enrolled:	3.2
Number of Offers:	428	Mean GMAT Enrolled:	618
Number Enrolled:	183		

Percentile GPA ranking			Percentile ranking by GMAT		
N/A	%	N/A	N/A	%	N/A
N/A	%	N/A	N/A	%	N/A
N/A	%	N/A	N/A	%	N/A

DEMOGRAPHICS

First-Year Students	183	Women	29%
Second-Year Students	176	Men	71%
International Students	56	Minorities	
		African American	8%
Mean Age	27	Native American	—
Mean Class Size	36	Asian American	18%
Mean Years Experience	4	Hispanic American	7%

% UNDERGRADUATE MAJOR		% HOME REGIONS	
Arts/Humanities	33%	New England	3%
Business/Management	25%	Mid-Atlantic	5%
Natural/ Physical		Southeast	3%
Sciences	14%	Southwest	3%
Technical/Engineering,		Mid West	N/A
Computer Science	14%	Rocky Mountain	1%
Economics	14%	Far West	84%

ACADEMIC STRENGTHS/FEATURES*

KEY	REPUTATION	RESOURCE COMMITMENT NEXT 2 YEARS
	A-exceptionally well known; national reputation	+ increase = same - less
	B-well respected	RELATIONSHIP TO CORE PROGRAM
	C-building; targeted as key area	1=Required 4=Not offered
	D-standard program	2=Elective 5=Plan to
	E- not provided	3=Part of offer
		other courses

BUSINESS FUNCTION	REPUTATION	RESOURCES COMMITTED
Consulting	A	=
Marketing	A	=
Management/Strategy	A	=
Operations-Service	A	=
Operations-Production	A	=
Finance/Accounting	A	=
HR/ILR/Organizational Behavior	A	=
Technology/Information Systems	A	=
Real Estate	A	=

SPECIAL INTERESTS	REPUTATION	RESOURCES COMMITTED	RELATIONSHIP TO CORE PROGRAM
International	A	+	2
Small Business	A	+	2
Entrepreneurial	A	+	2
Diversity	—	—	2
Communications	B	+	1
Manufacturing	—	—	1
Emerging Business	A	+	2
Family Business	—	—	3
Health Care	C	+	2
Public Administration	—	—	2
Ethics	—	—	1
Entertainment	A	+	2

TEACHING METHODOLOGIES	PERCENTAGE OF ALL COURSES	SKILLS DEVELOPMENT	PERCENTAGE OF ALL COURSES
Case Study	50%	Quantitative/	
Lecture	50%	Technical	20%
Experiential	—	Managerial	55%
Combination	—	Communication	15%
Other	—	Ethics	10%
		Other	—

*Reported by Dean's Office

University of Southern California

CAREER SERVICES

MBA Career Services has a fresh start under new director Tom Kozicki. There's little evidence of a major effort to educate and counsel on job-searching techniques through workshops, publications or individual assistance. Employer contacts and connections is the name of the game. The communications with employers are well done both in terms of published information and office systems.

DISTINGUISHED PROGRAM/RESOURCES

"Just-in-Time" faxed resume referral system for recruiting employers,

CAREER SERVICES

CAREER MANAGEMENT		RECRUITMENT	
Career Planning Program for First-Year Students	Yes	Employers Interviewing at School	83
Career Presentations in the Curricula	Yes	Interviews Conducted at School	N/A
Alumni Network	Yes	Marketing to Employers	N/A
Summer Jobs Program/ Internships	Yes	Resume Books	Yes
Employer Associates Program	Yes	Resume Database to Employers	Yes
Job Search Course	Yes	Resume Database/ Referral System	Yes
		Career Fairs	No

CAREER SERVICES STAFF

Professional	2	Graduate Assistants	3
Support	2	Peer Advisors	N/A

FIRST JOB STATISTICS AND SALARY DATA

	1993	1992	1991
Mean no. of Job Offers/Graduate	N/A	N/A	N/A
STARTING SALARY	MEAN	MEAN	MEAN
Acct/Finance	$49,300	$52,000	
Marketing	47,000	48,500	
Operations/Services	45,000	43,700	
Management/Strategy	49,400	52,000	
Health Care	—	—	
Consulting	50,000	48,800	
Operations/Production	—	—	N/A
Tech/Info Systems	44,000	51,000	
HR/LR/O. Dev/	40,000	—	
Public Admin.	—	—	
Other	47,000	40,400	
Other	—	—	
Small Business	—	—	
International	—	—	

TOP TEN EMPLOYERS BY HIRES

1. Ernst & Young Consulting
2. Arthur Andersen Consulting
3. Deloitte & Touche
4. Price Waterhouse Consulting
5. Kenneth Leventhal
6. Andersen Consulting
7. Standard Chartered Bank
8. Mattel
9. Allied Signal
10. Citibank

STUDENT LIFE

The USC Graduate School of Business Administration is home to a variety of professional associations. While most of these associations focus on career areas, others serve either social or community interests. Students tutor inner-city youth, assist in the management of an organization for the homeless and provide pro bono consulting services to minority-owned businesses. The Association of Graduate Business Students coordinates a variety of social activities, including weekly MBA Pub Nights, weekend ski trips and a visiting speaker series.

FACILITIES AND TECHNOLOGY

Set on the 150-acre USC campus, and next to the site of the 1984 Olympics, the Business School consists of three connected buildings, including the I.M. Pei-designed Hoffman Hall. The buildings house an auditorium, case rooms, seminar rooms, offices, computer labs and the Crocker Business Library. The Crocker Library contains corporate reports on over 5,000 companies and a special collection of accounting and taxation materials. Because the facilities are currently shared with undergraduate students, a dedicated MBA lounge and information center was added in 1992. Plans are underway to add an additional building by 1995.

Although they have access to both mainframe and super computers, students tend more frequently to utilize the three microcomputer networks that are installed, along with the 12 satellite centers. Laser printing and color graphics facilities are available, along with a large software library and consulting services. A 20-unit Macintosh computer lab was added to the Business School in 1992. All classrooms are equipped for sophisticated multimedia presentations, and five mini-studios are available to videotape mock interviews and presentations.

SCHOLARSHIPS AND FINANCIAL ASSISTANCE

A limited number of full-tuition fellowships are awarded to top incoming students. Partial fellowships are awarded on the basis of scholastic accomplishment and academic promise. Federal financial aid is also available.

COMMUNITY/CITY LIFE

Los Angeles Population: 3,000,000
Weather: Mild year-round, with temperatures ranging from the high 50's in the winter months to the 80's in summer.

Known as a major center for international trade, Los Angeles, along with Tokyo, is one of two great urban economies on the Pacific Rim. Its Gross National Product is exceeded by only 11 nations, and it accounts for close to half of the economy of California. While not in the safest neighborhood, the USC campus is less than 2 miles from downtown L.A., and is adjacent to the city's business hub. With its diverse population, Los Angeles supports numerous and varied cultural events, and is home to world-class museums, three of which are located across the street from the business school. Students enjoy attending professional sporting events from football to hockey, and sampling the wide variety of restaurants and nightclubs available. California beaches are only 20 minutes away, and mountains for skiing are within a 2 hour drive.

HOUSING AND LIVING COSTS

University Housing reserves several apartment buildings for graduate students. Because space is limited, housing is assigned on a first-come, first-served basis. All apartments are furnished and can house one, two or four students. During the 1993—94 academic year, studio and one-bedroom apartments ranged from $519 to $599 per month.

STANFORD UNIVERSITY

GRADUATE SCHOOL OF BUSINESS

Stanford, CA 94305-5015
Tel: 415-723-2716
Fax: 415-725-1668

AT A GLANCE

First-Year Students:	353	Employer Ranking:	#5 of 61
Second-Year Students:	359	Student/Faculty Ratio:	N/A
Location:	Medium size Town	Annual Tuition:	
No. of Employers		in-state:	$19,500
Recruiting on Campus	195	out-of-state:	$19,500

Strengths: Consistently viewed as one of the outstanding programs. Leaders in the marketplace. Excellent international emphasis throughout program. Teamwork and spirit are real.

Distinctions: Students are required to have greater quantitative facility to succeed but courses are not more quantitative than other top programs. Economics faculty has Nobel Laureate. Partnerships excel with Engineering. Grades are not made public.

Goals: Core values include rewarding risk taking, commitment to personal and professional development of students, faculty and staff, personal integrity, cooperative culture and commitment to service.

Words From the Dean: A. Michael Spence   Tenure: 4 years
"The School is committed to the principle that the best managers are also good citizens who recognize the value of leadership and who will be actively involved in public service throughout their lives."

OVERVIEW

Stanford's campus is "the farm" to students, so named for its plentiful and beautiful acreage. The stated goal of the Graduate School of Business is to be the best in the world; many say it already is. The faculty is first rate and their research is widely used in businesses everywhere. The Stanford Integrated Manufacturing Association, a collaboration with 16 top companies, is a leading example. Teamwork is stressed through class projects and team competitions. Palo Alto is an expensive place to live, but it has a great deal to offer in terms of services, culture, recreation and climate. And San Francisco is just an hour away.

ACADEMIC BRIEF

Students must take 12 required core courses and can choose from approximately 100 electives. One of the new core courses is in human resources management. The core courses are taken during the first year in the program and focus on organizational behavior, political economics, accounting, finance operations, computer modeling and decision analysis/statistics. During the second year, students are required to take 13 electives and are encouraged to experiment with subjects that are new to them.

KEYS TO ADMISSIONS AND APPLICATION

1-minimal   2-somewhat   3-significant

CRITERIA	IMPORTANCE	OTHER CONSIDERATIONS
GPA	—	
GMAT Scores	—	
Quality of Undergraduate Inst.	—	Academic
Quality of Undergrad. Major	—	accomplishments/abiltity;
Years Experience	2	management potential;
Recommendations	2	diversity among the entire
Activities	2	class being admitted.
Essay	3	
Interview	—	

PROFILE OF ENROLLED STUDENTS

Number Applicants:	4500	Mean GPA Enrolled:	N/A
Number of Offers:	N/A	Mean GMAT Enrolled:	75% above 650
Number Enrolled:	355		

Percentile GPA ranking			Percentile ranking by GMAT		
N/A	%	N/A	N/A	%	N/A
N/A	%	N/A	N/A	%	N/A
N/A	%	N/A	N/A	%	N/A

DEMOGRAPHICS

First-Year Students	353	Women	92
Second-Year Students	359	Men	620
International Students	1st-81	Minorities	149
	2nd-62	African American	N/A
Mean Age	27.2	Native American	N/A
Mean Class Size	N/A	Asian American	N/A
Mean Years Experience	3.89	Hispanic American	N/A

% UNDERGRADUATE MAJOR		% HOME REGIONS	
Arts/Humanities	12.5%	New England	N/A
Business/Management	15.3%	Mid-Atlantic	N/A
Natural/ Physical		Southeast	N/A
Sciences	5.1%	Southwest	N/A
Technical/Engineering,	25.8%	Rocky Mountain	N/A
Computer Science		Far West	N/A
Social Sciences	14.7%	International	20.4%

The Best Graduate Business Schools

ACADEMIC STRENGTHS/FEATURES*

KEY	REPUTATION	RESOURCE COMMITMENT NEXT 2 YEARS	
K **E** **Y**	A-exceptionally well known; national reputation	+ increase = same - less	
	B-well respected	RELATIONSHIP TO CORE PROGRAM	
	C-building; targeted as key area	1=Required 4=Not offered	
	D-standard program	2=Elective 5=Plan to	
	E- not provided	3=Part of offer	
		other courses	

BUSINESS FUNCTION	REPUTATION	RESOURCES COMMITTED
Consulting	E	N/A
Marketing	A	=
Management/Strategy	A	+
Operations-Service	A	=
Operations-Production	A	+
Finance/Accounting	A	=
HR/ILR/Organizational Behavior	A	+
Technology/Information Systems	A	+
Public Management	A	

SPECIAL INTERESTS	REPUTATION	RESOURCES COMMITTED	RELATIONSHIP TO CORE PROGRAM
International	B	+	1
Small Business	A	=	2
Entrepreneurial	A	+	2
Diversity	B	=	1
Communications	B	=	—
Manufacturing	A	+	1
Emerging Business	—	N/A	2
Family Business	E	N/A	4
Health Care	A	=	2
Public Administration	A	=	2
Ethics	A	=	1
Other	—	—	—

TEACHING METHODOLOGIES	PERCENTAGE OF ALL COURSES	SKILLS DEVELOPMENT	PERCENTAGE OF ALL COURSES
Case Study	N/A	Quantitative/	N/A
Lecture	N/A	Technical	N/A
Experiential	N/A	Managerial	N/A
Combination	N/A	Communication	N/A
Other	—	Other	—

*Reported by Dean's Office

Stanford University

CAREER SERVICES

The Career Management Center delivers an excellent range of educational and recruitment services to both first- and second-year students. The center offers workshops, individual counseling and a well stocked resource area. The center has done a particularly good job of developing effective alliances with other business school offices in helping students integrate broader issues and services into their career planning. Examples include the Public Management Program for summer opportunities; GSB Alumni Office, Bechtel International Center for International students; the Haas Center for Public Service; and the Law School Career Services Office.

DISTINGUISHED PROGRAM/RESOURCES

The CMC Resource Center contains a comprehensive variety of media and resources/handouts that assist students in assessment and goal setting.

CAREER SERVICES

CAREER MANAGEMENT

Career Planning Program for First-Year Students	Yes
Career Presentations in the Curricula	No
Alumni Network	Yes
Summer Jobs Program/ Internships	Yes
Employer Associates Program	No
Job Search Course	No

RECRUITMENT

Employers Interviewing at School	195
Interviews Conducted at School	9,400
Marketing to Employers	Yes
Resume Books	Yes
Resume Database to Employers	Yes
Resume Database/ Referral System	Yes
Career Fairs	Yes

CAREER SERVICES STAFF

Professional	4	Graduate Assistants	—
Support	4	Peer Advisors	10

FIRST JOB STATISTICS AND SALARY DATA

	1993	1992	1991
Mean no. of Job Offers/Graduate	2.63	N/A	N/A
STARTING SALARY	MEDIAN	MEDIAN	MEDIAN
Acct/Finance	$65,000		
Marketing	60,000		
Human Services	70,000		
Advertising/Marketing/ Public Relations	60,000		
Pharmautical/Medical Products	62,100		
Consumer Products	57,000		
Diversified Products	75,000	N/A	N/A
Computer Products Manufacturing	60,500		
HR/LR/O. Dev.	70,000		
Industry/Construction Trade	72,000		
Investment Banking	55,000		
Media Telecommunicatios	60,000		
Computer Services	63,500		
Natural/Refined Resources	56,000		

TOP TEN EMPLOYERS BY HIRES

1. Bain & Co.
2. Bankers Trust
3. Booz, Allen & Hamilton, Inc.
4. Boston Consulting Group
5. CSC Index Group
6. J.P. Morgan & Co.
7. McKinsey & Co. Inc.
8. Mercer Management Consulting
9. Mitsui & Co. LTD.
10. Montgomery Securities

STUDENT LIFE

Over the past several years, students have placed more and more emphasis on community involvement, with over two-thirds of the student body volunteering in one or more public service activities each year. Students raise money for the Special Olympics and the homeless, provide food to local soup kitchens and tutor at-risk elementary school children. One student commented that "...such activities help us to keep our perspective on the most important things in life."

Stanford also boasts more than 50 clubs and committees, coordinated by the Stanford Business School Student Association (SBSSA), which allow students to pursue their interest areas. In addition to an annual Business School holiday party, there are Friday afternoon school-wide parties known as Liquidity Preference Functions. A support group, Biz Partners, exists for Business School couples and families, and organizes activities for Biz Kids.

FACILITIES AND TECHNOLOGY

The Stanford campus is 8,200 acres of oak-studded foothills, towering eucalyptus trees and Spanish-style academic buildings with trademark red-tiled roofs. The Business School, consisting of two buildings near the center of the campus, has an open look with large patios and courtyards. The main building contains lecture classrooms and offices, as well as the Arbuckle Student Center. Adjacent to the main building is the Edmund W. Littlefield Center, which houses faculty offices and seminar rooms.

The J. Hugh Jackson Library, one of the most comprehensive academic business libraries in the world, is located within the Business School complex. The Rosenberg Corporate Research Center, added in 1992, allows business school students greater access to sources of corporate information through state-of-the-art electronic resources, traditional collections and support services. The Stanford Business School supports a multi-vendor computing environment, with four mainframe computers and close to 100 Macintosh and DOS-based microcomputers. Laser printers and scanners are also available, as well as an extensive software library.

SCHOLARSHIPS AND FINANCIAL ASSISTANCE

In the past few years, approximately 65% of students have received financial aid. After a candidate is admitted to the program, the Financial Aid Office reviews the candidate's application. If financial need is established, aid is offered.

COMMUNITY/CITY LIFE

Stanford Population:11,000
Metro San Francisco area Population: 6,000,000
Weather: Mild conditions year-round, with fall/spring temperatures in the 70's, and winter temperatures in the 50's.

Stanford is located on the residential San Francisco Peninsula, midway between the San Francisco financial and banking center and San Jose's high-tech business hub. Business School students enjoy the offerings of San Francisco, only one hour away. With its ethnic neighborhoods, beautiful views and diverse cultural life, San Francisco offers something of interest to students of all backgrounds. The Sierra Nevada mountains, Napa Valley wine country and the beaches of Monterey Bay are all within a day's drive. For longer outings, students are attracted to both Yosemite National Park and Lake Tahoe.

HOUSING AND LIVING COSTS

Approximately one-quarter of the students live in on-campus housing. Student housing is assigned through a lottery system. The average cost for a one-bedroom, on-campus apartment for the 1993-94 academic year was $2,955. Other students rent apartments or houses in nearby communities. The monthly rent for a one-bedroom apartment averages $600-850.

The Best Graduate Business Schools

UNIVERSITY OF TEXAS AT AUSTIN

GRADUATE SCHOOL OF BUSINESS

Austin, TX   78712-1170
Tel: 512-471-7612
Fax: 512-471-4243

AT A GLANCE

First-Year Students:	387	Employer Ranking:	—
Second-Year Students:	403	Student/Faculty Ratio:	N/A
Location:	City	Annual Tuition:	
No. of Employers		in-state:	$3,630
Recruiting on Campus	N/A	out-of-state:	$8,580

Strengths: Accounting, Information Systems Management, International Business/ Marketing, Entrepreneurship. Innovative programs with highly credentialed faculty. Great emphasis on entrepreneurial courses.

Distinctions: Market-driven concentrations in an aggressive program putting students in constant contact with industry. Teamwork promoted through first-year cohort system. Classroom 2000 is high-tech learning at its best. Received one of only five national grants for Center for International Research.

Words From the Dean: Robert E. Witt   Tenure: 8 years
"The successful manager of tomorrow will have to creatively and analytically challenge the management assumptions and practices of today. At Texas, we are dedicated to preparing managers to succeed and lead in such an environment."

OVERVIEW

The University of Texas Graduate School of Business has a proud history dating back to 1913 and has recently shown up on most major top-20 polls. The Systematic Business Relationships program has developed strong ties with corporate giants like Procter & Gamble, 3M and Motorola resulting in innovative opportunities for students. Classroom 2000, a high tech facility, resulted from one of these grants and developed into the ISM concentration. UT students seem to be more involved in the vision and daily mission of the school than are students at most other schools. They are active in getting their ideas heard on everything from curriculum to public relations. One of the main attractions of UT is its location in Austin, the state's capital and a progressive city of 800,000, smack in the middle of the lush Hill Country of central Texas. Yankees and others are drawn to the Tex-Mex cuisine, abundant recreational opportunities, climate and surrounding lakes.

ACADEMIC BRIEF

The goal of the University of Texas at Austin is to develop managers for "the early assumption of significant management and leadership responsibilities." UT's Systematic Business Relationships Program, sponsored by Procter & Gamble, 3M and Motorola, enables students to become part of a customer-focused team while working onsite with suppliers and retailers. Students can specialize in five academic areas: accounting, finance, management, management science and information systems, and marketing administration.

KEYS TO ADMISSIONS AND APPLICATION

1-minimal 2-somewhat 3-significant

CRITERIA	IMPORTANCE	OTHER CONSIDERATIONS
GPA GMAT Scores Quality of Undergraduate Inst. Quality of Undergrad. Major Years Experience Recommendations Activities Essay Interview	N/A	N/A

PROFILE OF ENROLLED STUDENTS

Number Applicants:	-	Mean GPA Enrolled:	-
Number of Offers:	-	Median GMAT Enrolled:	-
Number Enrolled:	-		

Percentile GPA ranking			Percentile ranking by GMAT		
35	%	3.51-4.0	9	%	700+
42	%	3.01-3.5	60	%	600-690
17	%	2.51-3.0	24	%	500-590

DEMOGRAPHICS

First-Year Students	387	Women	211
Second-Year Students	403	Men	579
International Students	128	Minorities	145
		African American	56
Mean Age	26	Native American	1
Mean Class Size	25	Asian American	21
Mean Years Experience	4	Hispanic American	67

% UNDERGRADUATE MAJOR		% HOME REGIONS	
Arts/Humanities	15%	New England	10%
Business/Management	36%	Mid-Atlantic	10%
Natural/ Physical		Southeast	5%
Sciences	7%	Southwest	40%
Technical/Engineering,		Mid West	8%
Computer Science	20%	Rocky Mountain	5%
Social Sciences	18%	Far West	8%

ACADEMIC STRENGTHS/FEATURES*

KEY	REPUTATION	RESOURCE COMMITMENT NEXT 2 YEARS
	A-exceptionally well known; national reputation	+ increase = same - less
	B-well respected	**RELATIONSHIP TO CORE PROGRAM**
	C-building; targeted as key area	1=Required 4=Not offered
	D-standard program	2=Elective 5=Plan to
	E- not provided	3=Part of offer
		other courses

BUSINESS FUNCTION	REPUTATION	RESOURCES COMMITTED
Consulting	B	=
Marketing	A	=
Management/Strategy	B	=
Operations-Service	A	=
Operations-Production	A	=
Finance/Accounting	A	=
HR/ILR/Organizational Behavior	B	=
Technology/Information Systems	A	+
Statistics	B	—

SPECIAL INTERESTS	REPUTATION	RESOURCES COMMITTED	RELATIONSHIP TO CORE PROGRAM
International	A	+	2/3
Small Business	A	=	2
Entrepreneurial	A	+	2
Diversity	B	=	2
Communications	E	=	2
Manufacturing	A	=	2
Emerging Business	A	=	2
Family Business	—	—	—
Health Care	—	—	—
Public Administration	—	—	—
Ethics	—	—	—
Risk Management	B	=	—

TEACHING METHODOLOGIES	PERCENTAGE OF ALL COURSES	SKILLS DEVELOPMENT	PERCENTAGE OF ALL COURSES
Case Study	—	Quantitative/	
Lecture	—	Technical	80%
Experiential	—	Managerial	100%
Combination	100%	Communication	75%
Other	—	Group Projects	80%
		Problem Solving	100%

*Reported by Dean's Office

CAREER SERVICES

UT-GSB CSO (Career Services Office) serves both undergraduate and graduate business students at Texas but has designated special services for MBAs. The programs are comprehensive and follow a traditional career development model, assisting students in all steps and stages. The weekly Job-line lists permanent, summer and internship positions for students. A full-time librarian is available to help students with research, a service not usually provided in MBA offices.

DISTINGUISHED PROGRAM/RESOURCES

The Job Club is a unique four-week program in which students join together in goal setting, networking and job-search activities.

CAREER SERVICES

CAREER MANAGEMENT		RECRUITMENT	
Career Planning Program for First-Year Students	No	Employers Interviewing at School	355*
Career Presentations in the Curricula	No	Interviews Conducted at School	11,838*
Alumni Network	Yes	Marketing to Employers	Yes
Summer Jobs Program/ Internships	Yes	Resume Books	Yes
Employer Associates Program	Yes	Resume Database to Employers	No
Job Search Course	Yes	Resume Database/ Referral System	Yes
		Career Fairs	Yes

CAREER SERVICES STAFF			
Professional	3	Graduate Assistants	4
Support	7	Peer Advisors	0

* Includes undergraduate.

FIRST JOB STATISTICS AND SALARY DATA

	1993	1992	1991
Mean no. of Job Offers/Graduate	1.5	N/A	N/A
STARTING SALARY	MEAN	MEAN	MEAN
Acct/Finance	$48,000	$42,000	
Marketing	49,000	42,000	
Operations/Services	64,000	45,000	
Management/Strategy	50,000	46,000	
Health Care	—	—	
Consulting	51,000	46,000	N/A
Operations/Production	—	—	
Tech/Info Systems	48,000	46,000	
HR/LR/O. Dev.	—	—	
Public Admin.	—	—	
Other	—	—	
Small Business	—	—	
International	—	—	

TOP TEN EMPLOYERS BY HIRES

1. Deloitte & Touche
2. Federal Express
3. Ford Motor Company
4. Andersen Consulting
5. Arthur Andersen
6. American Airlines
7. American Management Systems
8. Dell Computer Corp.
9. Procter & Gamble
10. IBM

STUDENT LIFE

Students strive to perform well academically and in activities that benefit the school. The Graduate Business Council is a student organization that works to expand the academic and social lives of graduate students. The council sponsors events like student orientation and the Distinguished Lecture Series. It is also involved in academic, alumni and placement activities. Other student organizations and groups include: the Black Graduate Business Association, the Environmental Management Group and the Graduate Business Women's Network. In addition, students can participate in various intramural and competitive team sports. The city of Austin offers theaters, clubs, museums and outdoor activities like hiking and fishing.

FACILITIES AND TECHNOLOGY

The Graduate School of Business is housed in the George Kosmetsky Center for Business Education, a 350,000-square-foot complex of four inter-linked buildings that contain classrooms, offices, research centers and computer laboratories.

The Computation Center supports academic computing with Digital Equipment Corporation (DEC) 5810's, DEC 6000-420's, 3 DEC VAX 11/780's, 3 Vaxstation II's, ENCORE Multimax, a cluster of Sun workstations and IBM 3081/KX-48 computer systems. All computers are accessible from computers both on and off campus and are connected to each other through a high-speed data communication network.

SCHOLARSHIPS AND FINANCIAL ASSISTANCE

Loans, grants and a work/study program are available for students who are U.S. citizens. International students who have established residency and who demonstrate outstanding academic performance may be considered for limited scholarships. Some fellowships are available for minority students.

COMMUNITY/CITY LIFE

Population: 600.000
Weather: Hot and dry. Summer temperatures in 90s. Average year-round temperatures in the 70s.

The city of Austin is a busy metropolis of approximately 800,000 residents. It is a cultural and entertainment center and home to major corporations such as Texas Instruments, 3M and Motorola. The surrounding area, The Hill Country, contains many hills, lakes and rivers. Here, students can enjoy the lush natural beauty of Central Texas through hiking, camping and other recreational activities.

HOUSING AND LIVING COSTS

Adequate housing is available for both single and married students on and off campus. The most cost-effective living accommodation for single students is in the on-campus dorm. Approximate cost for on-campus housing for the academic year is $1,558. For those who live off campus, there is a free university shuttle bus, available from the neighboring area.

VANDERBILT UNIVERSITY

OWEN GRADUATE SCHOOL OF MANAGEMENT

401 Twenty-first Avenue South
Nashville, TN 37203
Tel: 615-322-6469
Fax: 615-343-1175

AT A GLANCE

First-Year Students:	197	Employer Ranking:	#11 of 61
Second-Year Students:	180	Student/Faculty Ratio:	10:1
Location:	City	Annual Tuition:	
No. of Employers		in-state:	$18,000
Recruiting on Campus	200	out-of-state:	$18,000

Strengths: Finance, Services Marketing, Operations Research. Internationalized curriculum.

Distinctions: Financial Markets Research Center is exceptional. Creative experiential programs for leadership and communication skills development.

Goals: Continue to recruit world-class faculty. Continue to solicit useful feedback from students, employers, alumni and corporate friends.

Words From the Dean: Martin S. Geisel   Tenure: 9 years
"...And we will continue to distinguish ourselves through broadening partnerships with business, expanding international educational opportunities and widening the integration of our curriculum so that our graduates think and act cross-functionally."

OVERVIEW

"Owen at Vanderbilt" is a rising star in the crowded and competitive graduate business school night. With under 400 students and a student/faculty ratio of 10:1, it can back up its statement that "interaction with faculty is the norm." Located in businesslike, yet relatively "safe and sane" Nashville, Owen offers its students diverse cultural, recreational and educational opportunities. MBA students have the opportunity to work with executives in outstanding organizations, and to acquire the combination of international, quantitative and problem-solving skills expected from a top graduate business program.

ACADEMIC BRIEF

Owen speaks the same language as Harvard, Kellogg, Wharton, Stanford, Tuck, et al. Its students are well grounded in business theory, business skills and managerial problem-solving. Mathematics competency is tested by examination during the first year and a review course is offered in August for those who need it. Owen is in step with business education trends with new courses in Customer Service and Customer

Marketing. Owen has been and is still a leader in providing students with a global perspective. Twenty years ago when the enrollment was only 94 students, 15 foreign countries were represented in that class.

KEYS TO ADMISSIONS AND APPLICATION

1-minimal   2-somewhat   3-significant

CRITERIA	IMPORTANCE	OTHER CONSIDERATIONS
GPA	2	
GMAT Scores	2	
Quality of Undergraduate Inst.	2	
Quality of Undergrad. Major	2	
Years Experience	1	N/A
Recommendations	2	
Activities	1	
Essay	3	
Interview	3	

PROFILE OF ENROLLED STUDENTS

Number Applicants:	1048	Mean GPA Enrolled:	N/A
Number of Offers:	495	Mean GMAT Enrolled:	N/A
Number Enrolled:	197		

Percentile GPA ranking			Percentile ranking by GMAT		
17	%	3.3-3.5	15	%	500-540
26	%	3.0-3.3	37	%	550-590
26	%	2.7-3.0	14	%	650-690

DEMOGRAPHICS

First-Year Students	197	Women	101
Second-Year Students	180	Men	276
International Students	84	Minorities	
		African American	13
Mean Age	25.6	Native American	1
Mean Class Size	24	Asian American	18
Mean Years Experience	5-6	Hispanic American	1

% UNDERGRADUATE MAJOR		% HOME REGIONS	
Arts/Humanities	12.7%	New England	12%
Business/Management	30.5%	Mid-Atlantic	11%
Natural/Physical	8.1%	Southeast	30%
Sciences	19.9%	Southwest	14%
Technical/Engineering,	11.8%	Mid West	8%
Computer Science	22.8%	Far West	9%
Social Sciences	14.7%		

The Best Graduate Business Schools

ACADEMIC STRENGTHS/FEATURES*

<table>
<tr><th rowspan="6">K
E
Y</th><th>REPUTATION</th><th colspan="2">RESOURCE COMMITMENT
NEXT 2 YEARS</th></tr>
<tr><td rowspan="2">A-exceptionally well known;
  national reputation</td><td colspan="2">+ increase   = same   - less</td></tr>
<tr><td colspan="2">RELATIONSHIP TO CORE PROGRAM</td></tr>
<tr><td>B-well respected
C-building; targeted as
  key area</td><td>1=Required
2=Elective
3=Part of</td><td>4=Not offered
5=Plan to
  offer</td></tr>
<tr><td>D-standard program
E- not provided</td><td colspan="2"> other courses</td></tr>
</table>

BUSINESS FUNCTION	REPUTATION	RESOURCES COMMITTED
Consulting	B	=
Marketing	A	+
Management/Strategy	B	=
Operations-Service	A	+
Operations-Production	A	+
Finance/Accounting	A	+
HR/ILR/Organizational Behavior	A	+
Technology/Information Systems	B	=
Services Marketing	A	—

SPECIAL INTERESTS	REPUTATION	RESOURCES COMMITTED	RELATIONSHIP TO CORE PROGRAM
International	B	+	1
Small Business	B,C	+	2
Entrepreneurial	B,C	+	2
Diversity	B	+,=	1
Communications	B,C	+	1
Manufacturing	A	=	1
Emerging Business	E	+	4
Family Business	E	+	4
Health Care	C	+	2
Public Administration	E	-	4
Ethics	D	=	2
Environment	-	+	2

TEACHING METHODOLOGIES	PERCENTAGE OF ALL COURSES	SKILLS DEVELOPMENT	PERCENTAGE OF ALL COURSES
Case Study	50%	Quantitative/	
Lecture	20%	Technical	50%
Experiential	10%	Managerial	45%
Combination	20%	Communication	5%
Other	—	Other	—

*Reported by Dean's Office

CAREER SERVICES

The Career Planning and Placement Office at Owen successfully strikes the elusive balance between teaching students the "self-directed job search" and building personal relationships with employers, that significantly enhance students' career opportunities. Peter Veruki, Director, brings his varied background in corporate recruiting, university publishing and career planning and placement to bear on the design and delivery of career services.

The Career Planning and Placement Office is particularly successful in integrating career management with the larger Owen mission through a required four-session course for all first-year students as well as pre-enrollment planning sessions with prospective students. Veruki emphasizes that the student needs to be responsible for assessing and determining the right "person-opportunity fit." The office is miles ahead in cultivating contacts with smaller employers who do not desire to interview on campus.

DISTINGUISHED PROGRAM/RESOURCES

Profiles of Owen—a slick, substantial publication for all employers containing helpful recruiting "gab" but also a unique section of mini-student profiles with bulleted points, photos and career goals.

MBA Career Management Guidebook—an outstanding career guide for MBAs.

CAREER SERVICES

CAREER MANAGEMENT		RECRUITMENT	
Career Planning Program for First-Year Students	Yes	Employers Interviewing at School	200
Career Presentations in the Curricula	No	Interviews Conducted at School	12,000
Alumni Network	Yes	Marketing to Employers	Yes
Summer Jobs Program/ Internships	Yes	Resume Books	Yes
Employer Associates Program	Yes	Resume Database to Employers	Yes
Job Search Course	Yes	Resume Database/ Referral System	Yes
		Career Fairs	Yes

CAREER SERVICES STAFF

Professional	3	Graduate Assistants	0
Support	2	Peer Advisors	0

	1993	1992	1991
Mean no. of Job Offers/Graduate	267	198	201
STARTING SALARY	MEAN	MEAN	MEAN
Acct/Finance	$44,244	$39,410	
Marketing	46,118	43,980	
Operations/Services	—	—	
Management/Strategy	52,222	46,312	
Health Care	—	—	
Consulting	48,483	50,727	
Operations/Production	41,846	45,866	N/A
Tech/Info Systems	—	32,500	
HR/LR/O. Dev.	41,118	43,714	
Public Admin.	—	—	
Commercial Banking	39,438	—	
Investment Banking	68,053	53,111	
Small Business	—	—	
International	—	—	

TOP TEN EMPLOYERS BY HIRES

1. Andersen Consulting
2. Northern Telecom
3. Ernst & Young
4. Deloitte & Touche
5. Sara Lee Meats
6. Taco Bell
7. HCM
8. Coopers & Lybrand
9. GE
10. American Airlines

STUDENT LIFE

The small school atmosphere lends itself to a cooperative feeling among students. Students have the opportunity to lead in a wide range of groups and activities, including management of the Owen Lecture Series and the Owen Business Projects Group, a student-run consulting group for small local businesses.

Social activities are plentiful and include the usual mixers, social hours, flings and follies that characterize graduate student life. The Owen School Student Association sponsors a "Keg-in-the-Courtyard" party each Thursday evening—and students are grateful there are no classes on Fridays.

Athletic recreation has been enhanced significantly since the opening of a $14 million university recreation center, located just blocks away from the Owen School.

FACILITIES AND TECHNOLOGY

Owen is housed in Management Hall, a modern structure built in 1982 that has been merged with the Victorian Gothic "Old Mechanical," built for engineering students in 1888. Management Hall contains a central courtyard visible from all floors that provides an open environment for social and serious gatherings. The building's blend of Victorian Gothic and modern design makes for a unique and pleasing facility.

Because there is no undergraduate business program at Vanderbilt, Owen students have complete use of all the facilities of Management Hall, including seminar rooms, lounges, a computer lab and the Walker Management Library. Both the Walker Management Library and the Heard University Library provide graduate business students with extensive print and electronic resources. Computer facilities available in Management Hall include a variety of IBM-compatible and Macintosh personal computers. Scanners, laser and ink-jet printers, and plotters are also available. All of the computers are networked to the University's VAX 6620 and provide students with Bitnet, Internet and all university databases.

SCHOLARSHIPS AND FINANCIAL ASSISTANCE

The Owen School offers a full range of financial assistance programs. Last year, more than 100 scholarships and fellowships were awarded to first-year students. Approximately two out of every three students receive some form of financial aid, and 95% of all financial aid applicants receive assistance. Owen has allotted more than $1,300,000 for MBA scholarships for the 1993-94 year.

COMMUNITY/CITY LIFE

Nashville Population: 455,000
Weather: Hot summers. Mild the rest of the year. Year-round temperatures average is in the 70s.

Nashville, Tennessee ("Music City USA" or "the Athens of the South," depending upon your cultural leanings) is a metropolitan area and home to several Fortune 1000 companies. Students enjoy the balance between city and country. The climate is decidedly southern ("oppressively humid summers" and "almost heaven" the rest of the year). Nashville claims to lie within 600 miles of 50% of the population of the U.S. Its strong economy supports international giants like Northern Telecom and Bridgestone as well as a variety of small businesses. Vanderbilt University and Nashville appreciate their close ties in commerce and culture.

HOUSING AND LIVING COSTS

Campus housing is available for both single and married students. Approximately 10% of Owen students live on campus. The cost for on-campus housing in the 1993—94 academic year averages $200-650 per month, depending on location. Surrounding neighborhoods provide a wide range of choices for off-campus living. Rentals range from $300-450 per month for an efficiency, $350-575 for a one-bedroom apartment and $450+ for a two-bedroom apartment.

UNIVERSITY OF VIRGINIA

DARDEN GRADUATE SCHOOL
OF BUSINESS ADMINISTRATION

Box 6550
Charlottesville, VA   22906-6550
Tel: 804-924-3900
Fax: 804-924-4859

AT A GLANCE

First-Year Students:	251	Employer Ranking:	#5 of 61
Second-Year Students:	224	Student/Faculty Ratio:	8:1
Location:	Large Town	Annual Tuition:	
No. of Employers		in-state:	$7,000
Recruiting on Campus	150	out-of-state:	$15,000

Strengths: Ethics, Leadership Strategy; emphasis on case method pedagogy; teaching excellence.

Distinctions: Ethics, Management Strategy; action-oriented, applied teaching and research, well-connected to business interests.

Goals: New facilities in 1995 will reflect Jefferson's academic village concept as exists on the main campus (called "grounds"); increase balance between scholarship and teaching; international partnerships

Words From the Dean: Leo I. Higdon   Tenure: 2 years
"...the Darden School MBA program has always been designed as a unified curriculum rather than a collection of courses. Our MBA program has been recognized for this general management orientation, and is further distinguished by its courses in ethics and communications."

OVERVIEW

With a number of former Harvard faculty members, emphasis on "cases" and heavy workloads, Darden continues to move toward the top ranks of business schools. Its relatively small class size allows students a more personal, less competitive education, which is loudly applauded by its students. Group study is also very big as "cracking the case" is an ongoing theme—on and off campus. The Strategy, Leadership and Change course does a great job of tying things together in the second year as does the required Directed Study. Darden is located a mile or so from Thomas Jefferson's historic and inspiring campus, so you won't be able to stroll by Edgar Allen Poe's room on "the Lawn" between classes. Charlottesville is full of history, charm and country living.

ACADEMIC BRIEF

The first year of study combines general management programs and a required course in ethics. The second year allows students to select from a group of courses called Core Electives. These courses allow students to develop their interests in specific areas such as accounting, finance, marketing and business policy. This structure allows students to develop a strict, focused program or to design a broad one. Darden is also noted for its self-evaluated groups where peers evaluate and grade each other in select courses. Teamwork, cooperation, sensitivity and honest communication/feedback are some of the skills built through this process.

KEYS TO ADMISSIONS AND APPLICATION

1-minimal 2-somewhat 3-significant

CRITERIA	IMPORTANCE	OTHER CONSIDERATIONS
GPA	2	
GMAT Scores	2	
Quality of Undergraduate Inst.	1	
Quality of Undergrad. Major	1	
Years Experience	2	N/A
Recommendations	2	
Activities	2	
Essay	3	
Interview	3	

PROFILE OF ENROLLED STUDENTS

Number Applicants:	2192	Mean GPA Enrolled:	3.9
Number of Offers:	564	Mean GMAT Enrolled:	627
Number Enrolled:	252		

Percentile GPA ranking			Percentile ranking by GMAT		
18	%	2.5-2.9	27	%	500-590
40	%	3.0-3.49	53	%	600-690
18	%	3.5-4.0	15	%	700-790

DEMOGRAPHICS

First-Year Students	251	Women	162
Second-Year Students	224	Men	314
International Students	71	Minorities	73
		African American	31
Mean Age	27	Native American	2
Mean Class Size	N/A	Asian American	28
Mean Years Experience	4-6	Hispanic American	12

% UNDERGRADUATE MAJOR		% HOME REGIONS	
Arts/Humanities	15%	New England	15%
Business/Management	28%	Mid-Atlantic	45%
Natural/ Physical		Southeast	8%
Sciences	23%	Southwest	2%
Technical/Engineering,		Mid West	6%
Computer Science	23%	Rocky Mountain	N/A
Social Sciences	34%	Far West	10%

The Best Graduate Business Schools

ACADEMIC STRENGTHS/FEATURES*

K E Y	REPUTATION	RESOURCE COMMITMENT NEXT 2 YEARS
	A-exceptionally well known; national reputation	+ increase = same - less
	B-well respected	RELATIONSHIP TO CORE PROGRAM
	C-building; targeted as key area	1=Required 4=Not offered
	D-standard program	2=Elective 5=Plan to
	E-not provided	3=Part of offer other courses

BUSINESS FUNCTION	REPUTATION	RESOURCES COMMITTED
Consulting	E	=
Marketing	B	=
Management/Strategy	B	+
Operations-Service	B	=
Operations-Production	B	=
Finance/Accounting	A	=
HR/ILR/Organizational Behavior	B	=
Technology/Information Systems	E	=
Other	—	—

SPECIAL INTERESTS	REPUTATION	RESOURCES COMMITTED	RELATIONSHIP TO CORE PROGRAM
International	B	+	2
Small Business	B	=	2
Entrepreneurial	B	=	2
Diversity	—	—	—
Communications	A	=	1,2
Manufacturing	N/A	=	1,2
Emerging Business	N/A	=	2
Family Business	N/A	=	2
Health Care	N/A	=	2
Public Administration	N/A	=	1,2
Ethics	A	—	1,2
Other	—	—	—

TEACHING METHODOLOGIES	PERCENTAGE OF ALL COURSES	SKILLS DEVELOPMENT	PERCENTAGE OF ALL COURSES
Case Study	60%	Quantitative/	
Lecture	15%	Technical	30%
Experiential	10%	Managerial	50%
Combination	25%	Communication	20%
Other	—	Other	—

*Reported by Dean's Office

CAREER SERVICES

Career Services at Darden are comprehensive and based on solid career management concepts. The staff includes professionals with both counseling and business expertise—just the right combination for working with graduate business students. Services include a resume database referral system for employers, well-written publications on career transition and a nationally recognized West Coast Job Fair in San Francisco.

DISTINGUISHED PROGRAM/RESOURCES

Required Career Management Course—taken by more than 100 first-year students, this course provides students with strategies for intelligently setting goals and teaches career-search skills.

CAREER SERVICES

CAREER MANAGEMENT		RECRUITMENT	
Career Planning Program for First-Year Students	Yes	Employers Interviewing at School	150
Career Presentations in the Curricula	No	Interviews Conducted at School	N/A
Alumni Network	Yes	Marketing to Employers	Yes
Summer Jobs Program/ Internships	Yes	Resume Books	Yes
Employer Associates Program	Yes	Resume Database to Employers	Yes
Job Search Course	Yes	Resume Database/ Referral System	Yes
		Career Fairs	Yes

CAREER SERVICES STAFF

Professional	3	Graduate Assistants	0
Support	5	Peer Advisors	0

FIRST-JOB STATISTICS AND SALARY DATA

	1993	1992	1991
Mean no. of Job Offers/Graduate	1.5	1.5	1.7
STARTING SALARY	MEAN	MEAN	MEAN
Acct/Finance	$66,600	$59,800	
Marketing	55,200	60,000	
Operations/Services	57,000	58,500	
Management/Strategy	62,500	58,000	
Health Care	—	—	
Consulting	71,000	69,700	
Operations/Production	—	—	N/A
Tech/Info SysTems	57,500	55,500	
HR/LR/O. Dev.	—	55,500	
Public Admin.	—	—	
General Mangement	62,500	60,500	
Other	—	—	
Small Business	—	—	
International	—	—	

TOP TEN EMPLOYERS BY HIRES

1. Coopers & Lybrand
2. Carrier Corporation
3. A.T.&T. Company
4. Boston Consulting
5. Citibank N/A
6. Gemini Consulting
7. MBA Enterprise Corporation
8. Allied Signal
9. Booz, Allen & Hamilton, Inc.
10. Chase Manhattan Corporation

STUDENT LIFE

With the challenging pace of studies at Darden, one would think there would be little time for non-classroom-related work. It's all a matter of time management, say Darden students. Beginning with the Dean's receptions at the start of each year, students develop a sense of camaraderie, a feeling of "...we're all in this together." Students are also able to get acquainted with the faculty during the daily 9:25 coffee break and in casual games of basketball. In addition to numerous clubs that provide the opportunity to pursue a variety of interests, many Darden students volunteer through Darden Outreach, the school's community service umbrella, and Opportunity Consultants, Inc., a nonprofit corporation of students assisting small businesses in solving management problems.

FACILITIES AND TECHNOLOGY

Located on the North Grounds of the University of Virginia's campus, Darden is part of a complex that also includes the Law School and the Judge Advocate General's

School. Designed by Thomas Jefferson in 1819, the university's original campus has been designated as one of the ten most significant architectural structures built in the first 200 years of the nation's history by the American Institute of Architecture. While the current Darden facilities do not follow this architecture, a new building, scheduled for completion in 1994, was inspired by the original buildings. The current Darden facility, located about a mile from the central university grounds, houses ten case-method classrooms, seminar and study rooms and the Camp Library, which contains research collections in both business and economics.

Over 175 microcomputers at Darden are networked together and are linked to three VAX 4000 minicomputers. The school's computer lab contains 24 personal computers and 5 laser printers for student use. Darden students can also access the University's RS6000 minicomputers and an IBM 3090 through the Darden network. Each classroom contains a microcomputer that connects to a large-screen projector.

SCHOLARSHIPS AND FINANCIAL ASSISTANCE

Darden awards scholarships based on financial need and academic, personal and professional merit. Various educational loan programs are available to students, including Perkins Loans, Stafford Loans and the Supplemental/Plus Loan Program. Darden also receives corporate gifts that support the Minority Fellowship program from such sponsors as Bristol-Myers Squibb, CIGNA, Citibank and Exxon.

COMMUNITY/CITY LIFE

Charlottesville Population: 45,000
Weather: Hot summers. Humid, mild winters. Ideal in fall and spring.

Located near the foothills of the Blue Ridge Mountains and the Shenandoah Valley, Charlottesville is the quintessential college town. There is no problem with crime in this town, and the cost of living is lower than at many other business schools. Horseback riding and skiing are popular pastimes. Charlottesville is located only two hours away from Washington, D.C., and only three hours away from Atlantic Ocean beaches.

HOUSING AND LIVING COSTS

Darden provides housing for both single and married students. For single students, nearby accommodations are available in Copeley II and during their second year of study, the Ranges in the central university grounds. Married students are housed at the University Gardens and Copeley Hill, both within walking distance of the school. For single students, university housing requires that four students share a two-bedroom apartment. Most students choose to rent apartments in the nearby Charlottesville community. Approximate rent for the academic year averages $3,309.

The Best Graduate Business Schools

WASHINGTON UNIVERSITY

THE JOHN M. OLIN SCHOOL OF BUSINESS

John E. Simon Hall
One Brookings Drive
St. Louis, MO   63130-48990
Tel: 314-935-6344
Fax: 314-935-4074

AT A GLANCE

First-Year Students:	144	Employer Ranking:	—
Second-Year Students:	146	Student/Faculty Ratio:	17:1
Location:	Major City	Annual Tuition:	
No. of Employers		in-state:	$17,000
Recruiting on Campus	100	out-of-state:	$17,000

Strengths: Finance, Marketing, Operations and Manufacturing Management. Experiential teaching. Integration of research into classroom.

Distinctions: The Management Center and Career Resource Center provide excellent opportunities for case competitions and communication skills development. Number of contact hours with faculty is higher than most programs.

Goals: Continue development of all areas critical to being a world class business school.

Words From the Dean: Lyn D. Pankoff   Tenure: 1.5 years
"As business schools go, the Olin school is small, friendly, unbureaucratic, and an intellectually exciting place in the heart of the midwest."

OVERVIEW

Although its name may lead you to believe that Washington University is in our nation's capital or in the state of Washington, this school is actually located in St. Louis, home to 12 *Fortune* 500 headquarters and a huge variety of industries. Dean Robert Virgil has been the leader at Olin for 12 years has just retired. His achievements include incredible gains in faculty quality and endowment, a national reputation for the school and a beautiful building complex resembling Oxford University. Olin belongs to Consortium for Graduate Study, which includes such other notable business schools as Michigan, Indiana, and Darden (Virginia).

ACADEMIC BRIEF

Students are put through a rigorous program that provides the hands-on skills they need to develop into top managers. Courses stress practical management education and allow students to use their classroom learning to solve actual business problems. The Management Center has a unique 15-week course called the Practicum, in which students propose solutions to complex business problems.

KEYS TO ADMISSIONS AND APPLICATION

1-minimal 2-somewhat 3-significant

CRITERIA	IMPORTANCE	OTHER CONSIDERATIONS
GPA	2	
GMAT Scores	2	
Quality of Undergraduate Inst.	2	History of setting and
Quality of Undergrad. Major	3	achieving challenging
Years Experience	2	goals.
Recommendations	2	Foreign language
Activities	2	skills.
Essay	2	
Interview	2	

PROFILE OF ENROLLED STUDENTS

Number Applicants:	897	Mean GPA Enrolled:	3.16
Number of Offers:	367	Median GMAT Enrolled:	608
Number Enrolled:	144		

Percentile GPA ranking			Percentile ranking by GMAT		
	%			%	
80	%	490-680	80	%	2.60-3.60
	%			%	

DEMOGRAPHICS

First-Year Students	144	Women	79
Second-Year Students	146	Men	211
International Students	63	Minorities	38
		African American	24
Mean Age	26	Native American	0
Mean Class Size	145	Asian American	10
Mean Years Experience	—	Hispanic American	4

% UNDERGRADUATE MAJOR		% HOME REGIONS	
Arts/Humanities	14%	New England	11%
Business/Management	24%	Mid-Atlantic	22%
Natural/ Physical		Southeast	8%
Sciences	5%	Southwest	2%
Technical/Engineering,		Mid West	26%
Computer Science	25%	Rocky Mountain	—
Social Sciences	17%	Far West	4%

ACADEMIC STRENGTHS/FEATURES*

KEY	REPUTATION	RESOURCE COMMITMENT NEXT 2 YEARS	
	A-exceptionally well known; national reputation	+ increase = same - less	
	B-well respected	RELATIONSHIP TO CORE PROGRAM	
	C-building; targeted as key area	1=Required	4=Not offered
	D-standard program	2=Elective	5=Plan to
	E- not provided	3=Part of other courses	offer

BUSINESS FUNCTION	REPUTATION	RESOURCES COMMITTED
Consulting	B	N/A
Marketing	B	+
Management/Strategy	A	=
Operations-Service	A	=
Operations-Production	A	=
Finance/Accounting	A	=
HR/ILR/Organizational Behavior	B	=
Technology/Information Systems	D	N/A
Economics	A	=

SPECIAL INTERESTS	REPUTATION	RESOURCES COMMITTED	RELATIONSHIP TO CORE PROGRAM
International	B	=	1,2,3
Small Business	D	+	3
Entrepreneurial	B	+	2
Diversity	C	=	3
Communications	B	+	3
Manufacturing	A	+	1
Emerging Business	B	N/A	3
Family Business	E	N/A	4
Health Care	B	N/A	2
Public Administration	D	N/A	2
Ethics	D	=	2
Other	—	—	—

TEACHING METHODOLOGIES	PERCENTAGE OF ALL COURSES	SKILLS DEVELOPMENT	PERCENTAGE OF ALL COURSES
Case Study	—	Quantitative/	
Lecture	10%	Technical	40%
Experiential	10%	Managerial	20%
Combination	75%	Communication	40%
Simulation	5%	Other	—
Other	—		

*Reported by Dean's Office

CAREER SERVICES

Career management is an authentic program, not just a theoretical process, for Olin students through the Weston Business Placement Center. The program includes a series of individual sessions and group experiences starting in the first year. Groups of students work together on problems such as employer research and resume development. Results are presented to an audience at the end of the series. Each student has an industry mentor assigned for advice and support. The Center has an active internship program providing students with solid experience as part of their studies. The emphasis on "target marketing" and "bookless resumes" with employers who are searching for Olin candidates is also commendable.

DISTINGUISHED PROGRAM/RESOURCES

The Career Management Series—sessions and experiences moving students from assessment to job-search skill development.

CAREER SERVICES

CAREER MANAGEMENT

Career Planning Program for First-Year Students	Yes
Career Presentations in the Curricula	Yes
Alumni Network	Yes
Summer Jobs Program/ Internships	Yes
Employer Associates Program	No
Job Search Course	Yes

RECRUITMENT

Employers Interviewing at School	125
Interviews Conducted at School	2499
Marketing to Employers	Yes
Resume Books	Yes
Resume Database to Employers	No
Resume Database/ Referral System	No
Career Fairs	Yes

CAREER SERVICES STAFF

Professional	3	Graduate Assistants	3
Support	3	Peer Advisors	—

FIRST JOB STATISTICS AND SALARY DATA

	1993	1992	1991
Mean no. of Job Offers/Graduate	153	N/A	N/A
STARTING SALARY	MEAN	MEAN	MEAN
Acct/Finance	$35,500		
Marketing	42,000		
Operations/Services	—		
Management/Strategy	48,000		
Health Care	—		
Consulting	41,300		
Operations/Production	53,300	N/A	N/A
Tech/Info Systems	—		
HR/LR/O. Dev.	—		
Public Admin.	—		
Other	—		
Other	—		
Small Business	—		
International	—		

TOP TEN EMPLOYERS BY HIRES

1. Andersen Consulting
2. Ernst & Young
3. Procter & Gamble
4. Price Waterhouse
5. American Airlines
6. Arthur Andersen
7. —
8. —
9. —
10. —

STUDENT LIFE

Students comment that the combination of small class size and the open-door policy of the professors shows a greater concern for students at Olin than at other business schools. Friday afternoon keg parties for students and faculty and monthly lunches with the Dean are further indications of the friendly, close-knit atmosphere of Olin.

Olin has a number of student-based organizations, including the Women in Management Club, which hosted a national conference on women in the workplace; the Business Minority Council; and the Graduate Business Association. An example of creativity at Olin was seen when the Marketing Club published and distributed packages of MBA trading cards to marketing vice presidents across the country as part of a plan to market graduating MBA students.

FACILITIES AND TECHNOLOGY

John E. Simon Hall, built in 1986, is home to the Olin School of Business. The largest building on the Washington University hilltop campus, Simon Hall, with its slate roof and limestone-trimmed red granite walls, was inspired by the architecture of Oxford and Cambridge. The facility provides an excellent site for learning and socializing, with classrooms, the Kopolow Business Library, a computing center, small group-study rooms, offices, student lounges and an enclosed courtyard.

The business computing center contains 60 terminals for Olin student use, or students can dial in to the center from their own personal computers at their homes. Students are given E-mail accounts, and use this facility as one of the ways they communicate with faculty. Access is available to Bitnet and Internet, as well as the Washington University mainframes.

SCHOLARSHIPS AND FINANCIAL ASSISTANCE

Financial aid falls into three major categories: Dean's Scholarships, need-based aid and special scholarships. More than 85 Dean's Scholarships are awarded each year. These scholarships extend over two years and range from $1,000 to full tuition. Special Minority Fellowships and Women's Fellowships are available.

COMMUNITY/CITY LIFE

St. Louis Population: 460,000
Weather: Average July temperature is 81°; average in January is 27°.

St. Louis, the 15th largest metropolitan area in the United States, is just 15 miles north of the true U.S. population center. With the 500-mile radius around St. Louis containing 31% of the nation's total population, it's no wonder that St. Louis is undergoing an urban renaissance. The old post office area and the massive ro-manesque Union Station have been restored to their original beauty. St. Louis boasts the lowest cost of living among major metropolitan areas, and is number one in housing affordability. Within walking distance of the university are the world-famous St. Louis Zoo, skating rinks, a golf course and a botanical garden. Downtown St. Louis, only a ten-minute car ride away, offers professional sports, a riverfront entertainment district, a variety of restaurants, symphony and opera.

HOUSING AND LIVING COSTS

Washington University has no school-owned housing. Approximate cost of renting a one-bedroom apartment for the academic year is $5,400.

UNIVERSITY OF WISCONSIN

GRADUATE SCHOOL OF BUSINESS

975 University Ave.
Grainger Hall
Madison, WI 53706-1323
Tel: 608-262-9213
Fax: 608-265-4194

AT A GLANCE

First-Year Students:	246	Employer Ranking:	—
Second-Year Students:	292	Student/Faculty Ratio:	N/A
Location:	Medium size city	Annual Tuition:	
No. of Employers		in-state:	$9,700
Recruiting on Campus	125	out-of-state:	$16,000

Strengths: Marketing, Finance, Management. Extraordinary features in the new Grainger Hall. Creative faculty. Innovative use of technology/media in teaching.

Distinctions: Chosen recipient of the TQM Challenge—one of eight in the country—to collaborate with five major companies on applications. Diversity studies place students in action working with neighborhoods. Business Learning Center is unique program for matching students up for study and tutorial.

Goals: Increase diversity of graduate student body. Develop stronger programs, especially in "niche areas," which are Wisconsin's strengths.

Words From the Dean: Andrew J. Policano   Tenure: 4 years
"Wisconsin has nationally ranked programs in all business disciplines...and specialized master's programs such as real estate, arts administration, marketing research, distribution management and security analysis. A long tradition of emphasizing small, specialized programs provides a unique environment for students whose placement opportunities are based on a huge network of alumni and highly satisfied recruiters."

OVERVIEW

"Wisconsin" conjures up images of liberal politics, cold winters, the Green Bay Packers and a world-class university. People in the School of Business have a new image in mind—the newest and very best facility available anywhere to house its acclaimed business program. The 40-million-dollar Grainger Hall, complete with a 156-foot bell tower, opened for business in the fall of 1993. All indications are that this building is a symbol of great things to come for Wisconsin Business. Wisconsin has decreased the number of enrolled students in the past two years and has also seen its average GMAT score go up. A large percentage of graduates (about half) have always stayed in Wisconsin after completing the MBA. Now, with the awesome Grainger Hall as home, they might not leave the building.

ACADEMIC BRIEF

Major areas of study include accounting, business statistics, finance and banking, marketing and real estate. The Grainger Business Ethics Symposium has been integrated into the curriculum. The Symposium will explore a different ethical issue each year. The courses, which are held in Grainger Hall, provide a framework to help students identify and resolve ethical dilemmas. Lora, a second year student, commented on the "cross-industry" emphasis at Wisconsin. She noted that her classes use cases and examples from many industries.

KEYS TO ADMISSIONS AND APPLICATION

1-minimal   2-somewhat   3-significant

CRITERIA	IMPORTANCE	OTHER CONSIDERATIONS
GPA	3	
GMAT Scores	2	
Quality of Undergraduate Inst.	2	
Quality of Undergrad. Major	2	
Years Experience	3	N/A
Recommendations	3	
Activities	2	
Essay	3	
Interview	—	

PROFILE OF ENROLLED STUDENTS

Number Applicants:	908	Mean GPA Enrolled:	3.4
Number of Offers:	401	Median GMAT Enrolled:	595
Number Enrolled:	157		

Percentile GPA ranking			Percentile ranking by GMAT		
90	%	3.8	90	%	680
70	%	3.6	70	%	660
50	%	3.4	50	%	600

DEMOGRAPHICS

First-Year Students	246	Women	185
Second-Year Students	292	Men	353
International Students	86	Minorities	54
		African American	16
Mean Age	25	Native American	3
Mean Class Size	—	Asian American	21
Mean Years Experience	1-3	Hispanic American	14

% UNDERGRADUATE MAJOR		% HOME REGIONS	
Arts/Humanities	12%	New England	4%
Business/Management	38%	Mid-Atlantic	3%
Natural/ Physical		Southeast	3%
Sciences	14%	Southwest	1%
Technical/Engineering,		Mid West	63%
Computer Science	13%	Rocky Mountain	1%
Social Sciences	22%	Far West	4%

The Best Graduate Business Schools

ACADEMIC STRENGTHS/FEATURES*

KEY	REPUTATION	RESOURCE COMMITMENT NEXT 2 YEARS	
K E Y	A-exceptionally well known; national reputation B-well respected C-building; targeted as key area D-standard program E- not provided	+ increase = same - less	
		RELATIONSHIP TO CORE PROGRAM	
		1=Required 4=Not offered 2=Elective 5=Plan to 3=Part of offer other courses	

BUSINESS FUNCTION	REPUTATION	RESOURCES COMMITTED
Consulting	D	=
Marketing	A	=
Management/Strategy	B	=
Operations-Service	B	=
Operations-Production	B	=
Finance/Accounting	A	=
HR/ILR/Organizational Behavior	A	=
Technology/Information Systems	B	+
Other	—	—

SPECIAL INTERESTS	REPUTATION	RESOURCES COMMITTED	RELATIONSHIP TO CORE PROGRAM
International	B	+	1
Small Business	B	=	2
Entrepreneurial	B	+	2
Diversity	C	+	1
Communications	B	+	1
Manufacturing	C	=	2
Emerging Business	D	=	2
Family Business	D	=	2
Health Care	B	=	2
Public Administration	B	=	2
Ethics	B	=	1
Distribution Management	C	+	—

TEACHING METHODOLOGIES	PERCENTAGE OF ALL COURSES	SKILLS DEVELOPMENT	PERCENTAGE OF ALL COURSES
Case Study	—	Quantitative/	
Lecture	—	Technical	35%
Experiential	—	Managerial	45%
Combination	100%	Communication	20%
Other	—	Other	—

*Reported by Dean's Office

CAREER SERVICES

Career Services at Wisconsin's School of Business have always enjoyed a solid reputation. Although it's difficult to get significant numbers of recruiters to travel to smaller cities like Madison, Karen Staufacher and her staff go all out to provide services and resources for students. From well-run Career Forums to Job Fairs with other top MBA schools, and from major events like Business Career Awareness Month to practical little handouts like "Researching a Company," the office provides the best in assistance for students.

DISTINGUISHED PROGRAM/RESOURCES

VIEWnet—this pilot program applies video-conference technology to recruitment interviewing.

CAREER SERVICES

CAREER MANAGEMENT		RECRUITMENT	
Career Planning Program for First-Year Students	Yes	Employers Interviewing at School	125
Career Presentations in the Curricula	Yes	Interviews Conducted at School	1,200
Alumni Network	Yes	Marketing to Employers	Yes
Summer Jobs Program/ Internships	Yes	Resume Books	Yes
Employer Associates Program	Yes	Resume Database to Employers	Yes
Job Search Course	Yes	Resume Database/ Referral System	Yes
		Career Fairs	Yes

CAREER SERVICES STAFF

Professional	3	Graduate Assistants	—
Support	3	Peer Advisors	—

FIRST JOB STATISTICS AND SALARY DATA

	1993	1992	1991
Mean no. of Job Offers/Graduate	N/A	N/A	N/A
STARTING SALARY	MEAN	MEAN	MEAN
Acct/Finance	$38,300	$35,300	
Marketing	39,500	38,600	
Operations/Services	37,000	39,000	
Management/Strategy	46,000	—	
Health Care	—	—	
Consulting	38,000	35,300	
Operations/Production	—	—	N/A
Tech/Info Systems	36,500	32,500	
HR/LR/O. Dev.	36,100	—	
Public Admin.	—	—	
Actuarial	36,000	32,600	
Other	—	—	
Small Business	—	—	
International	—	—	

TOP TEN EMPLOYERS BY HIRES

1. Arthur Andersen & Co.
2. Ford Motor Company
3. Oscar Meyer
4. Coopers & Lybrand
5. Deloitte & Touche
6. KPMG Peat Marwick
7. Land O' Lakes
8. GE Medical Services
9. Principal Financial Group
10. A.C. Nielsen

STUDENT LIFE

Students enjoy the Big-Ten sporting events that are available at the university, including its championship football team. The campus also offers theater, music, movies, dance and choral events on a regular basis. Hundreds of student organizations are available, as well as ethnic societies and political organizations of every type.

FACILITIES AND TECHNOLOGY

The School of Business has recently moved into Grainger Hall, a 260,000-square-foot red-tile-roof and brick-facade building featuring the latest in classroom technology. This five-story building contains 30 classrooms, two large lecture halls, an auditorium and a library. Computer network docking stations are available to students in the commons areas, group study rooms, library and hallway seating areas.

The new library, three times the size of its predecessor, offers access to data bases across campus and across the nation. In addition to two full-service computer labs, the

University of Wisconsin

building boasts two computerized classrooms (one Macintosh, one DOS) with multi-media computers, where instructors may view or display student work from "master" computers at the front of the class.

SCHOLARSHIPS AND FINANCIAL ASSISTANCE

Students with exceptional grade point averages and GMAT scores may qualify for University scholarships. There are also a limited number of graduate fellowships, scholarships and teaching or project/research assistantships.

COMMUNITY/CITY LIFE

Madison Population: 250,000
Weather: 70's in the summer; long cold winters with temperatures in the teens and 20's.

Rated as the second-best metropolitan area in the country by *Money* magazine, Madison is the state capital, and, as a popular T-shirt states, it is "The Alternative To Reality." In addition to a low unemployment rate and a laid-back style, residents also boast about the health care available, particularly that provided by the University of Wisconsin Hospital and Clinics. Students enjoy over 20 diverse ethnic restaurants, as well as State Street's thriving pedestrian mall with its colorful street vendors, New Age stores and coffee shops. Cultural events take place at the Memorial Union Theatre, the Madison Civic Center, the Elvehjem Museum of Art and the Madison Art Center. Popular outdoor activities include biking, hiking and cross-country skiing.

HOUSING AND LIVING COSTS

There is limited school-owned housing available and Wisconsin residents are given priority. Only 2% of the students live in on-campus housing. The most cost-effective accommodation is a shared apartment near the school for around $3,000 a year.

YALE UNIVERSITY

YALE SCHOOL OF ORGANIZATION AND MANAGEMENT

Box 1A   New Haven, CT 06520-7368
Tel: 203 432-5932   Fax: 203 432-9991

AT A GLANCE

First-Year Students:	223	Employer Ranking:	—
Second-Year Students:	202	Student/Faculty Ratio:	N/A
Location:	City	Annual Tuition:	
No. of Employers		in-state:	$19,300
Recruiting on Campus	71	out-of-state:	$19,300

Strengths: Finance, General Management, Strategy. Combines business, government and non-profit issues into a single, multi-disciplinary curriculum. Emphasis on pro bono work with the Outreach Management Consulting Group is leading the way.

Distinctions: The Internship Fund is managed by the first-year class and supplements income for students. Runs a one-of-a-kind Career Day in Washington D.C. bringing SOM students together with over 50 non-profit and public employers.

Goals: "Develop in its students an intellectual mastery of management in its most general sense...."

Words From the Dean: Paul MacAvoy   Tenure: 2 years
"The School's small but diverse student body interacts with a distinguished faculty in an environment that stresses teamwork and facilitates innovative thinking."

OVERVIEW

It is apparent even from their public relations brochures—printed on expensive stock, with bold black and white photos, little gloss and no advertising pizzazz—that this program is steeped in Yale tradition. The approach to management relies heavily on the generalist view, which translates to requirements in political theory, economical analysis, and the like, along with regular business functions. Because the school has close ties to other Yale graduate and professional programs, management students can design individualized programs of great breadth and depth. The Yale program also prepares people to manage in all sectors—private, government and nonprofit. Yale SOM grades students only "proficient, pass or fail."

ACADEMIC BRIEF

Yale's program requires students to complete 18 courses over two academic years. The first-year curriculum includes a broad exposure to basic management principles and stresses the use of theory. The second-year curriculum includes the course Analysis of Institutions, which teaches students to think critically about complicated problems under the supervision of instructors. Second-year students can choose from several elective courses, including investment banking, nonprofit organizations and international trade.

KEYS TO ADMISSIONS AND APPLICATION

1-minimal 2-somewhat 3-significant

CRITERIA	IMPORTANCE	OTHER CONSIDERATIONS
GPA	2	
GMAT Scores	3	
Quality of Undergraduate Inst.	2	
Quality of Undergrad. Major	2	
Years Experience	3	N/A
Recommendations	2	
Activities	1	
Essay	2	
Interview	2	

PROFILE OF ENROLLED STUDENTS

Number Applicants:	1,134	Mean GPA Enrolled:	3.24
Number of Offers:	N/A	Mean GMAT Enrolled:	542
Number Enrolled:	223		

Percentile GPA ranking			Percentile ranking by GMAT		
90	%	3.80	90	%	720
70	%	3.49	70	%	690
50	%	3.30	50	%	640

DEMOGRAPHICS

First-Year Students	223	Women	33%
Second-Year Students	202	Men	67%
International Students	34%	Minorities	12%
		African American	2%
Mean Age	27.5	Native American	.25%
Mean Class Size	N/A	Asian American	8%
Mean Years Experience	4.5	Hispanic American	2%

% UNDERGRADUATE MAJOR		% HOME REGIONS	
Arts/Humanities	19%	New England	14%
Business/Management	14%	New York	10%
Natural/ Physical		Mid-Atlantic	18%
Sciences	14%	Southeast	5%
Technical/Engineering,		Southwest	14%
Computer Science	15%	Mid West	8%
Social Sciences	38%	International	31%

ACADEMIC STRENGTHS/FEATURES*

KEY	REPUTATION	RESOURCE COMMITMENT NEXT 2 YEARS	
	A-exceptionally well known; national reputation	+ increase = same - less	
	B-well respected	RELATIONSHIP TO CORE PROGRAM	
	C-building; targeted as key area	1=Required	4=Not offered
	D-standard program	2=Elective	5=Plan to offer
	E- not provided	3=Part of other courses	

BUSINESS FUNCTION	REPUTATION	RESOURCES COMMITTED
Consulting	A	=
Marketing	B	=
Management/Strategy	A	+
Operations-Service	E	=
Operations-Production	B	=
Finance/Accounting	A	+
HR/ILR/Organizational Behavior	A	=
Technology/Information Systems	E	=
Other	—	—

SPECIAL INTERESTS	REPUTATION	RESOURCES COMMITTED	RELATIONSHIP TO CORE PROGRAM
International	B	=	2
Small Business	D	=	3
Entrepreneurial	D	=	3
Diversity	D	=	3
Communications	D	=	3
Manufacturing	D	=	3
Emerging Business	D	=	3
Family Business	D	=	2
Health Care	B	=	3
Public Administration	E	=	3
Ethics	E	=	3
Other	—	—	—

TEACHING METHODOLOGIES	PERCENTAGE OF ALL COURSES	SKILLS DEVELOPMENT	PERCENTAGE OF ALL COURSES
Case Study	5%	Quantitative/	
Lecture	2%	Technical	50%
Experiential	85%	Managerial	45%
Combination	—	Communication	5%
Other	—	Other	—

*Reported by Dean's Office

CAREER SERVICES

Ivy League business schools haven't been noted for their emphasis on teaching students a practical job-search process. Yale's Career Development Office, however, offers students an impressive variety of workshops, lectures and publications to promote decision-making and job placement. Director Nancy Edmiston and her staff provide a variety of leading-edge services and strategies under the headings "Exploration Tools" and "Training Tools." CDO has developed a sophisticated program for bringing students and employers together on campus, from preliminary "brown bag" presentations to first- and then second-round interviews.

DISTINGUISHED PROGRAM/RESOURCES

Series of well-written publications, including *The CDO Workbook for Managing Career Transition,* that pull no punches in letting even the best and brightest Yale SMO students know that job search is hard work.

CAREER SERVICES

CAREER MANAGEMENT		RECRUITMENT	
Career Planning Program for First-Year Students	Yes	Employers Interviewing at School	71
Career Presentations in the Curricula	No	Interviews Conducted at School	1405
Alumni Network	Yes	Marketing to Employers	Yes
Summer Jobs Program/ Internships	Yes	Resume Books	Yes
Employer Associates Program	Yes	Resume Database to Employers	Yes
Job Search Course	No	Resume Database/ Referral System	No
		Career Fairs	Yes

CAREER SERVICES STAFF

Professional	3	Graduate Assistants	—
Support	4	Peer Advisors	—

FIRST JOB STATISTICS AND SALARY DATA

	1993	1992	1991
Mean no. of Job Offers/Graduate	N/A	N/A	N/A
STARTING SALARY	MEAN	MEAN	MEAN
Acct/Finance	$55,534	$53,500	
Marketing	50,167	—	
Operations/Services	45,000	—	
Management/Strategy	56,000	56,429	
Health Care	—	—	
Consulting	60,114	56,900	
Operations/Production	—	—	N/A
Tech/Info Systems	49,000	43,625	
HR/LR/O. Dev.	55,000	50,000	
Public Admin.	—	—	
Other	59,833	51,037	
Other	—	—	
Small Business	—	—	
International	—	—	

TOP TEN EMPLOYERS BY HIRES

1. Booz, Allen & Hamilton
2. Chemical Bank
3. Cosmair
4. GECapital
5. Goldman Sachs
6. IBM
7. Morgan Stanley
8. Procter & Gamble
9. Prudential
10. World Bank

STUDENT LIFE

Student organizations such as Nonprofit, Public Sector and Social Change reflect the fact that roughly 50% of the students come from a nonbusiness background at Yale. The School of Organization and Management (SOM) also supports extracurricular organizations such as the Outreach Management Consulting Group, which offers its services to local public and nonprofit organizations.

With the mean age of students at the Yale SOM being 27, many of the students are married. Much of the social life of the school takes place in the homes of the students, typically within a 15- minute walk of the campus. Informal gatherings of students and faculty are frequent, and students enjoy the fact that they have three-day weekends, with no classes on Fridays. Social highlights include an annual silent auction in support of the school's Internship Fund, twice-yearly talent nights, student-produced satirical reviews and black-tie events in December and May.

FACILITIES AND TECHNOLOGY

The Yale School of Organization and Management campus, a combination of historic houses and modern buildings in a contiguous complex, provides modern classrooms, study areas and common-room facilities. Across the street from the campus is Donaldson Commons, the SOM dining facility.

A fully equipped, functional and networked computer lab is available at SOM, with close to 80 IBM, Apple and AST personal computers. A variety of software is available, and lab personnel are on hand to assist students. Via the network, students also have access to a variety of external data sources, including the Dow Jones News Retrieval Service and LEXIS/NEXIS. Private rooms with personal computers and software are also available for group projects.

SCHOLARSHIPS AND FINANCIAL ASSISTANCE

More than 60% of students receive some form of financial assistance. Grants are awarded on the basis of financial need. Yale was the first school in the country to offer The Public Service Loan Forgiveness Program. This program offers assistance to students who accept pubic or non-profit positions upon graduation.

COMMUNITY/CITY LIFE

New Haven Population: 132,000
Weather: Climate is moderated by Long Island Sound; four distinct seasons with summers in the 70/80s and winters in the 30s.

New Haven, 75 miles from New York City and 135 miles from Boston, is the second largest city in Connecticut. A former manufacturing-based city, New Haven has changed to a service-based economy, with a multi-textured composite of students, workers, and professionals. New Haven offers over 700 restaurants, from lofty four-star establishments to lowly pizzerias. Yale and New Haven cooperate to offer both theater and music, including the Woolsey Hall Concert Series and the New Haven Symphony concerts. The New Haven harbor and public beaches are easily accessible from the city. Hiking, bicycling, sailing, and skiing in the winter are popular forms of recreation.

HOUSING AND LIVING COSTS

Tuition for the 1993-94 year averaged $20,000. Room and board, activities, computers, books, supplies, medical insurance and personal expenses averaged approximately $11,640. The total average cost for an academic year is approximately $31,860.

The Best Graduate Business Schools

TWENTY DISTINGUISHED PROGRAMS

UNIVERSITY OF ARIZONA

KARL ELLER GRADUATE SCHOOL OF MANAGEMENT

McClelland Hall
Tucson, AZ 85721
Tel: 602-621-2566
Fax: 602-621-2606

AT A GLANCE

First-Year Students:	65	Employer Ranking:	#12 of 61
Second-Year Students:	70	Student/Faculty Ratio:	30:1
Location:	Medium-size town	Annual Tuition:	
No. of Employers		in-state:	$1,600
Recruiting on Campus	68	out-of-state:	$7,000

Strengths: MIS and Entrepreneurship concentrations. Beautiful new building with all accompaniments; growing small business community in Tucson.

Distinctions: Special relationship with INTEL for TQM/CIP applications. Over $9 million from corporate support for new building.

Goals: Possible enrollment increase. Continue curriculum and placement innovations.

Words From the Dean: Dr. Kenneth Smith   Tenure: 12 years
"The MBA program at Eller has been carefully designed to facilitate the development of business leaders who function effectively in a continually changing environment. Successful leaders anticipate change, plan for it and readily adapt to it."

OVERVIEW

Tucson is booming and Eller with it. High-tech and optics industries abound in this region and Hughes Aircraft is moving its headquarters here after purchasing General Dynamics. Intel from Phoenix has adapted the program for special Total Quality Management applications. With the new McClelland Hall and outstanding programs in MIS and Entrepreneurship, Eller is poised for high success in the 90's. Class size is very small, and academic support in advising and tutorials are unusually strong for a graduate business school. The school's global outlook is particularly evident in its collaborative efforts with sister institutions in Mexico.

The University of Arizona offers students a functional education of field, core and elective courses that prepare them for real business issues. The first-year curriculum centers on decision-making and problem-solving skills. The second-year curriculum provides theory, project courses and interaction with local and national business leaders. The school's goal is for students to be able to identify business problems, develop practical solutions and make effective managerial decisions. These principles are the foundations of the program.

Neil, a first-year student in Marketing and Finance, lauded the Business Simulation Course, which allowed him to make hundreds of decisions in the total marketing of his product.

DEMOGRAPHICS

First-Year Students	65	Women	36
Second-Year Students	70	Men	99
International Students	19	Minorities	20
		African American	1
Mean Age	29	Native American	5
Mean Class Size	35	Asian American	4
Mean Years Experience	4-6	Hispanic American	10

PROFILE OF ENROLLED STUDENTS

Number Applicants:	391	Mean GPA Enrolled:	33.3
Number of Offers:	157	Median GMAT Enrolled:	600
Number Enrolled:	65		

Percentile GPA ranking			Percentile ranking by GMAT		
N/A %	N/A		40 %	600-690
N/A %	N/A		45 %	500-590
N/A %	N/A		4 %	400-490

FACILITIES AND TECHNOLOGY

One of the newest buildings on campus is McClelland Hall, a 200,000-square-foot facility, that is home to the Eller Graduate School of Management. There is also a new computer facility for graduate students with various software packages and on-line services. The Business Information Center has on-line retrieval of library reference materials and other databases. The technology classroom has 36 work stations that use group systems software for strategic planning and decision-making.

COMMUNITY/CITY LIFE

Tucson, with a population of more than 600,000, is located in the Sonoran desert valley and is surrounded by mountains. Because of its climate, it attracts visitors from around the world. Students enjoy many national attractions such as the Grand Canyon and Lake Mead. The city is known for its cultural diversity and offers many fine arts, including the Arizona Opera Company, the Tucson Symphony Orchestra and Ballet Arts.

ACADEMIC STRENGTHS/FEATURES*

KEY	REPUTATION A-exceptionally well known; national reputation B-well respected C-building; targeted as key area D-standard program E-not provided	RESOURCE COMMITMENT NEXT 2 YEARS + increase = same - less
		RELATIONSHIP TO CORE PROGRAM 1=Required 4=Not offered 2=Elective 5=Plan to 3=Part of offer other courses

BUSINESS FUNCTION	REPUTATION	RESOURCES COMMITTED
Consulting	E	=
Marketing	A	=
Management/Strategy	B	=
Operations-Service	B	=
Operations-Production	B	=
Finance/Accounting	B	=
HR/ILR/Organizational Behavior	B	=
Technology/Information Systems	A	=
Accounting	B	=

SPECIAL INTERESTS	REPUTATION	RESOURCES COMMITTED	RELATIONSHIP TO CORE PROGRAM
International	C	=	1/2
Small Business	A	=	—
Entrepreneurial	A	=	2
Diversity	E	=	—
Communications	A	+	1/2
Manufacturing	B	=	1
Emerging Business	—	=	1/2
Family Business	—	—	—
Health Care	B	+	2
Public Administration	B	—	—
Ethics	—	—	—
Other	—	+	—

TEACHING METHODOLOGIES	PERCENTAGE OF ALL COURSES	SKILLS DEVELOPMENT	PERCENTAGE OF ALL COURSES
Case Study	25%	Quantitative/ Technical	20%
Lecture	20%		
Experiential	25%	Managerial	25%
Combination	30%	Communication	20%
Other	—	Analytical	35%
		Other	—

*Reported by Dean's Office

CAREER SERVICES

The Graduate Placement Office provides effective services in both career management and recruitment. The number of employers who recruit on campus is respectable, and the office works overtime on employer development, marketing to Tucson's top 200 employers. The Placement Office offers a career course for first-year students and emphasizes career counseling for all students. Use of technology for resume referral and candidate tracking is on a par with most top MBA programs.

CAREER SERVICES

CAREER MANAGEMENT		RECRUITMENT	
Career Planning Program for First-Year Students	Yes	Employers Interviewing at School	68
Career Presentations in the Curricula	No	Interviews Conducted at School	604
Alumni Network	Yes	Marketing to Employers	Yes
Summer Jobs Program/ Internships	Yes	Resume Books	Yes
Employer Associates Program	Yes	Resume Database to Employers	Yes
Job Search Course	No	Resume Database/ Referral System	Yes
		Career Fairs	Yes

CAREER SERVICES STAFF

Professional	1	Graduate Assistants	2
Support	1	Peer Advisors	—

UNIVERSITY AT BUFFALO
STATE UNIVERSITY OF NEW YORK

SCHOOL OF MANAGEMENT
206 Jacobs Management Center
Buffalo, NY   14260
Tel: 716-645-3204
Fax: 716-645-2131

AT A GLANCE

First-Year Students:	151	Employer Ranking:	—
Second-Year Students:	173	Student/Faculty Ratio:	19:1
Location:	Suburb	Annual Tuition:	
No. of Employers		in-state:	$3,300
Recruiting on Campus	43	out-of-state:	$7,000

Strengths: Marketing, Finance, Accounting; great value for the price

Distinctions: Successful international programs in France, Finland, Mexico and Spain.   Good connections to manufacturing concerns in Buffalo and involved in Canadian commerce as well.

Goals: Decrease size of program for more personal learning and increase quality of some programs. Increase contacts with Buffalo industry as a whole.

Words From the Dean: Frederick W. Winter   Tenure: 1 year
"The School of Management at Buffalo has the ingredients to build an already very good school into a national leader. The faculty are first-rate; many are household names in scholarship."

OVERVIEW

UB's School of Management has been recognized as a great bargain in MBA education. Check the price tag. Buffalo is a city struggling economically, but progress is being made through cooperative efforts between the Management School, the Engineering School and local industry through the Center for Industrial Effectiveness. Before "globalization" became a buzzword, UB had developed strong ties with China, Japan, Mexico and France, where it offers courses at the School of International Studies in Montpellier. To counter Buffalo's well-known winter weather, the Jacobs Management Center and most other campus buildings are connected by protected walkways.   Niagara Falls is only 30 miles away and Buffalo has many cultural, recreational and entertainment offerings.

Since it's inception in 1927, the SUNY School of Management has provided students with a first-rate education. The School offers a full-time day program and a part-time evening program. The full-time program consists of 21 courses: 13 requirements and 8 electives. Students have a choice of 11 areas of specialization.

DEMOGRAPHICS

First-Year Students	151	Women	110
Second-Year Students	173	Men	214
International Students	81	Minorities	19
		African American	8
Mean Age	N/A	Native American	1
Mean Class Size	N/A	Asian American	1
Mean Years Experience	N/A	Hispanic American	1

PROFILE OF ENROLLED STUDENTS

Number Applicants:	629	Mean GPA Enrolled:	3.23
Number of Offers:	306	Median GMAT Enrolled:	586
Number Enrolled:	151		

Percentile GPA ranking			Percentile ranking by GMAT		
N/A	%	N/A	N/A	%	N/A
N/A	%	N/A	N/A	%	N/A
N/A	%	N/A	N/A	%	N/A

FACILITIES AND TECHNOLOGY

The University at Buffalo School of Management is located on the North Campus, which covers three square miles of woods and fields. The Jacobs Management Center, a red brick building built in 1985, houses the Business School. This modern building, which includes classrooms, office space, meeting rooms and a computer center, is connected to the central campus corridor, known as the Spine, by an enclosed overhead walkway, providing protection from the elements.

Library facilities are available through the University Library system, which includes the Lockwood Library, located adjacent to the Jacobs Management Center. A variety of computerized databases are available at no cost, with some services, such as the Dow Jones News/Retrieval service, being available for a fee.

The computer center in the Jacobs building is coordinated with the larger university computer facilities. The lab is open seven days a week for a total of 100 hours. A computer consultant is always on duty. IBM PS/2 model 30/286 computers are networked on a Novell LAN, with additional personal computers running in stand-alone mode.

COMMUNITY/CITY LIFE

While Buffalo brings harsh winters to mind, this city has much more to offer than just skating and skiing. Buffalo, the second largest city in New York State, sits at the end of Lake Erie at the point where it funnels into the Niagara River. Only minutes away from the city are the famous Niagara Falls, with recreational activities on either side of the river. Buffalo's ethnic diversity provides restaurants, entertainment and social events for almost all tastes. Sports fans can follow the Buffalo Bills in football and the Sabres in hockey. Amherst, New York is home to the University's North Campus, which is where the Business School is situated. Located just north of Buffalo, Amherst is a residential community of 125,000 with plenty of malls and movie theaters for students and residents.

ACADEMIC STRENGTHS/FEATURES*

KEY	REPUTATION	RESOURCE COMMITMENT NEXT 2 YEARS
	A-exceptionally well known; national reputation	+ increase = same - less
	B-well respected	**RELATIONSHIP TO CORE PROGRAM**
	C-building; targeted as key area	1=Required 4=Not offered
	D-standard program	2=Elective 5=Plan to
	E-not provided	3=Part of offer
		other courses

BUSINESS FUNCTION	REPUTATION	RESOURCES COMMITTED
Consulting	E	=
Marketing	A	=
Management/Strategy	D	=
Operations-Service	E	=
Operations-Production	C	=
Finance/Accounting	B	=
HR/ILR/Organizational Behavior	B	=
Technology/Information Systems	B	=
Other	A	-

SPECIAL INTERESTS	REPUTATION	RESOURCES COMMITTED	RELATIONSHIP TO CORE PROGRAM
International	C	+	2
Small Business	E	=	4
Entrepreneurial	D	+	2
Diversity	E	+	3
Communications	C	=	2
Manufacturing	D	=	1
Emerging Business	E	=	4
Family Business	E	=	4
Health Care	C	+	2
Public Administration	E	=	4
Ethics	E	=	3
Other	-	-	-

TEACHING METHODOLOGIES	PERCENTAGE OF ALL COURSES	SKILLS DEVELOPMENT	PERCENTAGE OF ALL COURSES
Case Study	35%	Quantitative/ Technical	60%
Lecture	50%	Managerial	10%
Experiential	15%	Communication	20%
Combination	-	Other	10%
Other	-		

*Reported by Dean's Office

State University at Buffalo

229

CAREER SERVICES

Because the Office of Career Development Services serves both graduate and undergraduate students, it does not specialize as much as some MBA career offices. However, it does provide the educational programs (career days, seminars, workshops, etc.) that come from an office that also serves undergraduate students. There are also a good number of services for MBAs, including the full smorgasbord of resume referral, job bulletin, information sessions, candidate screening and campus interviews.

CAREER SERVICES

CAREER MANAGEMENT

Career Planning Program for First-Year Students	Yes
Career Presentations in the Curricula	No
Alumni Network	Yes
Summer Jobs Program/ Internships	Yes
Employer Associates Program	No
Job Search Course	No

RECRUITMENT

Employers Interviewing at School	43
Interviews Conducted at School	704
Marketing to Employers	Yes
Resume Books	No
Resume Database to Employers	No
Resume Database/ Referral System	Yes
Career Fairs	Yes

CAREER SERVICES STAFF

Professional	2	Graduate Assistants	3
Support	4	Peer Advisors	0

CASE WESTERN RESERVE UNIVERSITY

WEATHERHEAD SCHOOL OF MANAGEMENT

310 Enterprise Hall
10900 Euclid Avenue
Cleveland, OH 44106-7235
Tel: 216-368-2069
Fax: 216-368-2845

AT A GLANCE

First-Year Students:	130	Employer Ranking:	—
Second-Year Students:	122	Student/Faculty Ratio:	14:1
Location:	Major City	Annual Tuition:	
No. of Employers		in-state:	$16,000
Recruiting on Campus:	—	out-of-state:	$16,000

Strengths: Management of Technology; Health Care Systems; one of the first MBA programs to emphasize international business; ongoing research on effectiveness of MBA programs.

Distinctions: Leading computer network of 80 work stations; Executive Advisor assigned to teams of 12 students in first year; links to business through mentoring program.

Goals: Expand Summer International Institute; develop valuable links with other Case schools; increase interaction with business community.

Words from the Dean: Scott S. Cowen   Tenure: 10 years
"Our unique MBA Program, which was introduced in 1990, was designed by Weatherhead faculty in consultation with executives of organizations that hire MBA graduates."

OVERVIEW

Weatherhead is named for Cleveland's entrepreneurial family who contributed significantly to the school. Case Western Reserve results from the combination of two schools—Case Institute of Technology and Western Reserve University. Weatherhead was a proponent of cross-discipline curricula and the "global view" long before these became buzzwords in business education. The school offers a superior first-year course called Management Assessment and Development, which helps students assess their management potential and then plan stategies for professional development. There is also a first-rate mentoring program that pairs students with Cleveland executives. Weatherhead is located in a rejuvenated area of Cleveland called University Circle. Cleveland offers culture, recreation and an inspiring new baseball stadium.

In the early 1990's, Weatherhead moved its curriculum "from a teaching process to a learning process," and instituted major changes in its program, reducing the number of required courses from 16 to 11 to make room for additions. The core courses provide students with a basic background on which to build more specific skills in areas such as accounting, labor and human relations, economics, finance and marketing.

231

Ellen, a second-year student, commented on the new orientation program, which she and 40 others developed in conjunction with the Dean's office. The week long program included the right balance between academic, social and team-building activities.

DEMOGRAPHICS

First-Year Students	130	Women	95
Second-Year Students	122	Men	157
International Students	45	Minorities	28
		African American	20
Mean Age	26.5	Native American	1
Mean Class Size	40	Asian American	4
Mean Years Experience	4-6	Hispanic American	3

PROFILE OF ENROLLED STUDENTS

Number Applicants:	618	Mean GPA Enrolled:	3.2
Number of Offers:	368	Median GMAT Enrolled:	574
Number Enrolled:	126		

Percentile GPA ranking			Percentile ranking by GMAT		
90	%	2.52-3.63	90	%	430-680
80	%	2.59-3.53	80	%	480-640
50	%	2.74-3.22	50	%	510-590

FACILITIES AND TECHNOLOGY

The graduate facilities are all under one roof, including classrooms, library, computer lab, lounge, faculty and administrative offices. Weatherhead's computer laboratory was the first in the country to provide a fully integrated network of personal computers for MBA instruction. The lab contains IBM-compatible and Macintosh computers that are connected to a local area network. The network provides various types of software and languages, electronic mail and a bulletin board. There are also two computer-supported classrooms that are used for computer instruction and teaching subjects such as finance, accounting and marketing. Computing resources include CWRUnet, which links more than 85 campus buildings and provides access to a variety of information resources. FREE-NET provides an electronic post office, a university calendar, the UPI News Wire and more than 280 other information services.

ACADEMIC STRENGTHS/FEATURES*

KEY	REPUTATION	RESOURCE COMMITMENT NEXT 2 YEARS	
	A-exceptionally well known; national reputation	+ increase = same - less	
	B-well respected	RELATIONSHIP TO CORE PROGRAM	
	C-building; targeted as key area	1=Required	4=Not offered
	D-standard program	2=Elective	5=Plan to
	E-not provided	3=Part of other courses	offer

BUSINESS FUNCTION	REPUTATION	RESOURCES COMMITTED
Consulting	C	=
Marketing	B	=
Management/Strategy	B	+
Operations-Service	C	+
Operations-Production	A	=
Finance/Accounting	B	=
HR/ILR/Organizational Behavior	A	=
Technology/Information Systems	A	+
Other	—	—

SPECIAL INTERESTS	REPUTATION	RESOURCES COMMITTED	RELATIONSHIP TO CORE PROGRAM
International	C	+	1,2,3
Small Business	B	=	2
Entrepreneurial	A	+	2
Diversity	B	+	1,2,3
Communications	C	=	1.3
Manufacturing	A	+	1,2,3
Emerging Business	A	+	2,3
Family Business	A	+	2
Health Care	A	+	2
Non-Profit Management	A	=	1,2
Ethics	C	+	1,2,3
Self Assessment	A	+	2

TEACHING METHODOLOGIES	PERCENTAGE OF ALL COURSES	SKILLS DEVELOPMENT	PERCENTAGE OF ALL COURSES
Case Study	20%	Quantitative/ Technical	
Lecture	20%	Managerial	
Experiential	40%	Communication	
Combination	20%	Team Building	
Other	—	Combination	100%

*Reported by Dean's Office

CAREER SERVICES

The Office of Career Planning and Placement (OCP&P) is traditional and offers students and employers a number of useful services. Campus interviewing is emphasized and resume books are provided to employers. The Weatherhead Computer Lab has a number of helpful corporate databases. Because classes are relatively small, students often receive career help from faculty in addition to placement staff.

CAREER SERVICES

CAREER MANAGEMENT		RECRUITMENT	
Career Planning Program for First-Year Students	Yes	Employers Interviewing at School	101
Career Presentations in the Curricula	Yes	Interviews Conducted at School	1,018
Alumni Network	Yes	Marketing to Employers	Yes
Summer Jobs Program/ Internships	Yes	Resume Books	Yes
Employer Associates Program	No	Resume Database to Employers	Yes
Job Search Course	Yes	Resume Database/ Referral System	Yes
		Career Fairs	Yes

CAREER SERVICES STAFF

Professional	2	Graduate Assistants	1
Support	2	Peer Advisors	—

COMMUNITY/CITY LIFE

Cleveland combines a busy metropolitan life with relaxed suburban living. It's the headquarters for 29 *Fortune* 500 companies and its location on the Cuyahoga River has made it a renowned international port. Case Western's University Circle campus is located close to the Cleveland Museum of Natural History, the home of the Cleveland Orchestra and the University Hospitals. University Circle attracts visitors from the northeast region of Ohio to its various events, which include musical performances, lectures and art shows. The University Circle also has dining, shopping and recreational facilities.

EMORY UNIVERSITY

EMORY BUSINESS SCHOOL

Office of Admissions
Atlanta, GA 30322
Tel: 404-727-6311
Fax: 404-727-4612

AT A GLANCE

First-Year Students:	126	Employer Ranking:	—
Second-Year Students:	138	Student/Faculty Ratio:	8:1
Location:	Major City	Annual Tuition:	
No. of Employers		in-state:	$17,000
Recruiting on Campus:	76	out-of-state:	$17,000

Strengths: Strategy, Marketing and Organization and Management. Beautiful suburban campus close to Atlanta.

Distinctions: High level of service and pro bono work by students. Satellite facility in uptown Atlanta business district.

Goals: Increase global programs and applications. Strive to maintain balance between knowledge and applied learning.

Words From the Dean: Ron Frank   Tenure: 5 years
"As EBS continues its surge to the top of the business school ranks, we attribute much of our success to our faculty's dedication to the educational needs of our students. Our recently revised mission statement exemplifies this orientation by valuing teaching, research and external interaction as independent components."

OVERVIEW

Known for its excellence in teaching and low student-faculty ratio of 6:1, EBS has "seized the day" and is integrating with the rising Atlanta economy. This includes sharing and providing resources for the 1996 Olympics. EBS is a member of the Olympic Force and looking forward to opportunities to serve Olympic committees. Student organizations are very active, especially the Community Action Committee. The Executive MBA program is one of the best anywhere and allows students to design projects with in-office applications. Like its Atlanta home, EBS is also growing on a number of international program fronts.

Sharon, a second-year student in Marketing, trumpeted the experience gained from her New Venture class, in which she took an idea from business plan through the beginning steps of raising capital.

DEMOGRAPHICS

First-Year Students	126	Women	87
Second-Year Students	138	Men	197
International Students	42	Minorities	34
		African American	17
Mean Age	26	Native American	1
Mean Class Size	-	Asian American	12
Mean Years Experience	1-2	Hispanic American	4

PROFILE OF ENROLLED STUDENTS

Number Applicants:	742	Mean GPA Enrolled:	3.2
Number of Offers:	261	Mean GMAT Enrolled:	620
Number Enrolled:	126		

Percentile GPA ranking			Percentile ranking by GMAT		
90	%	2.46-3.78	90	%	490-700
70	%	2.73-3.59	70	%	550-670
50	%	3.07-3.46	50	%	570-640

FACILITIES AND TECHNOLOGY

The Rich Building is the home of the Emory Business School. Originally built in 1942, the building has undergone numerous renovations. While the facility is adequate, its relatively small size keeps the day MBA program from expanding. Rich Building houses nine classrooms, the Computing Center, faculty and staff offices, the Career Services Office and the GBA office.

The Robert W. Woodruff Library, located next to the Rich Building, houses the Business School library collection and provides access to numerous outside databases.

The Emory Business Computing Center, located in the Rich Building, includes hands-on classroom instruction as well as facilities for individual computing. The Center supports a VAX 4000 Model 300 computer, and DEC station microcomputers, which run MS-DOS and Microsoft Windows. Apple Macintosh personal computers are also available. All personal computers have access to a variety of business software, and are connected via a local area network.

ACADEMIC STRENGTHS/FEATURES*

KEY	REPUTATION	RESOURCE COMMITMENT NEXT 2 YEARS	
	A-exceptionally well known; national reputation	+ increase = same - less	
	B-well respected	RELATIONSHIP TO CORE PROGRAM	
	C-building; targeted as key area	1=Required	4=Not offered
	D-standard program	2=Elective	5=Plan to
	E-not provided	3=Part of other courses	offer

BUSINESS FUNCTION	REPUTATION	RESOURCES COMMITTED
Consulting	B	=
Marketing	A	+
Management/Strategy	A	=
Operations-Service	C	+
Operations-Production	D	+
Finance/Accounting	B	+
HR/ILR/Organizational Behavior	A	=
Technology/Information Systems	C	+
Accounting	D	-

SPECIAL INTERESTS	REPUTATION	RESOURCES COMMITTED	RELATIONSHIP TO CORE PROGRAM
International	A	+	1
Small Business	-	+	3
Entrepreneurial	C	+	2
Diversity	B	+	2
Communications	C	+	1
Manufacturing	E	=	2
Emerging Business	B	+	2
Family Business	E	—	4
Health Care	A	+	2
Public Administration	E	—	4
Ethics	D	=	2
Other	-	-	-

TEACHING METHODOLOGIES	PERCENTAGE OF ALL COURSES	SKILLS DEVELOPMENT	PERCENTAGE OF ALL COURSES
Case Study	10%	Quantitative/	
Lecture	10%	Technical	30%
Experiential	20%	Managerial	60%
Combination	60%	Communication	10%
Other	—	Other	—

*Reported by Dean's Office

CAREER SERVICES

Emory's Office of Career Services offers a variety of useful career planning and recruitment services for students. There is an innovative course for first-year students in which 125 out of 200 students participate. The alumni network is large and used—networking receptions are held in a variety of cities. Emory is also well connected to consortia of local, regional and national schools for the purpose of Career/Job Fairs.

CAREER SERVICES

CAREER MANAGEMENT

Career Planning Program for First-Year Students	Yes
Career Presentations in the Curricula	Yes
Alumni Network	Yes
Summer Jobs Program/ Internships	Yes
Employer Associates Program	Yes
Job Search Course	Yes

RECRUITMENT

Employers Interviewing at School	76
Interviews Conducted at School	481
Marketing to Employers	Yes
Resume Books	Yes
Resume Database to Employers	Yes
Resume Database/ Referral System	No
Career Fairs	Yes

CAREER SERVICES STAFF

Professional	3	Graduate Assistants	1
Support	1	Peer Advisors	0

COMMUNITY/CITY LIFE

The Atlanta metropolitan area, with a population of 2.5 million people, was recently cited by *Fortune Magazine* as the best place in the U.S. to do business, based on quality of life and costs. Over 450 of the *Fortune* 500 companies have either a national or regional headquarters in Atlanta. The city has extensive social and cultural offerings, including the Atlanta Symphony and the Atlanta Ballet. Atlanta is also home to the Carter Presidential Library and the Centers for Disease Control. Students enjoy living in Atlanta because of its moderate climate, reasonable cost of living and accessibility to the rest of the country. Atlanta boasts three professional sports teams, and was chosen to be the site for the 1996 Summer Olympics.

UNIVERSITY OF FLORIDA

COLLEGE OF BUSINESS ADMINISTRATION

134 Bryan Hall
Gainesville, FL 32611-2017
Tel: 904-392-7992
Fax: 904-392-8791

AT A GLANCE

First-Year Students:	100	Employer Ranking:	#8 of 61
Second-Year Students:	116	Student/Faculty Ratio:	2:1
Location:	Large Town	Annual Tuition:	
No. of Employers		in-state:	$3,000
Recruiting on Campus:	70	out-of-state:	$9,000

Strengths: Finance, Marketing, Global Management. Relationship with a major research university, University of Florida.

Distinctions: Received national U.S. Department of Education grant to recruit outstanding minority candidates. Partnerships with international business schools.

Goals: Development of new facilities. Expansion of entrepreneurship studies and global management programs.

Words From the Dean: John Kraft   Tenure: 5 years
"There is a new emphasis at all academic levels on globalization issues, business ethics and cultural diversity. The College faculty and programs continue to receive honors."

OVERVIEW

Known for its entrepreneurial program, the Florida MBA Program is also experiencing success in finance and health sciences management. Students can experience an internship between their first and second years and several commented on its value for their career development. Academic options for students are plentiful, including international programs, an innovative Arts Administration program and a "three term" MBA. Class size is small and "R.O.I."—return on investment—is high, with low tuition and an affordable cost of living. Gainesville is a very liveable college town—and Florida weather is hard to beat.

The University of Florida is dedicated to "preparing students to excel in the business world of the twenty-first century." The faculty and staff are focusing on a threefold mission: education, research and service. The courses emphasize the changing conditions in the state, the nation and the world. There is a strong, new emphasis on global issues, business ethics and cultural diversity. Florida strives to increase its international recognition, to promote values and to improve the quality of life.

DEMOGRAPHICS

First-Year Students	100	Women	35%
Second-Year Students	116	Men	65%
International Students	26	Minorities	14%
		African American	8%
Mean Age	26	Native American	1%
Mean Class Size	20	Asian American	1%
Mean Years Experience	3-6	Hispanic American	4%

PROFILE OF ENROLLED STUDENTS

Number Applicants:	800	Mean GPA Enrolled:	3.4
Number of Offers:	163	Median GMAT Enrolled:	610-606
Number Enrolled:	100		

Percentile GPA ranking		Percentile ranking by GMAT	
	%		%
75%	% 3.1 - 3.7	75%	% 550 - 650
	%		%

FACILITIES AND TECHNOLOGY

Located in the popular "Sunbelt," the University of Florida campus is a mixture of palm trees, pine woods and palmettos along with Richardsonian Gothic halls and ultra-modern buildings. The large, 2,000-acre campus has numerous woods, ponds and lakes, including Lake Alice, a wildlife sanctuary that provides a home for the University's alligator mascots.

The MBA program is housed in the historic and recently renovated Bryan Hall, which is one of three buildings in the "Business Triangle," in the northeast corner of the University's campus. Bryan Hall contains graduate computer labs, several research centers and a microcomputer-based behavioral research lab. The Smathers Library, located next to the Business School and a depository for federal government publications, contains an extensive business reference section and provides access to electronic databases.

Computing facilities include a number of microcomputer labs across the campus, including one for graduate and faculty use in the business building. Seminars are held to train students on computer software and usage, and professionals are available to provide assistance.

ACADEMIC STRENGTHS/FEATURES*

KEY	REPUTATION	RESOURCE COMMITMENT NEXT 2 YEARS
	A-exceptionally well known; national reputation	A-increase B-same C-less
	B-well respected	RELATIONSHIP TO CORE PROGRAM
	C-building; targeted as key area	1=Required 4=Not offered
	D-standard program	2=Elective 5=Plan to
	E-not provided	3=Part of offer other courses

BUSINESS FUNCTION	REPUTATION	RESOURCES COMMITTED
Consulting	D	=
Marketing	B	+
Management/Strategy	B	+
Operations-Service	D	=
Operations-Production	D	=
Finance/Accounting	A	=
HR/ILR/Organizational Behavior	C	+
Technology/Information Systems	B	+
Other	—	—

SPECIAL INTERESTS	REPUTATION	RESOURCES COMMITTED	RELATIONSHIP TO CORE PROGRAM
International	C	+	1
Small Business	E	=	4
Entrepreneurial	B	+	2
Diversity	D	+	3
Communications	D	+	1
Manufacturing	D	=	1
Emerging Business	E	N/A	4
Family Business	E	=	4
Health Care	A	=	2
Public Administration	E	N/A	4
Ethics	D	+	2,3
Other	—	—	—

TEACHING METHODOLOGIES	PERCENTAGE OF ALL COURSES	SKILLS DEVELOPMENT	PERCENTAGE OF ALL COURSES
Case Study	30%	Quantitative/ Technical	40%
Lecture	—	Managerial	50%
Experiential	20%	Communication	10%
Combination	50%	Other	—
Other	—		

*Reported by Dean's Office

University of Florida

CAREER SERVICES

Florida MBAs can use both the university's centralized Career Resource Center and the MBA Placement Office. This "opportunity" sometimes indicates failure on the part of the business school to commit to career services—not at Florida. The MBA office delivers a full range of services just for MBA students and belongs to both the Chicago and Atlanta MBA Job Fair Consortiums. The campus Career Resource Center for all students is first-rate on all fronts and an added bonus for job hunting MBA's. The "Gator Alumni" program is as large and loyal as it gets, a leg up in these recessionary times.

CAREER SERVICES

CAREER MANAGEMENT

		RECRUITMENT	
Career Planning Program for First-Year Students	No	Employers Interviewing at School	70
Career Presentations in the Curricula	Yes	Interviews Conducted at School	N/A
Alumni Network	Yes	Marketing to Employers	Yes
Summer Jobs Program/ Internships	Yes	Resume Books	Yes
Employer Associates Program	No	Resume Database to Employers	Yes
Job Search Course	Yes	Resume Database/ Referral System	Yes
		Career Fairs	Yes

CAREER SERVICES STAFF

Professional	3	Graduate Assistants	25
Support	3	Peer Advisors	—

COMMUNITY/CITY LIFE

Southwest Gainesville, home to the University of Florida, is an urban area in the north-central part of Florida. While the community has a college town atmosphere, its tropical climate affords students recreational opportunities usually found only in much larger cities. Gainesville offers Victorian architecture, converted brick warehouses, horse farms and high-tech manufacturing. Noted by national magazines as one of the top ten places to live in America, Gainesville is only two hours away from Tampa, Orlando and Jacksonville, and just five hours from Miami and Atlanta.

HOFSTRA UNIVERSITY

GRADUATE BUSINESS SCHOOL

134 Hofstra University
Hempstead, NY 11550-1090
Tel: 516-463-5683
Fax: 516-463-5268

AT A GLANCE

First-Year Students:	110	Employer Ranking:	—
Second-Year Students:	108	Studen/Faculty Ratio:	16:1
Location:	Small Town	Annual Tuition:	
No. of Employers		in-state:	$10,000
Recruiting on Campus:	70	out-of-state:	$10,000

Strengths: Finance, Marketing, International Business, Accounting; emphasis on diversity in curriculum and in student body.

Distinctions: Has the only African-American Dean in a non-historically black college/university business school. Simulation games exist in most business functions. New state-of-the-art business building.

Goals: Broaden corporate support and expand offerings in international business.

Words from the Dean: Ambassador Ulric Haynes, Jr.   Tenure: 3.5 years
"Courses in the Hofstra MBA Program expose students to traditional learning experiences, innovative techniques, group interaction, simulated business situations and a thriving business community."

OVERVIEW

The Hofstra campus is only 25 miles from downtown Manhattan and students are offered a variety of resources for interacting with New York City business. Alumni contacts are strong and appear to have a loyalty to alma mater not seen in similar programs. Business facilities are impressive and the campus offers excellent recreation and athletic opportunities. The school is serious about diversity, which is addressed in a series of lectures presented by the Dean each year.

Hofstra encourages students to expand their horizons beyond traditional courses. The business program combines a traditional learning experience, high technology, group interaction and simulated business situations. It provides hands-on experience with computers and the study of environmental and ethical factors as they relate to business. Hofstra offers unique instructional methods both in and out of the classroom. There are seven areas of concentration offered in the MBA program, including accounting, banking/finance, business, computer information systems, management, marketing and international business.

Donna, an extremely active and enthusiastic president of the MBA Association and past president of the Hofstra Business Consulting Group, commented favorably on the open-door policy of the Dean and MBA Program Director. She cited nearness to Manhattan for off-campus learning and the actual work she did through the Consulting Group as big plusses in her program.

243

There's plenty of interaction between students and faculty at this east coast institution. Guylaine, a graduate from '93, could not say enough about how her professors encouraged her in studies as well as in activities. She regards this personal contact as "the most treasured" aspect of her work at Hofstra.

DEMOGRAPHICS

First-Year Students	110	Women	N/A
Second-Year Students	108	Men	N/A
International Students	35	Minorities	N/A
		African American	N/A
Mean Age	26.5	Native American	N/A
Mean Class Size	N/A	Asian American	N/A
Mean Years Experience	N/A	Hispanic American	N/A

PROFILE OF ENROLLED STUDENTS

Number Applicants:	1210	Mean GPA Enrolled:	3.2
Number of Offers:	714	Median GMAT Enrolled:	580
Number Enrolled:	221		

Percentile GPA ranking			Percentile ranking by GMAT		
17	%	3.5 - 4.0	44	%	600 - 390
64	%	3.0 - 3.49	40	%	500 - 590
19	%	<3.0	14	%	<490

FACILITIES AND TECHNOLOGY

Hofstra School of Business students have recently moved into a new, modern classroom building. The main business school building has also been extensively renovated, with computer labs, administrative and faculty offices, and student organization offices.

The Joan and Donald E. Axinn Library provides a full complement of business journals and periodicals, as well as a variety of company information databases. The library also provides access to outside databases.

The Hofstra computing facilities consist of a number of personal computer labs, including both IBM-compatible labs and Apple labs. Laser printers are available in all of the labs, and all major computer applications are supported, including WordPerfect, Lotus and Quattro. Students are also able to access the Hofstra mainframe computers, which include IBM and DEC machines.

COMMUNITY/CITY LIFE

Located in suburban Hempstead, Hofstra is easily accessible from New York City via mass transportation. While the surrounding area has some problems, Hofstra has excellent security and crime is not considered an issue. Students walk to the Nassau Coliseum, home to the NHL New York Islanders and site of many major entertainment and sporting events. They can also participate in water sports, such as sailing, water skiing and sailboarding on nearby Long Island Sound.

244

ACADEMIC STRENGTHS/FEATURES*

KEY	REPUTATION	RESOURCE COMMITMENT NEXT 2 YEARS	
K E Y	A-exceptionally well known; national reputation	+ increase = same - less	
	B-well respected C-building; targeted as key area D-standard program E-not provided	RELATIONSHIP TO CORE PROGRAM	
		1=Required 2=Elective 3=Part of other courses	4=Not offered 5=Plan to offer

BUSINESS FUNCTION	REPUTATION	RESOURCES COMMITTED
Consulting	E	+
Marketing	B	+
Management/Strategy	B	=
Operations-Service	E	N/A
Operations-Production	E	N/A
Finance/Accounting	A	=
HR/ILR/Organizational Behavior	B	=
Technology/Information Systems	D	+
Accounting	A	=

SPECIAL INTERESTS	REPUTATION	RESOURCES COMMITTED	RELATIONSHIP TO CORE PROGRAM
International	B	+	1
Small Business	C	+	2
Entrepreneurial	C	+	2
Diversity	C	+	3
Communications	B	+	1
Manufacturing	E	N/A	1
Emerging Business	C	+	3
Family Business	C	+	5
Health Care	E	-	4
Public Administration	E	-	5
Ethics	C	-	1
Accounting	A	=	—

TEACHING METHODOLOGIES	PERCENTAGE OF ALL COURSES	SKILLS DEVELOPMENT	PERCENTAGE OF ALL COURSES
Case Study	—	Quantitative/	
Lecture	—	Technical	30%
Experiential	—	Managerial	40%
Combination	100%	Communication	30%
Other	—	Other	—

*Reported by Dean's Office

CAREER SERVICES

The Hofstra MBA Placement office plays a significant role in orientation of incoming MBA students and encourages all students to stay actively involved with the placement office from entry through graduation. A full range of career development and placement services is offered, including individual career counseling, a series of seminars on job search strategies and interviewing skills, job postings mailed directly to final year students and on-campus interviews. Throughout the academic year MBA Career Forums bring to campus Hofstra MBA Alumni who hold managerial positions in leading firms.

CAREER SERVICES

CAREER MANAGEMENT

Career Planning Program for First-Year Students	Yes
Career Presentations in the Curricula	N/A
Alumni Network	Yes
Summer Jobs Program/ Internships	Yes
Employer Associates Program	No
Job Search Course	No

RECRUITMENT

Employers Interviewing at School	70
Interviews Conducted at School	N/A
Marketing to Employers	Yes
Resume Books	Yes
Resume Database to Employers	No
Resume Database/ Referral System	Yes
Career Fairs	No

CAREER SERVICES STAFF

Professional	1	Graduate Assistants	2
Support	2	Peer Advisors	—

THE UNIVERSITY OF IOWA

COLLEGE OF BUSINESS ADMINISTRATION

121 Phillips Hall
Iowa City, IA 52242
Tel: 319-335-1039
Fax: 319-335-3604

AT A GLANCE

First-Year Students:	117	Employer Ranking:	—
Second-Year Students:	122	Student/Faculty Ratio:	4:1
Location:	Medium-size town	Annual Tuition:	
No. of Employers		in-state:	$3,300
Recruiting on Campus:	53	out-of-state:	$8,200

Strengths: Finance, Operations Management, Marketing. Outstanding $36 million facility opened in 1993-94.

Distinctions: Solid programs in diversity training including simulations and a school commissioned play. Small Business Development Center works closely with Iowa business.

Goals: Expand international focus. Increase curriculum relevance in areas like TQM and technical management.

Words From the Dean: Gary Fethke   Tenure: interim
"At Iowa, we strive to recruit and retain a diverse faculty who are committed to their own and their students' intellectual pursuits.... . So while we encourage and provide many opportunities for faculty and student interactions, we also insist that our faculty pursue their personal intellectual agendas with focus and vigor."

OVERVIEW

Located in a quintessential college town in the rolling hills of eastern Iowa, the University of Iowa College of Business Administration has a new program that's moving and shaking. Emphasis on Total Quality Management and technical information management as well as expanded international resources for students are distinguishing features. Iowa City is 15 miles from prosperous Cedar Rapids, the state's second largest city and home to large international companies and surging small businesses alike.

The University of Iowa's program provides a strong foundation in the basics of business administration, including accounting, economics, finance, marketing and management. The "Iowa Advantage" is that although it is part of a Big Ten university, the College of Business Administration is a small, intimate college. It prides itself on the fact that classes average 35 students, allowing interaction between students and faculty.

Paul, an exchange student from the University of Frankfurt, reflected on the effectiveness of the Student MBA Association and especially the business trips to Denver that

247

it sponsored. He was also struck by the loyalty of Iowans—who were "always there when it counted."

DEMOGRAPHICS

First-Year Students	117	Women	69
Second-Year Students	122	Men	170
International Students	56	Minorities	21
		African American	11
Mean Age	27	Native American	0
Mean Class Size	40	Asian American	6
Mean Years Experience	1-3	Hispanic American	4

PROFILE OF ENROLLED STUDENTS

Number Applicants:	696	Mean GPA Enrolled:	3.30
Number of Offers:	276	Median GMAT Enrolled:	590
Number Enrolled:	117		

Percentile GPA ranking			Percentile ranking by GMAT		
90	%	2.63+	90	%	480+
70	%	2.94+	70	%	540+
50	%	3.28+	50	%	580+

FACILITIES AND TECHNOLOGY

The University of Iowa College of Business Administration moved to a new $36 million facility in the 1993-94 academic year. The building was designed to enhance interactive learning. It has a business library and a computer lab with 90 individualized workstations. There are also two behavioral labs and classrooms with video production equipment. Other interactive capabilities include the Simulated Securities Trading room with an electronic (real-time) feed of world markets.

COMMUNITY/CITY LIFE

Iowa City is a picturesque college town with a population of approximately 60,000. The Iowa River runs through the downtown area where musicians line the streets of the mall and provide a carnival atmosphere. Students can enjoy a waterfront stroll or a riverboat cruise along the Mississippi River, only 40 miles away.

ACADEMIC STRENGTHS/FEATURES*

KEY	REPUTATION	RESOURCE COMMITMENT NEXT 2 YEARS
	A-exceptionally well known; national reputation	+ increase = same - less
	B-well respected	**RELATIONSHIP TO CORE PROGRAM**
	C-building; targeted as key area	1=Required 4=Not offered
	D-standard program	2=Elective 5=Plan to
	E-not provided	3=Part of offer other courses

BUSINESS FUNCTION	REPUTATION	RESOURCES COMMITTED
Consulting	C	+
Marketing	B	+
Management/Strategy	C	+
Operations-Service	C	=
Operations-Production	B	=
Finance/Accounting	B	=
HR/ILR/Organizational Behavior	B	=
Technology/Information Systems	D	+
Other	—	—

SPECIAL INTERESTS	REPUTATION	RESOURCES COMMITTED	RELATIONSHIP TO CORE PROGRAM
International	C	+	2
Small Business	E	=	4
Entrepreneurial	D	=	2
Diversity	C	+	2,3
Communications	D	+	3
Manufacturing	D	=	1
Emerging Business	C	+	2
Family Business	E	=	4
Health Care	B	=	2
Public Administration	E	=	4
Ethics	D	+	1
Other	—	—	—

TEACHING METHODOLOGIES	PERCENTAGE OF ALL COURSES	SKILLS DEVELOPMENT	PERCENTAGE OF ALL COURSES
Case Study	—	Quantitative/ Technical	40%
Lecture	—	Managerial	30%
Experiential	—	Communication	30%
Combination	100%	Other	—
Other	—		

*Reported by Dean's Office

The University of Iowa

CAREER SERVICES

MBA Placement Services has a new initiative to serve exclusively MBA students at Iowa. The office has developed a solid program including useful educational components—a course for first years and a series of professional development seminars. The director and associate director also work personally with companies in a brokering function, screening and referring candidates to off-campus interview opportunities. MBA recruiting companies thrive on this kind of attention. Iowa is also well connected to valuable Big Ten Job Fair events.

CAREER SERVICES

CAREER MANAGEMENT

Career Planning Program for First-Year Students	Yes
Career Presentations in the Curricula	No
Alumni Network	Yes
Summer Jobs Program/ Internships	Yes
Employer Associates Program	No
Job Search Course	No

RECRUITMENT

Employers Interviewing at School	53
Interviews Conducted at School	272
Marketing to Employers	Yes
Resume Books	Yes
Resume Database to Employers	No
Resume Database/ Referral System	Yes
Career Fairs	Yes

CAREER SERVICES STAFF

Professional	2	Graduate Assistants	4
Support	1	Peer Advisors	—

UNIVERSITY OF MARYLAND

COLLEGE OF BUSINESS AND MANAGEMENT

Van Munching Hall
College Park, MD 20742-1815
Tel: 301-405-2278
Fax: 301-314-9862

AT A GLANCE

First-Year students:	120	Employer Ranking:	#9 of 61
Second-Year Students:	115	Student/Faculty Ratio:	N/A
Location:	Surburban	Annual Tuition:	
No. of Employers		in-state:	$6,000
Recruiting on Campus	66	out-of-state:	$10,000

Strengths: Finance, Management, Marketing. A program on the move under relatively new leadership.

Distinctions: Located in a great growth area with access to high-tech telecommunication and biomedical industries around D.C. beltway and Baltimore. Many faculty members consult and publish nationally.

Goals: To make the curriculum more experiential. To increase the flow of job information and to make the MBA experience more enjoyable.

Words from the Dean: William E. Mayer   Tenure: 2 years
"Maryland's primary customers are its students and the people who hire them. We pledge to provide those customers with outstanding value for their educational dollar. Our students receive an excellent product at an affordable price."

OVERVIEW

A new Dean and a new building are bringing new life to the College of Business and Management. Its location is second to none with access to Washington government and international organizations, Beltway high-technology companies, Baltimore commerce and the small companies developing in centers like Northern Virginia, Annapolis and Hunt Valley in Maryland. The new Dean literally hit the road and talked to his customers. As a result, innovations in curricula and programs have been made. It's tougher to get in, too—mean GMAT scores are up and only 120 full-time students were recently admitted from a pool of 1,600. Curriculum is a good blend of theory and practice, developing both analytical and leadership skills.

Maryland is a leader in working with companies who are planning to go international with their products. Peter, a second-year finance student, complimented Dr. Lee Preston's Center for International Business and its efforts to develop a database of international buyers for small companies.

DEMOGRAPHICS

First-Year Students	120	Women	78
Second-Year Students	115	Men	157
International Students	47	Minorities	59
		African American	26
Mean Age	25	Native American	2
Mean Class Size	38	Asian American	27
Mean Years Experience	1-3	Hispanic American	4

PROFILE OF ENROLLED STUDENTS

Number Applicants:	1570	Mean GPA Enrolled:	3.27
Number of Offers:	N/A	Mean GMAT Enrolled:	620
Number Enrolled:	N/A		

Percentile GPA ranking			Percentile ranking by GMAT		
N/A	%	N/A	N/A	%	N/A
N/A	%	N/A	N/A	%	N/A
N/A	%	N/A	N/A	%	N/A

FACILITIES AND TECHNOLOGY

The College of Business and Management is located in Van Munching Hall, a new building that opened in January 1993. The school boasts a glass atrium area that has become a campus focal point. The four-story building contains state-of-the-art classrooms, computer labs, office space and an auditorium.

Business library resources are concentrated in the McKeldin Library, the main university library.

The Office of Computing Services provides administration, instructional computing and coordination of the computer labs. The business school's computer lab contains both IBM and Macintosh personal computers. Other labs are available throughout the university. The university also supports a number of IBM mainframe computers and Unix machines.

COMMUNITY/CITY LIFE

Located in the 40-mile stretch known as the Washington-Baltimore corridor, College Park is afforded the opportunities of two large cities while maintaining a college-town atmosphere. Washington, just a short drive away, provides many historical places to visit, as well as numerous cultural events. Students have access to the many libraries in Washington, as well as the facilities of the Securities and Exchange Commission, the Federal Trade Commission and the Small Business Administration. Baltimore is a city rich in history that offers a variety of ethnic cuisines.

ACADEMIC STRENGTHS/FEATURES*

KEY	REPUTATION	RESOURCE COMMITMENT NEXT 2 YEARS
	A-exceptionally well known; national reputation	+ increase = same - less
	B-well respected	RELATIONSHIP TO CORE PROGRAM
	C-building; targeted as key area	1=Required 4=Not offered
	D-standard program	2=Elective 5=Plan to
	E-not provided	3=Part of offer
		other courses

BUSINESS FUNCTION	REPUTATION	RESOURCES COMMITTED
Consulting	A	+
Marketing	A	+
Management/Strategy	B	+
Operations-Service	B	+
Operations-Production	B	=
Finance/Accounting	A	+
HR/ILR/Organizational Behavior	A	=
Technology/Information Systems	B	+
Transportation	A	—

SPECIAL INTERESTS	REPUTATION	RESOURCES COMMITTED	RELATIONSHIP TO CORE PROGRAM
International	A	+	1
Small Business	E	—	4
Entrepreneurial	A	+	2
Diversity	A	+	1
Communications	A	+	1
Manufacturing	A	+	1
Emerging Business	A	—	2
Family Business	E	—	4
Health Care	E	—	4
Public Administration	A	=	2
Ethics	B	=	1
Quality Management	-	—	2

TEACHING METHODOLOGIES	PERCENTAGE OF ALL COURSES	SKILLS DEVELOPMENT	PERCENTAGE OF ALL COURSES
Case Study	20%	Quantitative/	
Lecture	30%	Technical	25%
Experiential	20%	Managerial	60%
Combination	30%	Communication	15%
Other	—	Other	—

*Reported by Dean's Office

CAREER SERVICES

The Graduate Career Management Center is headed by Dr. Glen Payne, who came to College Park with extensive MBA expertise from USC and Texas programs. He has implemented a number of changes, including a career course for first-year students with an invaluable three-day component on experiential learning. Career Fairs are plentiful and a national employer database, used mainly by international outplacement firms, has proven to be a valuable resource for students. The goal is always to increase employer participation in campus recruitment but other, more innovative ways of hooking students to the job market are being developed as well.

CAREER SERVICES

CAREER MANAGEMENT

Career Planning Program for First-Year Students	Yes
Career Presentations in the Curricula	Yes
Alumni Network	Yes
Summer Jobs Program/ Internships	Yes
Employer Associates Program	No
Job Search Course	Yes

RECRUITMENT

Employers Interviewing at School	66
Interviews Conducted at School	665
Marketing to Employers	Yes
Resume Books	Yes
Resume Database to Employers	No
Resume Database/ Referral System	Yes
Career Fairs	Yes

CAREER SERVICES STAFF

Professional	2	Graduate Assistants	4
Support	1	Peer Advisors	-

MICHIGAN STATE UNIVERSITY

ELI BROAD GRADUATE SCHOOL OF MANAGEMENT

215 Eppley Center
East Lansing, MI 48824-1121
Tel: 517-355-7604
Fax: 517-353-1649

AT A GLANCE

First-Year Students:	120	Employer Ranking:	—
Second-Year Students:	97	Student/Faculty Ratio:	3:1
Location:	Medium-Size City	Annual Tuition:	
No. of Employers		in-state:	$3,310.50
Recruiting on Campus:	120	out-of-state:	$6,436.00

Strengths: Materials and Logistics Management, Accounting, Hotel, Restaurant and Institutional Management. Emphasis on international connections and internationally recognized faculty.

Distinctions: Awarded federal grant for one of only five International Business Education and Research Centers. Located in capital of Michigan, affording access to public internships. New course "Competitor and Market Intelligence" allows intelligence study of the auto market.

Goals: Develop international exchange programs. Weave globalization, teamwork, diversity and ethics training into the curriculum.

Words From the Dean: Ken Bardach   Tenure: 2 years
"The curriculum is newly revised including greater internationalization of courses and enhancement of communication skills. Entering students are placed in cohort groups to build cooperation and teamwork."

OVERVIEW

Eli Broad Graduate Management has all the pieces in place to make a significant move in the MBA hierarchy. It combines significant resources from one of the world's finest state universities with $40 million from Mr. Broad and a vision for excellence. The curriculum is "globalized" and through "process management" business disciplines have been linked together. East Lansing winters are cold, but hardy students seem to thrive on the variety of year-round activities.

Each entering class is divided into cohort groups of approximately 40 students. These groups help build team skills by taking specific required courses together and by working on group assignments.

The full-time, two-year program includes courses in the following areas: core courses, required subjects, field of concentration and electives. Students are also encouraged to participate in paid or unpaid internships between their first and second year of study.

Kathleen, a second semester student, works at the MSU Center for International Business Education, which consults with business schools across the country on implementing international issues into their curricula and develops tools for companies going international. She feels the experience is giving her valuable insight into global complexities.

DEMOGRAPHICS

First-Year Students	120	Women	59
Second-Year Students	97	Men	158
International Students	50	Minorities	19
		African American	11
Mean Age	25	Native American	1
Mean Class Size	30	Asian American	5
Mean Years Experience	36%-0	Hispanic American	2

PROFILE OF ENROLLED STUDENTS

Number Applicants:	861	Mean GPA Enrolled:	3.34
Number of Offers:	271	Median GMAT Enrolled:	581
Number Enrolled:	120		

Percentile GPA ranking			Percentile ranking by GMAT		
22.9	%	<3.0	11.5	%	<500
31.3	%	3-3.49	47.9	%	500-599
45.8	%	3.5-4.0	37.5	%	600-699

FACILITIES AND TECHNOLOGY

The Eli Broad Graduate School of Management is located in the brick and sandstone Eppley Center, on the 5,239-acre Michigan State campus. Eppley Center, built in 1961 and designed to house 3,000 students, now houses 8,000 undergraduate and graduate business students. To relieve the crowding at Eppley, MSU is building a new 59,500 square foot facility to be used exclusively for the MBA program. This new $22.2 million building will include multilevel amphitheater lecture halls, multilevel classrooms, case-method classrooms, and an MBA Lounge. Administrators expect that the new building, and especially the case classrooms will encourage students to network and work together. The new building will be joined to Eppley by an elevated covered walkway.

Broad students have the use of both the MSU Computer Labs and a Broad Lab. The MSU Computer Lab offers 20 microcomputer labs across the campus, and numerous noncredit courses on personal computer hardware and software; it provides consulting as well as a reference library. The Broad Lab has a number of IBM-compatible personal computers and laser printers. All labs have access to the MSU IBM and DEC mainframe computers, the University Library and other networks.

ACADEMIC STRENGTHS/FEATURES*

KEY	REPUTATION	RESOURCE COMMITMENT NEXT 2 YEARS	
	A-exceptionally well known; national reputation	+ increase = same - less	
	B-well respected	RELATIONSHIP TO CORE PROGRAM	
	C-building; targeted as key area	1=Required	4=Not offered
	D-standard program	2=Elective	5=Plan to offer
	E-not provided	3=Part of other courses	

BUSINESS FUNCTION	REPUTATION	RESOURCES COMMITTED
Consulting	E	+
Marketing	B	=
Management/Strategy	B	=
Operations-Service	A	=
Operations-Production	A	=
Finance/Accounting	B	=
HR/ILR/Organizational Behavior	B	=
Technology/Information Systems	E	=
Hotel and Restaurant Management	A	—

SPECIAL INTERESTS	REPUTATION	RESOURCES COMMITTED	RELATIONSHIP TO CORE PROGRAM
International	C	+	1
Small Business	E	=	4
Entrepreneurial	E	=	4
Diversity	C	+	1
Communications	B	+	1
Manufacturing	A	=	1
Emerging Business	C	=	4
Family Business	E	=	4
Health Care	E	=	4
Public Administration	E	=	4
Ethics	C	+	2
Other	—	—	—

TEACHING METHODOLOGIES	PERCENTAGE OF ALL COURSES	SKILLS DEVELOPMENT	PERCENTAGE OF ALL COURSES
Case Study	10%	Quantitative/	
Lecture	45%	Technical	30%
Experiential	15%	Managerial	55%
Combination	30%	Communication	10%
Other	—	Team	5%
		Other	—

*Reported by Dean's Office

CAREER SERVICES

The MBA Placement and Career Center is gaining in reputation and resources as is the graduate management program at Broad. The ratio of campus recruiting employer to graduating student is close to 1:1— no mean feat given the marketplace and geography. Some credit is due to Jack Shingleton, former director of centralized placement services, who spent more than 25 years developing outstanding relationships with employers for MSU. The center's publications and programs on career management are excellent, and the MBA Pipeline program provides links with employers who do not come to campus. There is genuine spirit here—and excitement about the future.

CAREER SERVICES

CAREER MANAGEMENT

Career Planning Program for First-Year Students	Yes
Career Presentations in the Curricula	Yes
Alumni Network	Yes
Summer Jobs Program/ Internships	Yes
Employer Associates Program	Yes
Job Search Course	Yes

RECRUITMENT

Employers Interviewing at School	120
Interviews Conducted at School	1000
Marketing to Employers	Yes
Resume Books	Yes
Resume Database to Employers	Yes
Resume Database/ Referral System	Yes
Career Fairs	Yes

CAREER SERVICES STAFF

Professional	2	Graduate Assistants	4
Support	1	Peer Advisors	—

COMMUNITY/CITY LIFE

In the heart of an industrial section of Michigan, East Lansing is best known as home to Michigan State University. The town itself is a mere eight blocks long and one block wide. Its main street, Grand River Avenue, was part of an old Indian trail from Grand Rapids to Detroit. East Lansing sits next to Lansing, the capital of Michigan, which has a population of 130,000, many of whom are involved in the Michigan automotive industry.

UNIVERSITY OF NOTRE DAME

COLLEGE OF BUSINESS ADMINISTRATION

MBA Office
127 Hayes-Healey Center
South Bend, IN 46556
Tel: 219-631-8396
Fax: 219-631-5255

AT A GLANCE

First-Year Students:	106	Employer Ranking:	—
Second-Year Students:	164	Student/Faculty Ratio:	12:1
Location:	Medium-size town	Annual Tuition:	
No. of Employers		in-state:	$15,500
Recruiting on Campus:	90-95	out-of-state:	$15,500

Strengths: Finance, Marketing, Taxation. Reputation of the university itself. A leader in globalization and communication skill development.

Distinctions: New building to be dedicated in 1995. Strong small business association and connections to employers. Outstanding joint venture with Nippon and Inland Steel for students to study Japanese management.

Words from the Dean: John Koane   Tenure: 5 years
"...Notre Dame Business is a community with enviable international focus amid an atmosphere that fosters cooperation beyond competition. This program fosters self-defining values and ethics in a world that is increasingly complex, contradictory and confusing...".

OVERVIEW

In line with its Catholic service and scholarship ideals, Notre Dame Business School commits its students to service projects through local prisons and the community. As you might expect, ethics is important here; check out the mission statement and curriculum guide in the catalog. Students have the option of a two-year or three-semester MBA that includes strong involvement with international business and a wide choice of programs in London, Santiago, France and Austria. The new management complex to be completed in 1995 is just what this solid program in a nationally esteemed university needs.

The first-year program is designed to provide students with an introduction to the functional areas of business. During the second year, the program becomes more flexible and allows students to tailor their courses to their specific needs. All students are required to complete 62 hours of work for the degree of Master of Business Administration.

DEMOGRAPHICS

First-Year Students	106	Women	65
Second-Year Students	164	Men	205
International Students	54	Minorities	17
		African American	4
Mean Age	25	Native American	0
Mean Class size	40	Asian American	8
Mean Years Experience	1-3	Hispanic American	5

PROFILE OF ENROLLED STUDENTS

Number Applicants:	391	Mean GPA Enrolled:	3.06
Number of Offers:	253	Median GMAT Enrolled:	554
Number Enrolled:	142		

Percentile GPA ranking	Percentile ranking by GMAT
45 % 3.3+	65 % 580+

FACILITIES AND TECHNOLOGY

The Hayes-Healey Center, built in 1968, houses both the graduate and undergraduate business programs. While Hayes-Healey contains the standard case-discussion rooms, seminar rooms and a microcomputer lab, it does not provide all of the resources students need. Construction of a new 153,000 square-foot building, which will house both MBA and executive development classes, began in the summer of 1993 with a target completion date of 1995. This four-story building will include fiber-optic cabling, networked classrooms, a graduate electronic library and a multilevel MBA student lounge.

The Computing Center and Mathematics Building houses the main computing center of Notre Dame, which includes an IBM mainframe running MVS/TSO and VM/XA, and Convex mini-supercomputers. Ten public computing labs are available across the campus, each containing a variety of microcomputers and software.

COMMUNITY/CITY LIFE

The University of Notre Dame is located in South Bend, Indiana, 90 miles east of Chicago. Because South Bend is an industrial city, students conduct most of their activities within the Notre Dame campus, an essentially self-sufficient community.

The Best Graduate Business Schools

ACADEMIC STRENGTHS/FEATURES*

KEY	REPUTATION	RESOURCE COMMITMENT NEXT 2 YEARS	
	A-exceptionally well known; national reputation	+ increase = same - less	
	B-well respected	RELATIONSHIP TO CORE PROGRAM	
	C-building; targeted as key area	1=Required 4=Not offered	
	D-standard program	2=Elective 5=Plan to offer	
	E-not provided	3=Part of other courses	

BUSINESS FUNCTION	REPUTATION	RESOURCES COMMITTED
Consulting	D	=
Marketing	B	=
Management/Strategy	D	=
Operations-Service	E	=
Operations-Production	D	=
Finance/Accounting	B	=
HR/ILR/Organizational Behavior	C	=
Technology/Information Systems	D	+
Other	—	—

SPECIAL INTERESTS	REPUTATION	RESOURCES COMMITTED	RELATIONSHIP TO CORE PROGRAM
International	A	+	1
Small Business	D	=	3
Entrepreneurial	C	+	2
Diversity	D	+	3
Communications	A	=	1
Manufacturing	C	=	2
Emerging Business	D	=	3
Family Business	E	=	4
Health Care	E	=	4
Public Administration	E	=	4
Ethics	A	+	1
Other	—	—	—

TEACHING METHODOLOGIES	PERCENTAGE OF ALL COURSES	SKILLS DEVELOPMENT	PERCENTAGE OF ALL COURSES
Case Study	20%	Quantitative/ Technical	30%
Lecture	20%	Managerial	50%
Experiential	10%	Communication	20%
Combination	50%	Other	—
Other	—		

*Reported by Dean's Office

CAREER SERVICES

In conjunction with the nationally prominent central Career and Placement Services office, the MBA Career Development Office provides MBA's with all they need. Counseling and programming are of high quality. Services also include internship placement, an innovative Mentor Program connecting first years with alumni and the Chicago-based, consortium-run Job Fair with other top schools, which provides an excellent way to meet employers off campus.

Matthew, a second-year finance major, spoke enthusiastically about the opportunities for entrepreneurship. He was impressed by the many good ideas provided for "start-ups."

CAREER SERVICES

CAREER MANAGEMENT

Career Planning Program for First-Year Students	Yes
Career Presentations in the Curricula	Yes
Alumni Network	Yes
Summer Jobs Program/ Internships	Yes
Employer Associates Program	No
Job Search Course	No

RECRUITMENT

Employers Interviewing at School	95
Interviews Conducted at School	600
Marketing to Employers	Yes
Resume Books	Yes
Resume Database to Employers	No
Resume Database/ Referral System	Yes
Career Fairs	No

CAREER SERVICES STAFF

Professional	1	Graduate Assistants	3
Support	2	Peer Advisors	—

OHIO STATE UNIVERSITY

COLLEGE OF BUSINESS

163 Hagerty Hall
1775 College Road
Columbus, OH 43210-1309
Tel: 619-292-2666
Fax: 619-292-7999

AT A GLANCE

First-Year Students:	138	Employer Ranking:	—
Second-Year Students:	140	Student/Faculty Ratio:	2.6 :1
Location:	City	Annual Tuition:	
No. of Employers		in-state:	$4,000
Recruiting on Campus:	185	out-of-state:	$11,000

Strengths: Finance, Logistics. Scholarship and research—college houses several business-discipline journals. Initiatives in recruiting international scholars—25% of students are from Europe, Asia and Latin America.

Distinctions: Student investment program using $10 million of the school's endowment. TALL program teams faculty and students for business presentations. Success of case competition teams.

Goals: New business complex under construction. Increase quality in areas of functional knowledge, integration, international and leadership skills.

Words from the Dean: Joseph A. Alutto   Tenure: 4 years
"With new state-of-the-art buildings as enabling devices, continuously improving programs, new funding becoming available for innovations and a large base of active alumni and corporate supporters, the College provides an exciting and effective learning environment..."

OVERVIEW

The College of Business at Ohio State University in Columbus appears to have all the MBA bases covered. Taking advantage of its business partnerships with over 16 major companies with national headquarters in Ohio, the College of Business offers numerous opportunities for students to solve real business problems. The college emphasizes cooperation and hands-on leadership through a variety of approaches, including the required "Teamwork and Leadership Laboratory" and the highly successful Student Investment Class. This school provides top learning experiences, both in and outside the classroom.

During the first year, the MBA core curriculum is divided into three phases. Phase one provides a basis of accounting, economics, statistics and organizational behavior skills. Phase two exposes students to functional business areas such as finance, marketing, operations and human resource management. Phase three integrates practice and theory by allowing students to identify policy issues and develop strategies to resolve them.

The second year is more flexible. Students can elect nine of 12 courses. However, they must complete three electives in a key area of emphasis.

DEMOGRAPHICS

First-Year Students	138	Women	75
Second-Year Students	140	Men	205
International Students	73	Minorities	30
		African American	16
Mean Age	26	Native American	N/A
Mean Class Size	60	Asian American	2
Mean Years Experience	1-3	Hispanic American	12

PROFILE OF ENROLLED STUDENTS

Number Applicants:	681	Mean GPA Enrolled:	3.19
Number of Offers:	287	Median GMAT Enrolled:	602
Number Enrolled:	128		

Percentile GPA ranking			Percentile ranking by GMAT		
90	%	3.90 - 4.0	90	%	690 - 800
70	%	3.60 - 4.0	70	%	650 - 800
50	%	3.23 - 4.0	50	%	600 - 800

FACILITIES AND TECHNOLOGY

Page and Hagerty Halls are home to the College of Business at Ohio State. The buildings, featuring tiered seating and up-to-date audio visual equipment, are already overcrowded, and administrators recognize that to expand the business program at Ohio State, additional facilities will be needed. The school has raised $65 million for a new business school complex that should be completed by 1997.

The Business Library, located in Page Hall, houses over 175,000 business-related volumes, as well as reference materials. All MBA students are assigned a computer-based E-mail account. This account provides access to on-line database systems, as well as the *Wall Street Journal*, ABI Inform and other abstract services. The university has a microcomputer network of IBM, IBM-compatible and Macintosh personal computers, along with a variety of office and business software.

ACADEMIC STRENGTHS/FEATURES*

KEY	REPUTATION	RESOURCE COMMITMENT NEXT 2 YEARS	
	A-exceptionally well known; national reputation	+ increase = same - less	
	B-well respected	RELATIONSHIP TO CORE PROGRAM	
	C-building; targeted as key area	1=Required	4=Not offered
	D-standard program	2=Elective	5=Plan to offer
	E-not provided	3=Part of other courses	

BUSINESS FUNCTION	REPUTATION	RESOURCES COMMITTED
Consulting	E	=
Marketing	A	+
Management/Strategy	C	+
Operations-Service	A	+
Operations-Production	A	+
Finance/Accounting	A	+
HR/ILR/Organizational Behavior	A	=
Technology/Information Systems	A	=
Accounting	A	—

SPECIAL INTERESTS	REPUTATION	RESOURCES COMMITTED	RELATIONSHIP TO CORE PROGRAM
International	C	+	2
Small Business	D	=	2
Entrepreneurial	D	=	2
Diversity	C	=	3
Communications	D	=	1
Manufacturing	C	=	2
Emerging Business	E	-	2
Family Business	E	-	3
Health Care	D	=	2
Public Administration	A	-	2
Ethics	C	=	2
Other	—	—	—

TEACHING METHODOLOGIES	PERCENTAGE OF ALL COURSES	SKILLS DEVELOPMENT	PERCENTAGE OF ALL COURSES
Case Study	20%	Quantitative/ Technical	50%
Lecture	20%	Managerial	20%
Experiential	5%	Communication	20%
Combination	45%	Teamwork	10%
Teamwork	5%	Other	—
Other	5%		

*Reported by Dean's Office

CAREER SERVICES

The Career Services Office serves both undergraduate business students and MBA candidates. There is a separate director for MBA Career Services, and several programs—including seminars and a graduate Job Fair—are MBA-specific. The Office emphasizes career development and offers students a variety of opportunities through programs like the Student Investment Management Program and Internships. Connections with Eastern Europe are strong, with an excellent summer intern program with Russia.

CAREER SERVICES

CAREER MANAGEMENT

Career Planning Program for First-Year Students	Yes
Career Presentations in the Curricula	Yes
Alumni Network	Yes
Summer Jobs Program/ Internships	Yes
Employer Associates Program	No
Job Search Course	No

RECRUITMENT

Employers Interviewing at School	185
Interviews Conducted at School	585
Marketing to Employers	Yes
Resume Books	Yes
Resume Database to Employers	No
Resume Database/ Referral System	Yes
Career Fairs	Yes

CAREER SERVICES STAFF

Professional	5	Graduate Assistants	22
Support	4	Peer Advisors	—

COMMUNITY/CITY LIFE

Ohio State University is based in the growing city of Columbus, recently recognized as one of the top ten cities for entrepreneurial activity. In addition to a new $94 million Convention Center, the city also boasts a major art museum, a professional symphony, and ballet and opera companies. There are historic attractions close by, and Columbus offers plenty of affordable housing. While the city is a financial services center, it has a broad-based service-sector economy, a nationally recognized arts community and a sophisticated health-care network.

PENNSYLVANIA STATE UNIVERSITY

THE SMEAL COLLEGE OF BUSINESS ADMINISTRATION

106 Business Administration Building
University Park, PA 16802-3000
Tel: 814-863-0474
Fax: 814-863-8072

AT A GLANCE

First-Year Students:	118	Employer Ranking:	—
Second-Year Students:	143	Student/Faculty Ratio:	2.6 :1
Location:	Small Town	Annual Tuition:	
No. of Employers		in-state:	$5,100
Recruiting on Campus:	144	out-of-state:	$11,000

Strengths: Managerial Communications, Marketing, Finance. Close relationship with the University itself.

Distinctions: Received major grant from IBM to apply TQM principles to graduate business education. Close links to area small businesses. Evolving Research Park facility provides significant opportunities for students.

Goals: Maximize satisfaction level of student and employer customers.

Words From the Dean: J.D. Hammond   Tenure: 5.5 years
"The culture of the college and the university offer a superior living and learning environment and our corporate recruiters like the 'can do' approach of our graduates."

OVERVIEW

The Penn State Smeal College of Business Administration draws on the worldwide reputation of Penn State, considered one of the finest public universities anywhere, to attract students (1 in 700 Americans holds a Penn State Degree). The MBA program is gaining stature both regionally and nationally because of its recognized faculty, its multiple uses of corporate affiliations and alliances with this major research university. Located in the exact middle of the state, hours from Pittsburgh, Philadelphia and other populous places, the school works overtime to get companies to the campus for a variety of business, social, cultural and athletic events.

DEMOGRAPHICS

First-Year Students	118	Women	100
Second-Year Students	143	Men	161
International Students	55	Minorities	45
		African American	31
Mean Age	26.5	Native American	0
Mean Class Size	40	Asian American	6
Mean Years Experience	—	Hispanic American	8

PROFILE OF ENROLLED STUDENTS

Number Applicants:	1158	Mean GPA Enrolled:	3.06
Number of Offers:	310	Mean GMAT Enrolled:	N/A
Number Enrolled:	120		

Percentile GPA ranking			Percentile ranking by GMAT		
90	%	3.76	90	%	640
70	%	3.55	70	%	600
50	%	3.31	50	%	570

FACILITIES AND TECHNOLOGY

While the Penn State campus sprawls over 5,162 acres, the MBA program is concentrated in two buildings on the north end of the campus. The Business Administration Building and the Beam Building contain horseshoe-shaped classrooms with tiered seating, seminar and conference rooms, computer labs, offices and an MBA student lounge.

The school's business administration collection is housed in the Fred Lewis Pattee Library, which provides computerized access to a number of external databases. Business reference librarians are available for consultation.

The Penn State Center for Academic Computing has responsibility for university-wide computing resources. Personal computer labs are located at both the Beam and Business Administration Buildings. The labs contain AT&T, IBM, Hewlett-Packard and Macintosh computers, and a variety of printers and software. Dial-up access to the University's IBM and DEC VAX mainframes is available; the system is also connected to the John von Neumann Supercomputer Center and to a number of other systems outside the university.

ACADEMIC STRENGTHS/FEATURES*

KEY	REPUTATION	RESOURCE COMMITMENT NEXT 2 YEARS
	A-exceptionally well known; national reputation	+ increase = same - less
	B-well respected	**RELATIONSHIP TO CORE PROGRAM**
	C-building; targeted as key area	1=Required 4=Not offered
	D-standard program	2=Elective 5=Plan to
	E-not provided	3=Part of offer other courses

BUSINESS FUNCTION	REPUTATION	RESOURCES COMMITTED
Consulting	A	=
Marketing	A	+
Management/Strategy	B	+
Operations-Service	B	=
Operations-Production	A	+
Finance/Accounting	B	+
HR/ILR/Organizational Behavior	B	+
Technology/Information Systems	B	+
Real Estate	A	—

SPECIAL INTERESTS	REPUTATION	RESOURCES COMMITTED	RELATIONSHIP TO CORE PROGRAM
International	—	+	1
Small Business	—	—	2
Entrepreneurial	B	+	2
Diversity	B	=	1
Communications	A	+	1
Manufacturing	A	+	2
Emerging Business	—	=	4
Family Business	—	=	4
Health Care	—	=	4
Public Administration	—	=	4
Ethics	A	=	—
Business Marketing	A	=	2,3

TEACHING METHODOLOGIES	PERCENTAGE OF ALL COURSES	SKILLS DEVELOPMENT	PERCENTAGE OF ALL COURSES
Case Study	50%	Quantitative/	
Lecture	30%	Technical	35%
Experiential	20%	Managerial	40%
Combination	—	Communication	15%
Other	—	Software	10%
		Other	—

*Reported by Dean's Office

CAREER SERVICES

The Smeal School has established its own MBA Career Center through the MBA Association. The Dean's staff pitch in on various career advising responsibilities. The school also enjoys a productive relationship with the larger University Career Planning and Placement Office—a national model for high quality, centralized career service development and delivery. A number of Alumni Network, Employment Database and Job Search Skills programs are available for MBA students.

CAREER SERVICES

CAREER MANAGEMENT		RECRUITMENT	
Career Planning Program for First-Year Students	Yes	Employers Interviewing at School	144
Career Presentations in the Curricula	No	Interviews Conducted at School	955
Alumni Network	Yes	Marketing to Employers	Yes
Summer Jobs Program/ Internships	Yes	Resume Books	Yes
Employer Associates Program	Yes	Resume Database to Employers	No
Job Search Course	No	Resume Database/ Referral System	Yes
		Career Fairs	Yes

CAREER SERVICES STAFF

Professional	2	Graduate Assistants	3
Support	2	Peer Advisors	—

COMMUNITY/CITY LIFE

Located in central Pennsylvania, University Park, also known as "Happy Valley," is a college town surrounded by mountains. The area is popular for outdoor recreation, including fishing, hunting, hiking, biking and skiing. The Stone Valley Recreation Center, operated by the university, has a 72-acre lake, rental cabins, picnic areas, and a boat-rental facility. Citing a high standard of living and a low crime rate, *Psychology Today* magazine rated the area as the least stressful community in the nation. A number of outdoor festivals are held each year, including the Central Pennsylvania Festival of the Arts. University Park is located 120 miles east of Pittsburgh and 150 miles west of Philadelphia.

UNIVERSITY OF PITTSBURGH

JOSEPH M. KATZ GRADUATE SCHOOL OF BUSINESS

372 Mervis Hall
Pittsburgh, PA   15260
Tel.:   412-648-1510
Fax: 412-648-2571

AT A GLANCE

First-Year Students:	151	Employer Ranking:	#12 of 61
Second-Year Students:	150	Student/Faculty Ratio:	1:5
Location:	Major City	Annual Tuition:	
No. of Employers		in-state:	$12,500
Recruiting on Campus:	70	out-of-state:	$21,000

Strengths: Marketing, Finance, Management/Strategy. High-quality MBA in one year.

Distinctions: Recognized for top faculty with national research contributions. Required series of professional development workshops on key business topics. Location and connections to Pittsburgh business.

Goals: Continue internationalizing student body and curriculum. Use "value added" and "total quality management" principles to guide development.

Words From the Dean: H.J. Zoffer   Tenure: 26 years
" ...Thus prospective business students must rely on some mapping of their own needs with the attributes of the various schools. We at Katz view ourselves as 'niche marketers.' We are known for assessing our customers' needs...".

OVERVIEW

Katz has been known in the field for its 12-month, 52-credit program. However, under the leadership of Dean H.J. Zoffer, the Katz School has distinguished itself in a number of areas. Its international programs, partnerships with business and executive MBA programs have been nationally recognized.   Along with recent curriculum innovations, the school is also instituting a series of individual assessment efforts to help students determine strengths and weaknesses and subsequent professional and personal goals within the program. Pittsburgh provides a good business base for the school and Oakland offers a high-quality environment for the students.

First-Year Students	151	Women	93
Second-Year Students	150	Men	208
International Students	90	Minorities	31
		African American	19
Mean Age	27	Native American	N/A
Mean Class Size	N/A	Asian American	N/A
Mean Years Experience	1-3	Hispanic American	12

PROFILE OF ENROLLED STUDENTS

Number Applicants:	1061	Mean GPA Enrolled:	3.17
Number of Offers:	N/A	Median GMAT Enrolled:	603
Number Enrolled:	301		

Percentile GPA ranking			Percentile ranking by GMAT		
N/A	%	N/A	N/A	%	N/A
N/A	%	N/A	N/A	%	N/A
N/A	%	N/A	N/A	%	N/A

FACILITIES AND TECHNOLOGY

The University of Pittsburgh is located 10 minutes from downtown Pittsburgh on a 132-acre campus. The university's 90 buildings include the Cathedral of Learning, a 42-story ornate Gothic structure, known as the tallest school building in the western world. The Katz School occupies a sleek, reflective glass building that contains state-of-the-art computing facilities, a large business library and a cafeteria for MBA students. The classrooms are tiered and horseshoe-shaped.

COMMUNITY/CITY LIFE

With over 15 Fortune 500 companies calling Pittsburgh their home, this city has evolved from a steel town to one with a diversified economic base. The "Golden Triangle," located at the junction of three western Pennsylvanian rivers and only ten minutes from the Katz School, is an impressive collection of skyscraper office buildings, plazas and parks. Pittsburgh has been noted as one of the most liveable areas in the country, with a low crime rate and a range of cultural offerings, as well as nationally recognized universities and health facilities. The Katz School borders on the 450-acre Schenley Park, where students can walk, play tennis, golf, swim and ice skate.

ACADEMIC STRENGTHS/FEATURES*

KEY	REPUTATION	RESOURCE COMMITMENT NEXT 2 YEARS
	A-exceptionally well known; national reputation	+ increase = same - less
	B-well respected	**RELATIONSHIP TO CORE PROGRAM**
	C-building; targeted as key area	1=Required 4=Not offered
	D-standard program	2=Elective 5=Plan to
	E-not provided	3=Part of offer
		other courses

BUSINESS FUNCTION	REPUTATION	RESOURCES COMMITTED
Consulting	C	=
Marketing	A	=
Management/Strategy	A	=
Operations-Service	C	=
Operations-Production	B	+
Finance/Accounting	A	+
HR/ILR/Organizational Behavior	A	=
Technology/Information Systems	A	+
Accounting	A	

SPECIAL INTERESTS	REPUTATION	RESOURCES COMMITTED	RELATIONSHIP TO CORE PROGRAM
International	A	+	1
Small Business	N/A	=	2
Entrepreneurial	B	+	2
Diversity	C	+	3
Communications	B	+	1
Manufacturing	B	+	1
Emerging Business	N/A	=	2
Family Business	E	=	2
Health Care	A	=	1
Public Administration	E	=	2
Ethics	A	+	1
Other	—	—	—

TEACHING METHODOLOGIES	PERCENTAGE OF ALL COURSES	SKILLS DEVELOPMENT	PERCENTAGE OF ALL COURSES
Case Study	30%	Quantitative/	
Lecture	20%	Technical	30%
Experiential	20%	Managerial	30%
Combination	30%	Communication	30%
Other	—	Other	10%

*Reported by Dean's Office

CAREER SERVICES

Placement and Career Services have always been strong at Katz. The office is very proactive in its efforts to develop recruitment relationships with employers who do not come to campus. The direct mail campaign is exemplary. Education is also important and individual courses offered for both first-and second-year students enroll more than 300 students each. The American Assembly Dialogue program brings 12-15 CEOs to campus for discussion.

CAREER SERVICES

CAREER MANAGEMENT		RECRUITMENT	
Career Planning Program for First-Year Students	Yes	Employers Interviewing at School	70
Career Presentations in the Curricula	No	Interviews Conducted at School	—
Alumni Network	Yes	Marketing to Employers	Yes
Summer Jobs Program/ Internships	Yes	Resume Books	Yes
Employer Associates Program	Yes	Resume Database to Employers	No
Job Search Course	Yes	Resume Database/ Referral System	Yes
		Career Fairs	No

CAREER SERVICES STAFF

Professional	3	Graduate Assistants	1
Support	2	Peer Advisors	—

RICE UNIVERSITY

JESSE H. JONES GRADUATE SCHOOL OF ADMINISTRATION

225 Herring Hall
6100 South Main Street
Houston TX 77005
Tel: 713-527-4918
Fax: 713-285-5251

AT A GLANCE

First-Year Students:	120	Employer Ranking:	—
Second-Year Students:	100	Student/Faculty Ratio:	8:1
Location:	Major City	Annual Tuition:	
No. of Employers		in-state:	$8,000
Recruiting on Campus:	65	out-of-state:	$8,000

Strengths: Finance, Marketing, Accounting. Small size of program. Good balance between quantitative and communication skills development.

Distinctions: Only private school on *Forbes'* honor roll of affordable high-quality MBA programs. Flex-time arrangement allows students to remain fully employed.

Words From the Dean: Benjamin F. Bailar   Tenure: 7 years
"The curriculum is rigorous, the work intense. But our students are rewarded with an education that provides them with the background, the confidence and the skills to welcome the challenges of the global marketplace...".

OVERVIEW

Located in a safe, luxurious area of Houston, Jones (and Rice University) appear on many lists of "best buys in education." Indeed, at that tuition level, it is difficult to realize that Rice University is as fine a private university as there is—and Jones is making its mark in the MBA world as well. With exemplary programs in entrepreneurship and ethics, Jones has ranked in the "top 20—40" in most surveys. It is also serious about integrating liberal education, including communications, with its business curricula. Jones observes academic tradition with the "investiture" ceremony at graduation; the Dean places the academic hood on each graduate.

The first-year curriculum focuses on the development of analytical, organizational, quantitative and communication skills. In addition to standard accounting and management courses, students must study Organizational Behavior and Quantitative Methods.

During the second year, students take the skills they have learned and apply them to various policy issues. Most of the second-year courses are electives and the students can explore areas of particular interest. Required course work includes a case-method seminar called Management Strategy I and II. Here, students work in small groups to develop oral case presentations and written reports.

275

DEMOGRAPHICS

First-Year Students	120	Women	60
Second-Year Students	100	Men	160
International Students	33	Minorities	30
		African American	0
Mean Age	26.9	Native Indian American	0
Mean Class Size	12	Asian American	24
Mean Years Experience	1-3	Hispanic American	6

PROFILE OF ENROLLED STUDENTS

Number Applicants:	882	Mean GPA Enrolled:	3.25
Number of Offers:	304	Median GMAT Enrolled:	623
Number Enrolled:	120		

Percentile GPA ranking			Percentile ranking by GMAT		
90	%	3.81 - 4.0	90	%	701 - 800
70	%	3.47 - 4.0	70	%	646 - 800
50	%	3.36 - 4.0	50	%	632 - 800

FACILITIES AND TECHNOLOGY

The Rice campus is situated in an upscale residential Houston area, across the street from Hermann Park and the Texas Medical Center. Large stands of oak trees shade the lawns and fields. The academic halls are built of red brick and marble, and covered walkways allow for easy passage between many of the buildings.

Herring Hall, designed by internationally acclaimed architect Cesar Pelli, is home to the Jones School. Constructed of red brick and white limestone, the building is nestled in a grove of oak trees and harmonizes with the rest of the 300-acre Rice campus. Herring Hall includes seminar rooms, case rooms, a large lecture hall, a small microcomputer lab and a student-faculty lounge. An onsite business information center provides a collection of current management and accounting literature.

ACADEMIC STRENGTHS/FEATURES*

KEY	REPUTATION	RESOURCE COMMITMENT NEXT 2 YEARS	
	A-exceptionally well known; national reputation	+ increase = same - less	
	B-well respected	RELATIONSHIP TO CORE PROGRAM	
	C-building; targeted as key area	1=Required	4=Not offered
	D-standard program	2=Elective	5=Plan to offer
	E-not provided	3=Part of other courses	

BUSINESS FUNCTION	REPUTATION	RESOURCES COMMITTED
Consulting	C	=
Marketing	B	=
Management/Strategy	B	=
Operations-Service	E	N/A
Operations-Production	C	=
Finance/Accounting	A	+
HR/ILR/Organizational Behavior	C	=
Technology/Information Systems	B	=
Other	—	—

SPECIAL INTERESTS	REPUTATION	RESOURCES COMMITTED	RELATIONSHIP TO CORE PROGRAM
International	B	+	2
Small Business	E	N/A	4
Entrepreneurial	B	=	2
Diversity	A	+	1
Communications	C	=	1
Manufacturing	E	N/A	4
Emerging Business	E	—	4
Family Business	E	—	4
Health Care	E	—	4
Public Administration	B	+	1
Ethics	B	+	1
Other	—	—	—

TEACHING METHODOLOGIES	PERCENTAGE OF ALL COURSES	SKILLS DEVELOPMENT	PERCENTAGE OF ALL COURSES
Case Study	30%	Quantitative/ Technical	30%
Lecture	20%		
Experiential	40%	Managerial	30%
Combination	10%	Communication	20%
Other	—	Other	20%

*Reported by Dean's Office

Rice University

CAREER SERVICES

Placement at The Jones Graduate School focuses on a variety of ways of bringing employers and students together. The emphasis is on campus activity and includes traditional campus interviews, a successful summer internship recruiting initiative, resume books, receptions, presentations and job notifications. Director Spence Warren encourages employers to allow him personally to contact qualified students for the companies—an approach not often evident in MBA placement.

CAREER SERVICES

CAREER MANAGEMENT

Career Planning Program for First-Year Students	Yes
Career Presentations in the Curricula	Yes
Alumni Network	Yes
Summer Jobs Program/ Internships	Yes
Employer Associates Program	No
Job Search Course	No

RECRUITMENT

Employers Interviewing at School	70
Interviews Conducted at School	900
Marketing to Employers	Yes
Resume Books	Yes
Resume Database to Employers	No
Resume Database/ Referral System	Yes
Career Fairs	Yes

CAREER SERVICES STAFF

Professional	3	Graduate Assistants	N/A
Support	N/A	Peer Advisors	N/A

COMMUNITY/CITY LIFE

Rice University is located in Houston, the nation's fourth-largest city and headquarters for over 1,000 major corporations. A major center for both finance and agribusiness, Houston is the energy capital of the world, accounting for more than half of the United States' petrochemical manufacturing. Rice occupies a safe, upscale section of Houston, and students can enjoy the nationally renowned Houston Symphony, Houston Grand Opera, Houston Ballet and Alley Theater, as well as the professional sports teams that make Houston their home. Students comment that the relatively low cost of living enables them to take advantage of a variety of cultural, recreational and leisure activities, including Gulf Coast beaches only one hour away.

UNIVERSITY OF SOUTH CAROLINA

COLLEGE OF BUSINESS ADMINISTRATION
GRADUATE DIVISION

Office of Admissions
Columbia, SC 29208
Tel: 803-777-4346
Fax: 803-777-0414

AT A GLANCE

First-Year Students:	221	Employer Ranking:	—
Second-Year Students:	227	Student/Faculty Ratio:	N/A
Location:	Medium-size city	Annual Tuition:	
No. of Employers		in-state:	$10,000
Recruiting on Campus:	49	out-of-state:	$19,000

Strengths: International Business, Marketing, Accounting, Employment and Personnel. International MBA requires seven-months' study in Vienna. *U.S. News and World Report* ranks #1 in international business four consecutive years.

Distinctions: Recognized for faculty publishing and research. Leader in language skills development.

Words From the Dean: Susie H. VanHuss   Tenure: 1 year
"Long before terms like global economics, ethics, international business and TQM were commonplace in business curriculum, they were in place at the University of South Carolina."

OVERVIEW

The list of credentials for USC's MIBS (Master of International Business Studies) program is impressive, including high GMAT scores (mean of 620) and GPAs of entering students, winning case competitions against other international program students, collaborative programs with Austria's best schools and an international conference run by MIBS faculty. An outstanding feature of this program is the intensive study of the language and culture of most foreign countries. Marketing, Accounting and Personnel/Employment are also strong at USC. South Carolina offers a warm climate, bountiful recreational opportunities and a thriving economy. However, access to major cities is a challenge since Columbia is hundreds of miles from anywhere.

DEMOGRAPHICS

First-Year Students	221	Women	161
Second-Year Students	227	Men	287
International Students	43	Minorities	58
		African American	40
Mean Age	25.5	Native American	0
Mean Class Size	40	Asian American	18
Mean Years Experience	1-3	Hispanic American	N/A

PROFILE OF ENROLLED STUDENTS

Number Applicants:	1054	Mean GPA Enrolled:	3.29
Number of Offers:	465	Median GMAT Enrolled:	597
Number Enrolled:	221		

Percentile GPA ranking			Percentile ranking by GMAT		
90	%	3.79 - 4.0	90	%	680 - 740
70	%	3.46 - 3.78	70	%	620 - 670
50	%	3.26 - 3.45	50	%	590 - 610

FACILITIES AND TECHNOLOGY

Located in downtown Columbia, the College of Business Administration is part of USC's 242-acre main campus. The college occupies the H. William Close and Francis M. Hipp buildings, a nine-story complex.

Business students have access to the Elliot White Springs Library as well as to ABI-INFORM, COMPACT DISCLOSURE and USCAN databases.

The Computer Center occupies 12,000 square feet on the first floor of the Francis M. Hipp Building. Over 125 microcomputers are available for students in the computer lab, and the center has a separate entrance and security system to allow after-hours use. Access to the school's IBM 4381 mainframe computer is provided, along with a variety of software packages and other networks.

ACADEMIC STRENGTHS/FEATURES*

KEY	REPUTATION	RESOURCE COMMITMENT NEXT 2 YEARS
K E Y	A-exceptionally well known; national reputation B-well respected C-building; targeted as key area D-standard program E-not provided	+ increase = same - less
		RELATIONSHIP TO CORE PROGRAM 1=Required 4=Not offered 2=Elective 5=Plan to 3=Part of offer other courses

BUSINESS FUNCTION	REPUTATION	RESOURCES COMMITTED
Consulting	B	=
Marketing	A	=
Management/Strategy	A,B	=
Operations-Service	B	=
Operations-Production	B	=
Finance/Accounting	A	=
HR/ILR/Organizational Behavior	A	=
Technology/Information Systems	B	+
Other	—	—

SPECIAL INTERESTS	REPUTATION	RESOURCES COMMITTED	RELATIONSHIP TO CORE PROGRAM
International	A	+	1
Small Business	A	+	2
Entrepreneurial	A	+	2
Diversity	B	+	3
Communications	C	+	3
Manufacturing	C	=	2
Emerging Business	A	N/A	2
Family Business	C	N/A	N/A
Health Care	E	N/A	N/A
Public Administration	E	—	N/A
Ethics	C	—	3
Other	-	—	—

TEACHING METHODOLOGIES	PERCENTAGE OF ALL COURSES	SKILLS DEVELOPMENT	PERCENTAGE OF ALL COURSES
Case Study	15%	Quantitative/	
Lecture	5%	Technical	30%
Experiential	10%	Managerial	35%
Combination	70%	Communication	20%
Other	—	Team Building	15%
		Other	—

*Reported by Dean's Office

CAREER SERVICES

The companies recruiting USC graduates represent a healthy cross-section of industries. The Graduate Placement Office teams up with the centralized Career Counseling
Service for the campus to provide services. A number of specialized services for
MBAs exist, however, including resume books, referral networks and an alumni job
bank for MIBS students. Workshops are provided on a number of job search topics.

CAREER SERVICES

CAREER MANAGEMENT		RECRUITMENT	
Career Planning Program for First-Year Students	Yes	Employers Interviewing at School	N/A
Career Presentations in the Curricula	Yes	Interviews Conducted at School	N/A
Alumni Network	Yes	Marketing to Employers	N/A
Summer Jobs Program/ Internships	Yes	Resume Books	N/A
Employer Associates Program	Yes	Resume Database to Employers	N/A
Job Search Course	No	Resume Database/ Refrral System	N/A
		Career Fairs	N/A

CAREER SERVICES STAFF

Professional	5	Graduate Assistants	11
Support	—	Peer Advisors	—

COMMUNITY/CITY LIFE

Columbia, the state capital, is rich in culture and history. Beautiful, historic southern
mansions add character to the city and are open to the public. *Inc. Magazine* ranked
Columbia as one of the 20 fastest-growing metropolitan areas in the U.S., with its
population increasing 10.1% since 1980 and job opportunities increasing by 25%. The
construction and development of public areas, such as Sydney Park, Riverfront Park,
Historic Columbia Canal and the Riverbanks Zoo, provide further indications of
Columbia's growth. The Koger Center for the Arts sponsors numerous events,
including opera, theatre and dance productions. Within a two-hours drive students can
enjoy sunning on coastal beaches or hiking in the Blue Ridge Mountains.

SOUTHERN METHODIST UNIVERSITY

EDWIN L. COX SCHOOL OF BUSINESS

Office of Admissions
Dallas, TX 75275-0333
Tel: 214-768-3678
Fax: 214-768-4099

AT A GLANCE

First-Year Students:	114	Employer Ranking: —
Second-Year Students:	113	Student/Faculty Ratio: 28:1
Location:	Medium-size town	Annual Tuition:
No. of Employers		in-state: $16,000
Recruiting on Campus:	52	out-of-state: $16,000

Strengths: Finance, Management of Information Science, Leadership Development/ Assessment. Outstanding mentoring program.

Distinctions: Business Leadership Center is thriving with productive relationships with Dallas/Fort Worth major corporations. MBA Community Partners program is an excellent example of giving back to the community through free consultation.

Words From the Dean: David H. Blake   Tenure: 5 years
"To excel in business, you need to go beyond the fundamentals. To be a business leader, one who helps shape the organization's future, you must approach the challenges with a global perspective, a commitment to quality, and an ability to leverage your personal skills and resources to mobilize the talents and energies of others."

OVERVIEW

Founded in 1920, SMU's School of Business was renamed in 1978 for its principal donor, oilman Edwin L. Cox. Leadership development and assessment is a strong suit for this school; the Business Leadership Center is a unique program and delivers a host of services and resources that enhance student skill development—management, communications and career search. SMU-Cox offers a variety of international options and boasts an enrollment consisting of more than 20 % international students. The MBA Enterprise Corps provides opportunities for students to work with international companies in countries moving from socialist to free-market economies.

DEMOGRAPHICS

First-Year Students	114	Women	63
Second-Year Students	112	Men	164
International Students	33	Minorities	18
		African American	5
Mean Age	25	Native American	0
Mean Class Size	45	Asian American	6
Mean Years Experience	1-3	Hispanic American	7

PROFILE OF ENROLLED STUDENTS

Number Applicants:	409	Mean GPA Enrolled:	3.11
Number of Offers:	274	Median GMAT Enrolled:	613
Number Enrolled:	114		

Percentile GPA ranking			Percentile ranking by GMAT		
N/A	%	N/A	N/A	%	N/A
N/A	%	N/A	N/A	%	N/A
N/A	%	N/A	N/A	%	N/A

FACILITIES AND TECHNOLOGY

The Cox School complex is comprised of three primary buildings set in the shape of a horseshoe. The original building, the Fincher Building, built in 1952, houses administrative and faculty offices, along with conference and meeting rooms. The Maguire Building and the Crow Building contain classrooms and study rooms.

The Cox School has the Business Information Center (BIC) as its hub. The BIC combines the features of a university library with on-line computer systems, providing access to the latest business periodicals, market information and news retrieval services. Approximately 60 IBM-compatible personal computers and 16 Macintosh computers, with a variety of software, are available at the center.

COMMUNITY/CITY LIFE

Dallas has become a dynamic and diverse city over the past several decades. Because of its mild year-round climate, its comprehensive transportation system and its selection as the headquarters for many *Fortune* 500 companies, the city has grown into one of the largest metropolitan areas in the country. Dallas offers great dining, five-star hotels, first-run plays and world-class museums and symphonies. There are live musical performances daily in the Dallas/Fort Worth "Metroplex," numerous shopping malls and amusement parks. For sports fans, Dallas offers the Super Bowl champion Dallas Cowboys as well as college sports.

ACADEMIC STRENGTHS/FEATURES*

KEY	REPUTATION	RESOURCE COMMITMENT NEXT 2 YEARS
	A-exceptionally well known; national reputation	+ increase = same - less
	B-well respected	**RELATIONSHIP TO CORE PROGRAM**
	C-building; targeted as key area	1=Required 4=Not offered
	D-standard program	2=Elective 5=Plan to
	E-not provided	3=Part of offer other courses

BUSINESS FUNCTION	REPUTATION	RESOURCES COMMITTED
Consulting	B	=
Marketing	A	+
Management/Strategy	A	+
Operations-Service	B	=
Operations-Production	B	=
Finance/Accounting	A	+
HR/ILR/Organizational Behavior	A	+
Technology/Information Systems	A	+
Accounting	A	=

SPECIAL INTERESTS	REPUTATION	RESOURCES COMMITTED	RELATIONSHIP TO CORE PROGRAM
International	A	+	1,2,3
Small Business	A	+	2
Entrepreneurial	A	+	2
Diversity	A	+	1
Communications	A	+	1
Manufacturing	E	=	1,2,3
Emerging Business	D	=	2
Family Business	A	=	2
Health Care	E	+	2
Public Administration	E	=	2
Ethics	A	=	1,2,3
Consulting	—	—	1

TEACHING METHODOLOGIES	PERCENTAGE OF ALL COURSES	SKILLS DEVELOPMENT	PERCENTAGE OF ALL COURSES
Case Study	50%	Quantitative/	
Lecture	35%	Technical	30%
Experiential	—	Managerial	85%
Combination	—	Communication	100%
Group Projects	15%	Other	—
Other	—		

*Reported by Dean's Office

CAREER SERVICES

The Office of Career Services operates on the sound philosophy that students need to research and proactively contact employers in this changing MBA market. Several programs and publications are provided to assist students. The office is well connected to Dallas business and participates in a number of consortia to increase students' contact with employers from other parts of the country.

CAREER SERVICES

CAREER MANAGEMENT

Career Planning Program for First-Year Students	Yes
Career Presentations in the Curricula	No
Alumni Network	Yes
Summer Jobs Program/ Internships	Yes
Employer Associates Program	Yes
Job Search Course	Yes

RECRUITMENT

Employers Interviewing at School	52
Interviews Conducted at School	492
Marketing to Employers	Yes
Resume Books	Yes
Resume Database to Employers	No
Resume Database/ Referral System	Yes
Career Fairs	Yes

CAREER SERVICES STAFF

Professional	2	Graduate Assistants	3
Support	1	Peer Advisors	0

UNIVERSITY OF TENNESSEE AT KNOXVILLE

COLLEGE OF BUSINESS ADMINISTRATION

Office of Graduate Business Programs
527 Stokely Management Center
Knoxville, TN   37996-0550
Tel: 615-974-5033
Fax: 615-974-3826

AT A GLANCE

First-Year Students:	74	Employer Ranking:	—
Second-Year Students:	73	Student/Faculty Ratio:	17.5:1
Location:	City	Annual Tuition:	
No. of Employers		in-state:	$2,200
Recruiting on Campus:	N/A	out-of-state:	$6,000

Strengths: MBA Core Curriculum, HR/Organizational Behavior/Industrial Psychology, Marketing/Logistical Transportation. An up-and-coming program seeking and getting national attention.

Distinctions: Emphasis on Total Quality Management throughout curriculum. Management Development Center does impressive work with the business community. Placement is a part of a leading center headed by one of the best. Both services and statistics reflect this top quality.

Goals: Attain national profile with employers. Increase involvement globally.

Words from the Dean: C. Warren Neel   Tenure: 15 years
"Employing 'just in time' method of education, the program helps students learn what they need to know when they need to apply it to a problem arising from their business."

OVERVIEW

With impressive placement statistics, innovative ideas like having all first-year students involved in a fully integrated 30-hour curriculum in which they run their own hypothetical company, and a Management Development Center that sends first-hand knowledge into business classrooms, the Tennessee MBA program is gaining in national stature. Knoxville is a thriving business community with a wealth of entrepreneurial, manufacturing and financial services—perfect for internships and summer experiences. Excitement is running high at UTK-MBA; Tennessee's goal is national recognition for bold innovations, especially in experiential education. Feedback from students and employers indicates that this goal is within reach.

DEMOGRAPHICS

First-Year Students	74	Women	46
Second-Year Students	73	Men	101
International Students	5	Minorities	9
		African American	7
Mean Age	26	Native American	1
Mean Class Size	40	Asian American	1
Mean Years Experience	1-3	Hispanic American	0

PROFILE OF ENROLLED STUDENTS

Number Applicants:	501	Mean GPA Enrolled:	3.24
Number of Offers:	144	Mean GMAT Enrolled:	580
Number Enrolled:	80		

Percentile GPA ranking			Percentile ranking by GMAT		
N/A	%	N/A	N/A	%	N/A
N/A	%	N/A	N/A	%	N/A
N/A	%	N/A	N/A	%	N/A

FACILITIES AND TECHNOLOGY

The College of Business Administration is located in the heart of the university's 526-acre Knoxville campus. Plans are underway for a new graduate school facility fully equipped with electronic classrooms, team meeting rooms and satellite conference capabilities. Directly across the street from the College is the John C. Hodges Library, the largest library in Tennessee. The library includes 400 study carrels for graduate students.

MBA students utilize the UTK Computing Center, which houses multiple mainframe computers, both IBM and DEC, IBM PS/2's, a Macintosh lab with 16 Macintosh SE/30s and two Apple Laser Writers, as well as other printers and plotters.

COMMUNITY/CITY LIFE

Knoxville is part of a metropolitan area with a population of 600,000. Surrounded by the Great Smoky Mountains, the most visited national park in America, Knoxville offers a high quality of life, low crime rate and low cost of living. Knoxville, a center of educational and cultural opportunities, commerce, finance, high-tech research and industry, is home to such companies as Whittle Communications and the Aluminum Company of America. Knoxville residents enjoy many outdoor sports such as hiking, biking, skiing in the Smoky Mountains and boating and water skiing on nearby lakes. Knoxville's "funky Old City" is a popular attraction, as is the former World's Fair site with its jogging track, the Knoxville Museum of Art and an amphitheater for summer entertainment.

ACADEMIC STRENGTHS/FEATURES*

KEY	REPUTATION	RESOURCE COMMITMENT NEXT 2 YEARS
K E Y	A-exceptionally well known; national reputation B-well respected C-building; targeted as key area D-standard program E-not provided	+ increase = same - less **RELATIONSHIP TO CORE PROGRAM** 1=Required 4=Not offered 2=Elective 5=Plan to 3=Part of offer other courses

BUSINESS FUNCTION	REPUTATION	RESOURCES COMMITTED
Consulting	B	=
Marketing	B	+
Management/Strategy	B	=
Operations-Service	B	+
Operations-Production	B	=
Finance/Accounting	B	=
HR/ILR/Organizational Behavior	A	=
Technology/Information Systems	B	+
Accounting	A	—

SPECIAL INTERESTS	REPUTATION	RESOURCES COMMITTED	RELATIONSHIP TO CORE PROGRAM
International	C	+	1
Small Business	E	=	4
Entrepreneurial	A	+	2
Diversity	B	=	1
Communications	B	=	1
Manufacturing	B	=	1
Emerging Business	B	=.	2
Family Business	E	=	4
Health Care	D	+	2
Public Administration	E	=	2
Ethics	B	=	1
Environmental Mgt.	A	+	—

TEACHING METHODOLOGIES	PERCENTAGE OF ALL COURSES	SKILLS DEVELOPMENT	PERCENTAGE OF ALL COURSES
Case Study	20%	Quantitative/	
Lecture	20%	Technical	30%
Experiential	60%	Managerial	40%
Combination	—	Communication	30%
Other	—	Other	—

*Reported by Dean's Office

CAREER SERVICES

Career services for MBA students are offered through a centralized, campus-wide office for all students. Dr. Robert Greenburg heads up this top centralized "career shop," and MBAs benefit from many of the general programs. Resume referral is done electronically, as is often the case in top MBA programs.

CAREER SERVICES

CAREER MANAGEMENT		RECRUITMENT	
Career Planning Program for First-Year Students	Yes	Employers Interviewing at School	360
Career Presentations in the Curricula	Yes	Interviews Conducted at School	6541
Alumni Network	Yes	Marketing to Employers	Yes
Summer Jobs Program/ Internships	Yes	Resume Books	Yes
Employer Associates Program	No	Resume Database to Employers	Yes
Job Search Course	Yes	Resume Database/ Referral System	Yes
		Career Fairs	Yes

CAREER SERVICES STAFF

Professional	1	Graduate Assistants	2
Support	1	Peer Advisors	—

TULANE UNIVERSITY

A.B. FREEMAN SCHOOL OF BUSINESS

Goldring/Woldenberg Hall—Suite 200
New Orleans, LA 70118-5669
Tel: 504-865-5400
Fax: 504-865-6751

AT A GLANCE

First-Year Students:	120	Employer Ranking:	—
Second-Year Students:	97	Studen/Faculty Ratio:	13:1
Location:	City	Annual Tuition:	
No. of Employers		in-state:	$17,500
Recruiting on Campus:	59	out-of-state:	$17,500

Strengths: International Business, TQM, doctoral studies.

Distinctions: The Goldring Institute of International Business. One of 11 original, founding members of the American Assembly of Collegiate Schools of Business.

Goals: Strengthen faculty in core areas. Continue to build international programs in developing countries.

Words From the Dean: James W. McFarland   Tenure: 6 years
"Dedication to excellence and continuous improvement, and commitment to students are what make the Freeman School great." (Louis P. Mattis, Chairman of the Business School Council)

OVERVIEW

Famous for its separate, distinctive Goldring Institute for International Business, the Freeman School has built a nationally recognized program for international management. Several Institute programs exist abroad, including an Executive MBA in Taiwan. Freeman also offers first-year students a unique week-long program that focuses on executive skills. The Freeman Center for Doctoral Studies has an outstanding research reputation. Freeman's new seven-story building is first class. The school emphasizes partnerships and cultivates relationships with Tulane alumni in key business positions throughout the country. Following a recent comprehensive review, Freeman is now concentrating on global business, the manager's role and social and political business environments.

DEMOGRAPHICS

First-Year Students	120	Women	54
Second-Year Students	97	Men	163
International Students	72	Minorities	28
		African American	15
Mean Age	26	Native American	1
Mean Class Size	35	Asian American	3
Mean Years Experience	1-3	Hispanic American	9

PROFILE OF ENROLLED STUDENTS

Number Applicants:	485	Mean GPA Enrolled:	3.10
Number of Offers:	297	Mean GMAT Enrolled:	598
Number Enrolled:	118		

Percentile GPA ranking			Percentile ranking by GMAT		
80	%	2.5-3.7	80	%	480-700
70	%	2.6-3.6	70	%	500-690
50	%	2.7-3.4	50	%	540-650

FACILITIES AND TECHNOLOGY

Built in 1986, Goldring/Woldenberg Hall is home to the Freeman School. Goldring/ Woldenberg is a seven-story building designed specifically for the business school. It contains all business school classrooms, an auditorium, group study rooms, faculty offices and a three-story atrium.

At the Lillian A. and Robert L. Turchin Library, also located in Goldring/Woldenberg Hall, students can access a number of on-line databases, as well as the Tulane computer system. The Media Services facility provides a television studio and a viewing room to help students develop their business presentation skills. The Management Communication Center provides professional writing assistance to help students communicate more effectively.

The library also includes the Management Technology Center, which is equipped with IBM and Apple personal computers, laser printers and a variety of software applications. Students also have access to University computing resources, which include an IBM mainframe and Unix computers. A recent addition to the facility is a 44-networked laptop computer classroom for hands-on computer instruction. A Computer-Integrated Manufacturing (CIM) laboratory is utilized for simulating and teaching manufacturing processes and techniques.

The Best Graduate Business Schools

ACADEMIC STRENGTHS/FEATURES*

KEY	REPUTATION	RESOURCE COMMITMENT NEXT 2 YEARS	
K E Y	A-exceptionally well known; national reputation B-well respected C-building; targeted as key area D-standard program E-not provided	+ increase = same - less	
		RELATIONSHIP TO CORE PROGRAM 1=Required 2=Elective 3=Part of other courses	4=Not offered 5=Plan to offer

BUSINESS FUNCTION	REPUTATION	RESOURCES COMMITTED
Consulting	C	=
Marketing	D	+
Management/Strategy	D	+
Operations-Service	D	-
Operations-Production	D	-
Finance/Accounting	B	+
HR/ILR/Organizational Behavior	B	=
Technology/Information Systems	D	=
Accounting	B	—

SPECIAL INTERESTS	REPUTATION	RESOURCES COMMITTED	RELATIONSHIP TO CORE PROGRAM
International	B	+	1
Small Business	D	=	2
Entrepreneurial	C	=	2
Diversity	D	=	1
Communications	D	=	1
Manufacturing	D	=	1
Emerging Business	D	=	2
Family Business	C	=	2
Health Care	B	=	2
Public Administration	D	=	2
Ethics	D	=	1
Other	—	—	—

TEACHING METHODOLOGIES	PERCENTAGE OF ALL COURSES	SKILLS DEVELOPMENT	PERCENTAGE OF ALL COURSES
Case Study	30%	Quantitative/ Technical	45%
Lecture	50%	Managerial	45%
Experiential	10%	Communication	10%
Combination	10%	Other	—
Other	—		

*Reported by Dean's Office

Tulane University

CAREER SERVICES

Freeman has an active Career Service Office that offers a comprehensive program of services. There are courses for students and computer resources that include a financial information database. The 600-member alumni network is effectively utilized by students. The number of employers recruiting on campus is about average, but the office is well connected to New York and Atlanta Consortium Job Fairs.

Recently, the Career Service Office received a grant to install the Bloomberg System, an on-line financial news retrieval system. This tool enables students and faculty to gain up-to-the-minute news and financial data on thousands of companies.

CAREER SERVICES

CAREER MANAGEMENT		RECRUITMENT	
Career Planning Program for First-Year Students	Yes	Employers Interviewing at School	59
Career Presentations in the Curricula	Yes	Interviews Conducted at School	N/A
Alumni Network	Yes	Marketing to Employers	Yes
Summer Jobs Program/ Internships	Yes	Resume Books	Yes
Employer Associates Program	Yes	Resume Database to Employers	No
Job Search Course	Yes	Resume Database/ Referral System	Yes
		Career Fairs	Yes

CAREER SERVICES STAFF

Professional	4	Graduate Assistants	1
Support	5	Peer Advisors	—

COMMUNITY/CITY LIFE

Its location near the mouth of the Mississippi River is largely responsible for the historical and economic significance of New Orleans. Today, New Orleans is the second busiest port in the world, one of the most popular U.S. convention cities, and the state's business, banking, judicial and cultural center. New Orleans still exhibits the European influence of its early French and Spanish governors through its architecture, food and festivals. The most famous festival, Mardi Gras, attracts visitors from around the world. The city also prides itself on the diversity of its musical talent, which includes world-famous jazz artists, classical musicians and opera singers. The business school campus is located in residential, uptown New Orleans, approximately 15 minutes from the downtown area.

WAKE FOREST UNIVERSITY

BABCOCK GRADUATE SCHOOL OF MANAGEMENT

7659 Reynolds Station
Winston-Salem, NC 27109
Tel: 919-759-5422
Fax: 919-759-5830

AT A GLANCE

First-Year Students:	106	Employer Ranking:	—
Second-Year Students:	110	Student/Faculty Ratio:	7:1
Location:	Suburb	Annual Tuition:	
No. of Employers		in-state:	$14,000
Recruiting on Campus:	35	out-of-state:	$14,000

Strengths: International Business, Accounting, doctoral studies and research, TQM emphasis.

Distinctions: Business School Council consists of national and international representatives; Corporate Partner's Program and Family Business Forum are unique programs in MBA education. Babcock has its own world business simulation game.

Goals: Strengthen faculty in core areas. Continue development in international programs.

Words From the Dean: John B. McKinnon   Tenure: 6 years
"Having identified trends that affect business management in the 21st century...we will strive to enhance our curriculum to meet the needs of future business leaders."

OVERVIEW

Located in the "golden triangle"of North Carolina, Babcock shares the same economic resources as its more prestigious MBA neighbors in Chapel Hill (UNC, Kenan-Flagler) and Durham (Duke-Fuqua). Opportunities are plentiful for students to connect to and learn from the area's many emerging smaller businesses. Although Babcock is relatively new, beginning in 1969, it has developed solid programs in Finance and International Business. Worrel Professional Center for Law and Management is second to none, and Babcock's required course in communications has gained national prominence. Field studies are integral to the curriculum and involve local businesses. Winston-Salem enjoys a high quality of life; as one student said, "It's not heaven but you can see it from here."

First-year students study basic disciplines and learn to view problems from a general management perspective. Courses concentrate on organizational and behavioral sciences as well as functional disciplines such as finance and marketing. During the second year, students can choose up to 13 half-semester electives. This allows students the opportunity to focus on career-based interests.

Linda, a marketing student with no undergraduate business background, chose Babcock for its small size and support for non-business majors. The required study groups were challenging to work in but beneficial, she adds.

DEMOGRAPHICS

First-Year Students	106	Women	51
Second-Year Students	110	Men	165
International Students	24	Minorities	5
		African American	4
Mean Age	25	Native American	0
Mean Class Size	35	Asian American	0
Mean Years Experience	1-3	Hispanic American	1

PROFILE OF ENROLLED STUDENTS

Number Applicants:	358	Mean GPA Enrolled:	2.96
Number of Offers:	227	Median GMAT Enrolled:	602
Number Enrolled:	110		

Percentile GPA ranking			Percentile ranking by GMAT		
90	%	3.5-4.0	90	%	670-770
70	%	3.1-4.0	70	%	630-770
50	%	2.9-4.0	50	%	600-770

FACILITIES AND TECHNOLOGY

The Worrell Professional Center for Law and Management was opened in January of 1993. The 178,000-square-foot building was designed to encourage the association between students and faculty of the School of Law and the Babcock Graduate School of Management. Each school has its own wing with classrooms, offices and computer labs. The 2,200-square-foot computer lab has 32 Apple Macintosh Centris 610s, 15 IBM 386 PC compatibles, ten PowerBook docking stations, four Apple LaserWriters and ten Hewlett Packard laser printers.

Classrooms contain computer, audiovisual and telephone equipment controlled by a touch pad on the instructor's desk and through remote control. Each classroom and study room is connected to an information services network that allows students access to databases and external services such as LEXIS/NEXIS and satellite broadcasts from around the world.

ACADEMIC STRENGTHS/FEATURES*

KEY	REPUTATION	RESOURCE COMMITMENT NEXT 2 YEARS
	A-exceptionally well known; national reputation	+ increase = same - less
	B-well respected	**RELATIONSHIP TO CORE PROGRAM**
	C-building; targeted as key area	1=Required 4=Not offered
	D-standard program	2=Elective 5=Plan to
	E-not provided	3=Part of offer
		other courses

BUSINESS FUNCTION	REPUTATION	RESOURCES COMMITTED
Consulting	B	=
Marketing	A	=
Management/Strategy	B	=
Operations-Service	B	=
Operations-Production	B	=
Finance/Accounting	A	=
HR/ILR/Organizational Behavior	B	=
Technology/Information Systems	A	+
Other	—	—

SPECIAL INTERESTS	REPUTATION	RESOURCES COMMITTED	RELATIONSHIP TO CORE PROGRAM
International	B	+	1
Small Business	B	=	2
Entrepreneurial	B	=	2
Diversity	B	=	1
Communications	A	=	1
Manufacturing	B	=	1
Emerging Business	B	=	2
Family Business	B	=	2
Health Care	B	=	2
Public Administration	E	N/A	4
Ethics	A	=	1
Law and Economics	—	—	2

TEACHING METHODOLOGIES	PERCENTAGE OF ALL COURSES	SKILLS DEVELOPMENT	PERCENTAGE OF ALL COURSES
Case Study	—	Quantitative/	
Lecture	—	Technical	40%
Experiential	—	Managerial	40%
Combination	100%	Communication	20%
Other	—	Other	—

*Reported by Dean's Office

CAREER SERVICES

Career Services has formed effective alliances with area employers. The Corporate Affiliates program includes local "giants" Sara Lee, Nabisco, CIBA and Glaxo. Workshops are offered on all key career management topics and more than 100 first-year students enrolled in the career planning course. Career presentations are made to academic classes demonstrating Babcock's commitment to helping students in the career transition. Campus recruiting is light, but there are many other services like job posting, resume referral and a number of specialty resume books.

CAREER SERVICES

CAREER MANAGEMENT		RECRUITMENT	
Career Planning Program for First-Year Students	Yes	Employers Interviewing at School	35
Career Presentations in the Curricula	Yes	Interviews Conducted at School	600
Alumni Network	Yes	Marketing to Employers	Yes
Summer Jobs Program/ Internships	Yes	Resume Books	Yes
Employer Associates Program	Yes	Resume Database to Employers	No
Job Search Course	Yes	Resume Database/ Referral System	Yes
		Career Fairs	Yes

CAREER SERVICES STAFF

Professional	2	Graduate Assistants	3
Support	1	Peer Advisors	—

COMMUNITY/CITY LIFE

The community of Winston-Salem is rich in cultural, entertainment, sports and social events. Students enjoy the city symphony and Reynolds House, which has a collection of American arts and regularly hosts musicians and scholars. More than 250 industries including tobacco, textiles and electronic equipment are located in the area. Winston-Salem is the home of RJR Tobacco USA, the Hanes Group and Sara Lee Corp.

UNIVERSITY OF WASHINGTON

GRADUATE SCHOOL OF BUSINESS ADMINISTRATION

110 Mackenzie Hall, DJ-10
Seattle, WA 98195
Tel: 206-543-2056
Fax: 206-685-9392

AT A GLANCE

First-Year Students:	140	Employer Ranking:	—
Second-Year Students:	230	Student/Faculty Ratio:	25:1
Location:	City	Annual Tuition:	
No. of Employers		in-state:	$4,000
Recruiting on Campus:	27	out-of-state:	$9,000

Strengths: Finance, Accounting, Environmental Management. Atmosphere of cooperation and peer support is unique among MBA programs.

Distinctions: Exceptional new entrepreneurship program that brings students together with local start-ups. Opportunity to specialize in second year and Conversations with Executives program are helpful.

Words from the Dean: Robert S. Leventhal   Tenure: 5 years
"...Ours is an interactive learning environment in which you will be encouraged to use your understanding of the economic, political, and special arenas in which business operates...".

OVERVIEW

Diversity is the watchword at University of Washington School of Business Administration—it's written in script right across the cover of the latest annual report and backed up with programs and evidence. UW has made a major effort to gain prestige in the MBA market—and the results are beginning to show. There are new programs in international business, environmental management and manufacturing. The Centers for Retail Strategy and Pacific Coast Banking School are leaders. The school is also forging productive ties with executives who contribute their expertise in "skill development modules" and in a variety of campus speaking opportunities. Seattle is a beautiful city and the campus on Lake Washington, in view of the Cascade Mountains, is a scenic delight.

Students are put through a rigorous program in which they develop the hands-on skills needed to become managers. Courses stress practical management education and allow students to use their classroom learning to solve actual business problems.

The Management Center has a unique 15-week course called the Practicum, where students, both separately and in teams, are required to propose solutions to complex business problems.

DEMOGRAPHICS

First-Year Students	140	Women	159
Second-Year Students	230	Men	310
International Students	70	Minorities	61
		African American	10
Mean Age	27.5	Native American	2
Mean Class Size	25	Asian American	41
Mean Years Experience	4-6	Hispanic American	8

PROFILE OF ENROLLED STUDENTS

Number Applicants:	1026	Mean GPA Enrolled:	3.24
Number of Offers:	327	Median GMAT Enrolled:	622
Number Enrolled:	140		

Percentile GPA ranking			Percentile ranking by GMAT		
N/A	%	N/A	N/A	%	N/A
N/A	%	N/A	N/A	%	N/A
N/A	%	N/A	N/A	%	N/A

FACILITIES AND TECHNOLOGY

Located in a park-like setting with the Olympic and Cascade Mountains looming in the background, the University of Washington is a mixture of classic old buildings and contemporary new ones. The business school occupies three buildings: Balmer Hall, which houses the library and classrooms; Mackenzie Hall, the faculty and administrative center; and Lewis Hall, which houses the MBA career center. Now more than 30 years old, these buildings are no longer adequate for the demands of business management education. Construction of a new facility is under way.

ACADEMIC STRENGTHS/FEATURES*

KEY	REPUTATION	RESOURCE COMMITMENT NEXT 2 YEARS
	A-exceptionally well known; national reputation	+ increase = same - less
	B-well respected	RELATIONSHIP TO CORE PROGRAM
	C-building; targeted as key area	1=Required 4=Not offered
	D-standard program	2=Elective 5=Plan to
	E-not provided	3=Part of offer
		other courses

BUSINESS FUNCTION	REPUTATION	RESOURCES COMMITTED
Consulting	B	+
Marketing	B	+
Management/Strategy	B	+
Operations-Service	B	+
Operations-Production	B	+
Finance/Accounting	A	=
HR/ILR/Organizational Behavior	B	=
Technology/Information Systems	B	+
Accounting	A	—

SPECIAL INTERESTS	REPUTATION	RESOURCES COMMITTED	RELATIONSHIP TO CORE PROGRAM
International	B	+	1
Small Business	B	+	2
Entrepreneurial	B	+	2
Diversity	C	=	1
Communications	C	+	1
Manufacturing	C	+	2
Emerging Business	B	+	2
Family Business	C	+	2
Health Care	B	+	2
Public Administration	B	=	2
Ethics	B	=	1
Environment Management	A	—	—

TEACHING METHODOLOGIES	PERCENTAGE OF ALL COURSES	SKILLS DEVELOPMENT	PERCENTAGE OF ALL COURSES
Case Study	45%	Quantitative/	
Lecture	10%	Technical	60%
Experiential	—	Managerial	30%
Combination	—	Communication	10%
Other	45%	Other	—

*Reported by Dean's Office

CAREER SERVICES

Business cutbacks in the Northwest have affected campus recruiting at Washington. JoAnn Starr, Director of the Business Career Center, has effectively initiated contacts with diverse smaller companies to make up for those large company absences. A good number of *Fortune* 500 companies do recruit on campus, and employers are well served through a variety of systems and programs for interviews and student communication.

CAREER SERVICES

CAREER MANAGEMENT		RECRUITMENT	
Career Planning Program for First-Year Students	Yes	Employers Interviewing at School	42
Career Presentations in the Curricula	No	Interviews Conducted at School	N/A
Alumni Network	Yes	Marketing to Employers	Yes
Summer Jobs Program/ Internships	Yes	Resume Books	Yes
Employer Associates Program	No	Resume Database to Employers	No
Job Search Course	Yes	Resume Database/ Referral System	No
		Career Fairs	No

CAREER SERVICES STAFF

Professional	2	Graduate Assistants	2-4
Support	2	Peer Advisors	—

COMMUNITY/CITY LIFE

Seattle is one of the most sought-after places to live in the country. With a climate similar to that of San Francisco, Seattle offers scenic natural beauty along with big-city benefits. Students enjoy strolling the waterfront, visiting the many nearby islands, hiking through the rain forest on the Olympic Peninsula and climbing majestic Mount Rainier. Salmon is the famous local delicacy, and many local restaurants specialize in tempting ways to prepare it. For those who want to venture beyond the city limits, Portland, Oregon and Vancouver, British Columbia are popular weekend destinations.

SIXTEEN
RECOMMENDED PROGRAMS

ARIZONA STATE UNIVERSITY

COLLEGE OF BUSINESS
MBA Program Office
Tempe, AZ 85287-3506
Tel: 602-965-3332 Fax: 602-965-8569

AT A GLANCE

First-Year Students:	125	Employer Ranking:	—
Second-Year Students:	74	Student/Faculty Ratio:	5:1
Location:	Suburb	Annual Tuition:	
No. of Employers		in-state:	$1.600
Recruiting on Campus:	50	out-of-state:	$7,000

Strengths: Accounting, Marketing; joint international program with Thunderbird School; Phoenix location.

Distinctions: Considered very competitive "second tier" program by ranking organizations; Leadership Development Program is recognized as outstanding; new MBA computer room.

Goals: Increase enrollment to 600; maintain diversity of 25% minority and 40% women; expand placement services.

Words From the Dean: Dr. Larry Penley   Tenure: 4 years
"The objective of the program is to produce ASU MBA graduates who are comfortable dealing with state-of-the-art technology in a team-based work environment."

BARUCH COLLEGE

CITY UNIVERSITY OF NEW YORK
Office of MBA Programs   17 Lexington Ave.
New York, NY 10010   Tel: 212-447-3920

AT A GLANCE

First-Year Students:	370	Employer Ranking:	—
Second-Year Students:	361	Student/Faculty Ratio:	N/A
Location:	Major City	Annual Tuition:	
No. of Employers		in-state:	$1,700
Recruiting on Campus:	75	out-of-state:	$2,300

Strengths: Accounting. Location in the heart of midtown Manhattan; the largest business school in the country including undergraduates. Diversity of students and graduates.

Distinctions: Nobel Prize winner in Economics, Harry M. Markowitz, on faculty. Outstanding Center for the Study of Business and Government.

Goals: The long- awaited "Site A," the fifth building of the Business Complex, opens in 1994 and houses a new library and computer labs.

Words From the President: Matthew Goldstein   Tenure: 3 years
"We want this institution to become a larger influence in public policy debates. Our faculty expertise in health care, education and regulatory policy is considerable and it needs to be engaged in the issues that confront our society."

BOSTON COLLEGE

WALLACE E. CARROLL GRADUATE SCHOOL OF MANAGEMENT

Fulton Hall   Boston, MA   02167-3808
Tel: 617-552-3920

AT A GLANCE

First-Year Students:	100	Employer Ranking:	—
Second-Year Students:	63	Student/Faculty Ratio:	N/A
Location:	Suburb	Annual Tuition:	
No. of Employers		in-state:	$19,000
Recruiting on Campus:	N/A	out-of-state:	$19,000

Strengths: Finance and Operations Management. Access to financial services industry in Boston, New York City and east coast. Hands-on learning through consulting.

Distinctions: $24 million renovation to building.

Goals: Keep emphasis on general management skills while meeting needs of the business community.

Words From the Dean: Lovis S. Corsini   Tenure: 5 years
"The Carroll School of Management can give you an edge in your management career within an environment that is both demanding and humane."

BOSTON UNIVERSITY

BOSTON UNIVERSITY SCHOOL OF MANAGEMENT

685 Commonwealth Ave.
Boston, MA   02215
Tel: 617-353-2670

AT A GLANCE

Total Full/Part-time		Employer Ranking:	—
Students:	1247	Student/Faculty Ratio:	30:1
Location:	Major City	Annual Tuition:	
No. of Employers		in-state:	$17,000
Recruiting on Campus:	35	out-of-state:	$17,000

Strengths: General MBA and Health Care/Public Management; extensive team-building; location in Boston.

Distinctions: Recognized for its Executive MBA and Leadership Institute.

Goals: Implement fully integrated curriculum, "Management as a System—Creating Value." Move into new building.

Words From the Dean: Louis E. Lataif   Tenure: 3 years
"SMG graduates are trained to deal with the management control systems and with the human resource systems required for operating competitively, for innovating, for leading."

UNIVERSITY OF CALIFORNIA-IRVINE

GRADUATE SCHOOL OF MANAGEMENT

Office of Admissions
Irvine, CA 92717
Tel: 714-856-5232

AT A GLANCE

First-Year Students:	93	Employer Ranking:		—
Second-Year Students:	104	Student/Faculty Ratio:		N/A
Location:	Suburb	Annual Tuition:		
No. of Employers		in-state:		$4,756
Recruiting on Campus:	35	out-of-state:		$12,457

Strengths: Health Care Management, Information Technology; access to Orange County small businesses; Corporate Partners program.

Distinctions: Integrated communication skills with the curriculum; excellent computing facility.

Goals: Increase partnerships with Orange County and San Diego County businesses; become a major player in MBA marketplace with local and Pacific Rim influence.

Words From the Dean: Dennis J. Aigner   Tenure: 6 years
"...you will receive preparation for an interdependent, global economy that will frame the business challenges of the next decade and the next century."

UNIVERSITY OF CONNECTICUT

SCHOOL OF BUSINESS ADMINISTRATION

368 Fairfield Road U-41D
Storrs, CT 06269-2041
Tel: 203-486-2872

AT A GLANCE

First-Year Students:	113	Employer Ranking:	—
Second-Year Students:	125	Student/Faculty Ratio:	30:1
Location:	Small Town	Annual Tuition:	
No. of Employers		in-state:	$5,000
Recruiting on Campus:	53	out-of-state:	$11,000

Strengths: Accounting, General Management. Partnerships with Connecticut and New England businesses.

Distinctions: Emphasis on teaching. Rural setting with access to east coast cities.

Goals: Continue emphasis on business partnerships including Executive MBA program. Increase research; upgrade physical facilities.

Words From the Dean: Thomas G. Gutteridge   Tenure: 2 years
"The four-phase approach (contemporary management skills, applications, individual concentration, integrated business functions) to graduate business education is one of the distinguishing features of the program."

UNIVERSITY OF COLORADO AT BOULDER

GRADUATE SCHOOL OF BUSINESS ADMINISTRATION

Campus Box 419
Boulder, Colorado 80309-0419
Tel: 303-492-1831

AT A GLANCE

First-Year Students:	72	Employer Ranking:	—
Second-Year Students:	74	Student/Faculty Ratio:	7:1
Location:	Large Town	Annual Tuition:	
No. of Employers		in-state:	$3,300
Recruiting on Campus:	60	out-of-state:	$12,000

Strengths: Marketing, Technology, Innovation Venturing; Boulder provides good market for interns.

Distinctions: London Banking Seminar; increased number of cases using women and minorities as role models. Program for first-year students involving team-building and taking certain courses together. Centralized Placement Office makes notable effort to assist MBAs. Innovative employer outreach programs.

Goals: Bring more nationally prominent faculty to CU.

Dean: Larry Singell   Tenure: 1 year

UNIVERSITY OF GEORGIA

TERRY GRADUATE SCHOOL OF BUSINESS

351 Brooks Hall Athens, GA 30602
Tel: 706-542-5671

AT A GLANCE

First-Year Students:	54	Employer Ranking:	—
Second-Year Students:	98	Student/Faculty Ratio:	N/A
Location:	Large Town	Annual Tuition:	
No. of Employers		in-state:	$2,200
Recruiting on Campus:	N/A	out-of-state:	$6,000

Strengths: Risk Management, Real Estate, Entrepreneurship. Career development service provides personal traits—career path program.

Distinctions: Consulting with local businesses. Winner of numerous national business plan competitions. MBA-plus program combines leadership and service.

Goals: Revision of curriculum to focus on cross-functional skills. New Business Student Center to house case-type classrooms and career services.

Words From the Dean: Albert W. Niemi, Jr.   Tenure: 11 years
"To meet our objectives, we will continue to emphasize the variable that is most important to our bottom lines, admissions quality. We are not in a race to produce the most MBAs, only the best."

GEORGE MASON UNIVERSITY

SCHOOL OF BUSINESS ADMINISTRATION

Fairfax, VA 22030-4444
Tel: 703-983-2163

AT A GLANCE

First-Year Students:	70	Employer Ranking:	—
Second-Year Students:	65	Student/Faculty Ratio:	N/A
Location:	Suburb	Annual Tuition:	
No. of Employers		in-state:	$3,888
Recruiting on Campus:	30	out-of-state:	$10,056

Strengths: Finance with World Bank connections; Management with The Small Business Institute. Top regional program.

Distinctions: Winner of several Small Business Institute Case Awards. Proximity to Washington, D.C. and thriving northern Virginia economy. Integrated communications emphasis throughout the curriculum.

Goals: Continue effective partnerships with businesses and other organizations in its quest to be a nationally recognized program.

Words From the Dean: Cornelius de Kluyver   Tenure: 4 years
"At GMU, we realize that business as usual is no longer an option and are determined to equip tomorrow's leaders with the skills they need to succeed."

GEORGIA INSTITUTE OF TECHNOLOGY

SCHOOL OF MANAGEMENT

Room 212 Atlanta, GA 30332-0520
Tel: 404-894-2604

AT A GLANCE

First-Year Students:	105	Employer Ranking:	—
Second-Year Students:	—	Student/Faculty Ratio:	N/A
Location:	Major City	Annual Tuition:	
No. of Employers		in-state:	$2,300
Recruiting on Campus:	50	out-of-state:	$7,000

Strengths: Computer Integrated Manufacturing Systems, Management Technology.

Distinctions: Master of Science in Management. Small program size; location; connection to leading engineering program and large number of companies already recruiting there.

Goals: Continue development of business partnerships in Atlanta and the world.

Words From the Dean: Arthur Kraft   Tenure: 2.5 years
"The School of Management at Georgia Tech provides a unique educational experience that goes beyond teaching basic business skills. The use of microcomputers is integrated throughout the curriculum as a tool for solving complex problems."

UNIVERSITY OF KENTUCKY

MBA CENTER, COLLEGE OF BUSINESS AND ECONOMICS

103 B & E Building Lexington, KY 40506
Tel: 606-257-4627

AT A GLANCE

First-Year Students:	173	Employer Ranking:	—
Second-Year Students:	113	Student/Faculty Ratio:	4:1
Location:	Medium-size town	Annual Tuition:	
No. of Employers		in-state:	$2,200
Recruiting on Campus:	25	out-of-state:	$6,000

Strengths: Management Information Systems, Accounting, Economics. Curriculum reflects integration and teamwork, leadership and communication skills development.

Distinctions: New building and renovation programs just completed. Partnerships with business are successful, including $10,000,000 construction project. Local major companies encourage employees to enroll.

Goals: Increase number of African-Americans in program. Implement combined degree with Engineering.

Words From the Dean: Richard W. Furst   Tenure: 13 years
"Our curriculum was recently revised after an extensive three-year review. The new curriculum is demanding and will challenge you to carefully synthesize a large and diverse set of concepts and ideas." (Michael Tearney, Assoc. Dean)

UNIVERSITY OF MASSACHUSETTS AT AMHERST

SCHOOL OF MANAGEMENT

Room 209 Amherst, MA 01003
Tel: 413-545-5608

AT A GLANCE

First-Year Students:	40	Employer Ranking:	—
Second-Year Students:	30	Student/Faculty Ratio:	N/A
Location:	Medium-size town	Annual Tuition:	
No. of Employers		in-state:	$2,755
Recruiting on Campus:	35	out-of-state:	$6,000

Strengths: Consulting, Finance, Marketing. New England's largest business Ph.D. program.

Distinctions: The S.O.M. has a vital cooperative education program. Delivers on its commitment to diversity. Heavy involvement with small businesses and financial service industry.

Words From the Dean: Thomas O'Brien   Tenure: 8 years
"We are pleased to announce a $1 million gift which will endow a chair and allow the S.O.M. to attract an outstanding senior faculty member."

310

NORTHEASTERN UNIVERSITY

GRADUATE SCHOOL OF BUSINESS ADMINISTRATION

205 Huntington Hall   360 Huntington Ave
Boston, Massachusetts 02115
Tel: 617-437-2714

AT A GLANCE

First-Year Students:	163	Employer Ranking:		—
Second-Year Students:	121	Student/Faculty Ratio:		N/A
Location:	Major City	Annual Tuition:		
No. of Employers		in-state:		$16,000
Recruiting on Campus:	66	out-of-state:		$16,000

Strengths: Finance/Accounting, Small Business/Entrepreneurship, International Business. Experiential learning based in Northeastern's cooperative education excellence.

Distinctions: Use of executives for mentoring and teaching—150 CEOs participate. New 75,000 square-foot building with leading technologies. Boston location.

Goals: Enhance quality in all significant areas—build on excellence of experiential learning focus.

Words From the Dean: David Boyd   Tenure: 8 years
"...we offer five "different" MBA programs responding to different market segments...EMBA—executives, High Tech MBA, Coop MBA (for less experienced students), full-time MBA and part-time MBA... ."

TEXAS A & M UNIVERSITY

COLLEGE OF BUSINESS ADMINISTRATION

College Station, TX 77843-4113
Tel: 409-221-2900

AT A GLANCE

First-Year Students:	182	Employer Ranking:		—
Second-Year Students:	179	Student/Faculty Ratio:		35:1
Location:	Small Town	Annual Tuition:		
No. of Employers		in-state:		$1,300
Recruiting on Campus:	N/A	out-of-state:		$4,100

Strengths: Management Strategy, Marketing, Technology/Information Systems. New commitment to business education excellence.

Distinctions: Access to major resources of larger university. New facilities and business building are outstanding. Intense A & M spirit and loyalty.

Goals: Work hard to connect to Houston and Dallas markets. Increase contacts for employment and recruitment using the university's technical reputation. Implement numerous international programs.

Words From the Dean: Gary Trennepohl   Tenure: 2 years
"...To learn group dynamics, students spend the first year in cohorts and problem-solving teams. Seminars are offered to enhance leadership and team-building skills."

UNIVERSITY OF TEXAS AT ARLINGTON

COLLEGE OF BUSINESS ADMINISTRATION

Box 19376 Arlington, TX 76019-0376
Tel: 817-273-3004

AT A GLANCE

First-Year Students:	152	Employer Ranking:	—
Second-Year Students:	416	Student/Faculty Ratio:	35:1
Location:	Suburb	Annual Tuition:	
No. of Employers		in-state:	$900
Recruiting on Campus:	165	out-of-state:	$3,000

Strengths: Accounting, Infomation Systems. One of 12 schools to receive accreditation at both bachelor's and master's level and all levels of Accounting by AACSB.

Distinctions: Small Business Institute has accomplished many projects in conjunction with local businesses. Economics and Accounting have nationally prominent faculty. Excellent working relationships with Technical Center including Automation and Robotics Research Institute.

Goals: Continue to take advantage of resources in Dallas-Ft. Worth metropolitan area. Continue development of national profile and effective use of University of Texas System resources. Develop joint programs with Engineering and Technology.

Words From the Dean: Robert E. Witt   Tenure: 8 years
"The successful manager of tomorrow will have to creatively and analytically challenge the management assumptions and practices of today."

THE COLLEGE OF WILLIAM AND MARY

GRADUATE SCHOOL OF BUSINESS

Blow Memorial Hall, Williamsburg,VA
23187   Tel: 804-221-2900

AT A GLANCE

First-Year Students:	90	Employer Ranking:	—
Second-Year Students:	85	Student/Faculty Ratio:	4:1
Location:	Medium-size town	Annual Tuition:	
No. of Employers		in-state:	$4,000
Recruiting on Campus:	63	out-of-state:	$10,000

Strengths: Finance, Operations/Information Technology, Marketing. Faculty have outstanding credentials and contributions in their disciplines.

Distinctions: Excellent, modern facilities within beautiful and historic campus of the oldest college in the country. Computer labs and services above average. Close ties with growing eastern Virginia economy.

Goals: Recruit more minorities and women; increase international students programs.

Words From the Dean: Alfred N. Page   Tenure: 5 years
"Your MBA studies will enhance your ability to be an intelligent manager, an effective decision-maker and an international citizen."

CHAPTER SEVEN

CANADIAN AND INTERNATIONAL PROGRAMS

THE MBA IN CANADA

In Canada, graduate business schools face all the same issues as their counterparts in the United States—though on a somewhat smaller scale. There are 26 graduate business programs in Canada compared to over 700 in the United States. The challenge to improve the "product," increase customer satisfaction and recruit both the best students and corporations is just as intense, however.

One important difference between Canadian and U.S. schools is that the Canadians must work with much smaller budgets. The April 1992 issue of *Canadian Business* compared The University of Toronto with the University of Michigan and yielded the following disparities:

SCHOOL	ENROLLMENT	BUDGET	FACULTY	COMPUTER BUDGET
MICHIGAN	700	$55M	110	$1.3M
TORONTO	700	$9M	55	$.3M

Canadian MBA schools, like their southern neighbors, once believed that business was largely number crunching and thus emphasized economics, finance, and quantitative model building. They forgot the "management" part of business management. Henry Mintzberg, professor at McGill University put it this way, "Our MBA programs take people who have hardly ever made anything or sold anything and then make damn sure they never will" (*Mintzberg on Management*, 1992).

The downsizing of large corporations together with the pressure to compete globally has forced Canadian businesses to re-think their strategy. Like their U.S. counterparts, Canadian business leaders recognized the need for managers who are generalists, and who can speak, write, motivate, and work on a team as well as lead. And the business schools are responding to that need.

Top programs like Calgary, Toronto, Queens, UBC, Western, York, McGill, Dalhousie and Ecole des Hautes Etudes Commerciales among others are instituting "soft skills" courses and listening to corporate Canada. Advisory Boards consisting of business leaders are appearing on campus, and partnerships are being formed to work on issues from research to fund raising. Corporate Canada seems to be cooperating, especially in the development of new Executive Education programs which benefit their employees as well as the schools.

Financing an MBA in Canada is distinctly different from financing an MBA in the U.S. The combination of private and government financing allows the student to pay only a fraction of the actual costs of the program, thus providing more students with access to the MBA, but also placing a severe burden on the institution and the government who have to subsidize the balance.

UNIVERSITY OF ALBERTA, Edmonton, Alberta
Tuition: $1,877
Full-time enrollment: 55
Distinction: Accredited by AACSB, main accrediting body for U.S. MBA schools; teaching excellence.

UNIVERSITY OF BRITISH COLUMBIA, Vancouver, B.C.
Tuition: $1,877
Full-time enrollment: 280
Distinction: Emphasis on global management; connections to a number of international schools.

UNIVERSITY OF CALGARY, Calgary, Alberta
Tuition: $2,604
Full-time enrollment: 130
Distinction: Accredited by AACSB in 1993.

CONCORDIA UNIVERSITY, Montreal, Quebec
Tuition: $1,600
Full-time enrollment: 180
Distinction: Founded national case competition for Canadian MBA schools.

DALHOUSIE UNIVERSITY, Halifax, Nova Scotia
Tuition: $2,474
Full-time enrollment 169
Distinction: Liberal policy on electives and useful cooperation with other schools on campus.

ECOLE DES HAUTES ETUDES COMMERCIALES, Montreal, Quebec
Tuition: $1,528
Full time enrollment: 130
Distinction: For managers having 5 plus years of experience.

LAURENTIAN UNIVERSITY, Sudbury, Ontario
Tuition: $1,800
Full-time enrollment: 8
Distinction: Best known for its part-time program.

UNIVERSITE DE LAVAL, Quebec City, Quebec
Tuition: $22 per course
Full-time enrollment: 41
Distinction: Emphasis on soft skills; designed for experienced managers.

UNIVERSITY OF MANITOBA, Winnepeg, Manitoba
Tuition: $2,240
Full-time enrollment: 85
Distinction: Very competitive environment; everyone takes the toughest courses.

MCGILL UNIVERSITY, Montreal, Quebec
Tuition: $891/term
Full-time enrollment: 240
Distinction: Published research of faculty.

McMASTER UNIVERSITY, Hamilton, Ontario
Tuition: $889/term
Full-time enrollment: 238
Distinction: Cooperative Education program is unique and first rate.

MEMORIAL UNIVERSITY, St. John's, Newfoundland
Tuition: $501/semester
Full-time enrollment: 34
Distinction: Won the national case competition 3 out of 4 years.

UNIVERSITE DE MONCTON, Quebec
Tuition: $1,915
Full-time enrollment: 30
Distinction: International and environmental studies.

UNIVERSITY OF NEW BRUNSWICK, Fredericton, New Brunswick
Tuition: $1,840
Full-time enrollment: 49
Distinction: Excellence in teaching.

UNIVERSITY OF OTTAWA, Ontario
Tuituion: $962/semester
Full-time enrollment: 267
Distinction: Courses in French and English.

UNIVERSITE DE QUEBEC A MONTREAL, Montreal, Quebec
Tuition: $2,000
Full-time enrollment: 70
Distinction: Entrepreneurship and global applications.

QUEEN'S UNIVERSITY, Kingston, Ontario
Tuition: $1,776
Full-time enrollment: 109
Distinction: Exchange programs with schools in Europe and Asia.

SAINT MARY'S UNIVERSITY, Halifax, Nova Scotia
Tuition: $2,264
Full-time enrollment: 58
Distinction: Required thesis/research project.

UNIVERSITY OF SASKATCHEWAN, Saskatoon, Saskatchewan
Tuition: $2,130
Full-time enrollment: 62
Distinction: Joint program with Japan's Nanzan University.

UNIVERSITE DE SHERBROOKE, Sherbrooke, Quebec
Tuition: $1,531
Full-time enrollment: 71
Distinction: Required cooperative/work program.

SIMON FRASER UNIVERSITY, Burnaby, B.C.
Tuition: $710/semester
Full-time enrollment: 95
Distinction: Emphasis on specializing in business functions; not generalists.

UNIVERSITY OF TORONTO, Toronto, Ontario
Tuition: $2,517
Full-time enrollment: 209
Distinction: Ranked #1 in *Canadian Business* study.

UNIVERSITY OF WESTERN ONTARIO, London, Ontario
Tuition: $2,150
Full-time enrollment: 500
Distinction: Case study patterned on Harvard; international prominence.

WILFRED LAURIER UNIVERSITY, Waterloo, Ontario
Tuition: $900/term
Full-time enrollment: 42
Distinction: Applied approach using cases and projects.

UNIVERSITY OF WINDSOR, Windsor, Ontario
Tuition: $884/semester
Full-time enrollment: 138
Distinction: Small group learning and personal relationships with faculty.

YORK UNIVERSITY, Toronto, Ontario
Tuition: $889/term
Full-time enrollment: 550
Distinction: Offers the only international MBA in Canada including foreign language requirement and study abroad.

Tuition and enrollment figures from *Canadian Business*, April, 1992. "The Blackboard Jungle".

U.S. graduate business schools have lagged behind the rest of the world in developing international exchange programs. We're catching up in a hurry, however, due to pervasive "globalism" in business and new standards from The American Assembly of Collegiate Schools of Business. (Thunderbird got this one right long before the others; it was the first U.S. school to get serious about international business.) You won't find many competitive MBA programs today without an international focus and exchange programs for their students.

European universities have always prized the international view, largely due to their history and geography. Today, this is reflected by intense collaboration and networking among the European business schools. The promise of a common European currency and more favorable trade agreements provides even greater impetus for strengthening these relationships.

Long recognized for its intellectual, philosophical and cultural impact throughout the world, France has also played a significant role in shaping international business. On the management education front, the French "Grandes Ecoles" of Management have pooled resources to better meet the needs of European and world markets. This consortium consisting of the top five French business schools (ESC LYON, ESC NICE SPOHIA-ANTIPOLIS, ESCP, ESSEC and HEC) is also marketing its programs to an international audience through collaborative materials. A slick, smart publication, "A New Breed of Managers," can be found in the career services offices and academic departments of every Ivy League university and other select institutions like Stanford, Chicago, Amherst, Smith, and Carleton.

The point for U.S. students convinced they want a "real international MBA" is that they will be competing against "real international students," students who grew up speaking two or three languages and who come from families with generations of experience in international trade.

In Europe, Australia, Asia, and South America, some business schools are affiliated with a university and some are not. The business schools that are part of a large university most closely resemble U.S. business schools in programs and in emphasis. The others are schools that were started by individual companies or groups of companies. Such schools usually offer more practical business training, with less emphasis on theory and research.

By attending a foreign business school, U.S. students may gain greater insight into international issues and, perhaps, a better chance for jobs with international banks or other companies that have close ties to foreign business schools. However, there are several disadvantages as well. First, there's the very real possibility of a language problem. Then, there is the lack of student support, advising and tutorial services. Although these services are common in U.S. schools, they are not as available abroad.

Many U.S business schools have faculty members who have studied and taught abroad. Seek them out and question them about their experiences. The GMAC FORUMS mentioned previously also have international representatives present to meet with U.S. students.

If you are considering a foreign business school, be sure to get answers to all of the following questions.

- How will this program make a significant difference for me given my career goals?

- What will the biggest challenges be for being admitted—and once there, for succeeding?

- How many U.S. students apply each year—and how many are accepted? What do the student profiles look like?

- What percentage of classes are taught in which languages?

- How proficient do I need to be in writing and speaking the language(s) to be successful?

- Can you provide examples of U.S. students who have done well at your school and have attained top positions after graduation. Can I call some of these students?

- What about those students who didn't do well—what happened? Where did they wind up?

- How will my career options differ from those of students at top U.S. schools?

ADDITIONAL SOURCES OF INFORMATION:

European Master's Degrees in Management
IMEC
P.O. Box 34, NL-1400AA Bussum,
The Netherlands

International Education Information Center
809 United Nations Plaza
New York, NY 10017-3580 (visit; don't write)

Which MBA?
—A Critical Guide to the World's Best Programmes
The Economist Intelligence Unit
40 Duke Street
London WIA 4DW
England

INTERNATIONAL SCHOOLS

UNIVERSITY OF PUERTO RICO
Rio Piedras, Puerto Rico

Graduate School of Business Administration
University of Puerto Rico
Box 23325, University Station
San Juan, Puerto Rico 00931

EXPENSES: Nonresident students pay $3,500 per year.

PROGRAM: Standard business disciplines. Part of mission is to develop
social responsibility.

UNIVERSITY OF PUERTO RICO AT MAYAGUEZ
Mayaguez, Puerto Rico

Graduate Studies Office
University of Puerto Rico
Mayaguez, Puerto Rico 00680

EXPENSES: Nonresidents pay $1,750 per semester.

PROGRAM: Analysis and application; use of technology in all management areas.

CZECHOSLOVAK MANAGEMENT CENTER
Celakovice, Czech Republic

MBA Director
Czechoslovak Management Center
Namesti 5. kvetna 2
250 88 Celakovice, Czech Republic

EXPENSES: First year is $8,000; second year is at Katz School, University of
Pittsburgh.

PROGRAM: Team teaching emphasized during first year. Program accredited
by AACSB.

LONDON BUSINESS SCHOOL
London, England

Information Officer
London Business School, Box G
Sussex Place, Regent's Park
London, England NW1 4SA

EXPENSES:Tuition - $6,200 per year. Additional expenses - $6,900 per year.

PROGRAM: Cross-discipline skills and learning. One semester spent at
another international program. Considered in top 5 programs worldwide.

HELSINKI SCHOOL OF ECONOMICS AND BUSINESS ADMINISTRATION
Helsinki, Finland

Helsinki School of Economics and Business Administration
International Center, Hietaniemenkatu 7 A
SF-00100 Helsinki, Finland

EXPENSES: Tuition-$7,000 per year. Additional expenses - $12,000 per year.

PROGRAM: Focus is on international business. Many courses taught by visiting faculty.

INSEAD - THE EUROPEAN INSTITUTE OF BUSINESS ADMINISTRATION
Fontainebleau, France

INSEAD
MBA Information Service
Boulevard de Constance
F-77305 Fontainebleau Cedex, France

EXPENSES: Tuition and fees for one year-$21,500. Additional expenses - $18,000.

PROGRAM: One of the top programs in world; total emersion into international business; one year, intensive program.

IMD INTERNATIONAL
Lausanne, Switzerland

MBA Information Service
IMD International
P.O. Box 915
1001 Lausanne, Switzerland

EXPENSES: Approximate total cost per year is $12,000.

PROGRAM: Intensive, selective program; balance between analytical and communication/leadership skill development; students are a little older—average age is 30. Total international emphasis.

INTERNATIONAL UNIVERSITY OF JAPAN
Yamato-Machi, Nigata, Japan

Admissions, MBA
International University of Japan
Yamato-machi, Niigata 949-72 Japan

EXPENSES: Tuition - $11,850. Additional expenses - $11,000 per year.

PROGRAM: Close ties with Tuck School, Dartmouth. Involvement with Japanese business. Second year in U.S.

UNIVERSITY OF OXFORD
Oxford, England

Academic Secretary (Postgraduate)
Management & Industrial Relations
Graduate Studies Committee
Templeton College
Oxford, OXI 5NY, England

EXPENSES: University fee, overseas student - $3,500. Minimum estimated
maintenance cost - $3,500

PROGRAM: Distinguishing features of Oxford University applied to graduate management education.

ESSEC GRADUATE SCHOOL OF MANAGEMENT
Cergy-Pontoise Cedex, France

Director of Admissions
ESSEC
BP 105
95021 Cergy-Pontoise Cedex, France

EXPENSES: Tuition - $7,200, Living Expenses - $9,500

PROGRAM: Highly analytic program; several options including a three-year program
for students without an undergraduate degree.

LYON GRADUATE SCHOOL OF BUSINESS
Groupe ESC Lyon
Lyon, France

Groupe ESC Lyon
23 avenue Guy de Collongue - BP 174
69132 ECULLY Cedex, France

EXPENSES: Tuition - $5,700 all students
        CESMA MBA tuition - S15,500
        Living expenses -$6,900 - $8,600

PROGRAM: Program is research driven and internationally focused. Diverse teaching methods are employed; close partnerships with the European business community exist.

IESE
Barcelona, Spain

MBA Admissions
IESE, University of Navarra
Avenida, Pearson, 21
08034
Barcelona, Sapin

EXPENSES: Tuition - $12,000 per year. Additional expenses - $9,600 per year.

PROGRAM: Two-year program; bi-lingual; diverse teaching methods including projects.

UNIVERSITY COLLEGE DUBLIN
Michael Smurfit Graduate School of Business
Blackrock, Dublin, Ireland

MBA Programme Director
Michael Smurfit Graduate School of Business
Blackrock, County Dublin, Ireland

EXPENSES: $2,300

PROGRAM: Known for its Executive MBA program—one of the first in Europe. Emphasis on team-building and group skills.

NIJENRODE, THE NETHERLANDS SCHOOL OF BUSINESS
Breukelen, The Netherlands

International MBA Office
Straatweg 25
3621 BG Breukelen
The Netherlands

EXPENSES: International MBA Programme fee for EC citizen -
        $11,700, non-EC citizen $15,300,
        living expenses per month $750.

PROGRAM: Emphasis on European business within a 13-month MBA program for students with undergraduate and/or business experience.

UNIVERSITY OF STIRLING
MBA Programme
Stirling, Scotland, United Kingdom

Director, MBA Programme
Stirling, FK9 4LA
Scotland, United Kingdom

EXPENSES: Tuition $8,900. Room, food, books, etc. $6,500.

PROGRAM: Program abides by AACSB guidelines and faculty are dedicated
 to graduate management teaching and research.

ESADE (Escuela Superior de Administracion y Direccion
de Empresas)
Barcelona, Spain

MBA Program Director
ESADE
Avenue de Pedralbes 60-62
08034 Barcelona, Spain

EXPENSES: Tuition - $24,000. Living expenses per year - $11,400.

PROGRAM: High stress, high quality program focusing on developing expertise
in several business functional areas.

EUROPEAN UNIVERSITY
Belgium, France, Germany, Greece, Italy, The Netherlands, Portugal, Spain, and
Switzerland

Amerikalei 131
B-2000 Antwerp, Belgium

Rue de L'Industrie 45 - CP 310
CH-1950 Sion, Switzerland

137 Ave Jean Jaures
F-92140 Clamart, France

Nassauplein 25-27
2585 EC The Hague
The Netherlands

c/o San Juan de la Salle 8
E-08022 Barcelona, Spain

12 Makri Str.
117 42 Makrigianni
Athens, Greece

Palazzo Municipale
7, Peazza Aosta
110027 St. Vincent
Valle d'Aosta, Italy

Lisboa Business Center, 17
Rua Aexandre Herculano No. 5
1100 Lisbon, Portugal

c/o Euro-Internatsberatung
Grillparzerstrasse 46
8000 Munich 80
Germany

EXPENSES:

Belgium	$ 8,400
France	$ 7,900
Germany	$15,600
Greece	$ 6,700
Italy	$16,000
Portugal	$ 9,500
Spain	$14,300
Switzerland	$17,200
The Netherlands	$13,000

PROGRAM: Europe's largest private business school offering good balance between
theory and practice with a thorough international orientation.

Data on expenses are from *The Official Guide to MBA Programs*, 1992-94.

The Best Graduate Business Schools

APPENDIX

AMERICAN ASSEMBLY OF COLLEGIATE SCHOOLS OF BUSINESS ACCREDITATION COUNCIL MEMBERS LISTING BY STATE 1993-94

B=Baccalaureate   M=Masters

ALABAMA

University of Alabama	BM
University of Alabama at Birmingham	BM
Auburn University	BM
Auburn University at Montgomery	BM
University of Montevallo	B
University of South Alabama	BM

ALASKA

University of Alaska-Fairbanks	BM

ARIZONA

American Graduate School of International Mgt. -Thunderbird	M
University of Arizona	BM
Arizona State University	BM
Northern Arizona University	BM

ARKANSAS

University of Arkansas at Fayetteville	BM
University of Arkansas at Little Rock	BM
Arkansas State University	BM
University of Central Arkansas	BM

CALIFORNIA

University of California, Berkeley	BM
University of California, Davis	M
University of California, Irvine	M
University of California at Los Angeles	M
California Polytechnic State University, San Luis Obispo	BM
California State University, Bakersfield	BM
California State University, Chico	BM

CALIFORNIA

California State University, Fresno	BM
California State University, Fullerton	BM
California State University, Hayward	BM
California State University, Long Beach	BM
California State University, Los Angeles	BM
California State University, Northridge	BM
California State University, Sacramento	BM
Claremont Graduate School	M
Loyola Marymount University	BM
University of San Diego	BM
San Diego State University	BM
University of San Francisco	BM
San Francisco State University	BM
San Jose State University	BM
Santa Clara University	BM
University of Southern California	BM
Stanford University	M
University of the Pacific	B

COLORADO

University of Colorado-Boulder	BM
University of Colorado at Colorado Springs	BM
University of Colorado-Denver	BM
Colorado State University	BM
University of Denver	BM
Fort Lewis College	B
University of Northern Colorado	B

CONNECTICUT

University of Bridgeport	BM
University of Connecticut	BM
Yale University	M

DELAWARE

University of Delaware	BM

DISTRICT OF COLUMBIA

American University	BM
George Washington University	BM
Georgetown University	BM
Howard University	BM

FLORIDA

University of Central Florida	BM
University of Florida	BM
Florida Atlantic University	BM
Florida International University	BM
Florida State University	BM
University of Miami	BM
University of North Florida	BM
Rollins College	M
University of South Florida	BM

GEORGIA

Clark Atlanta University	M
Emory University	BM
University of Georgia	BM
Georgia Institute of Technology	BM
Georgia Southern University	BM
Georgia State University	BM
Valdosta State College	B
West Georgia College	BM

HAWAII

University of Hawaii at Manoa	BM

IDAHO

Boise State University	BM
University of Idaho	B
Idaho State University	BM

ILLINOIS

Bradley University	BM
University of Chicago	M
DePaul University	BM
Eastern Illinois University	BM
University of Illinois at Chicago	BM
University of Illinois at Urbana/Champaign	BM
Illinois State University	BM
Loyola University, Chicago	BM
Northern Illinois University	BM
Northwestern University	M
Southern Illinois University at Carbondale	BM
Southern Illinois University at Edwardsville	BM
Western Illinois University	BM

INDIANA

Ball State University	BM
Indiana State University	BM
Indiana University	BM
Indiana University-Northwest	BM
Indiana University, South Bend	BM
Indiana University Southeast	B
Indiana University-Purdue University Fort Wayne	BM
University of Notre Dame	BM
Purdue University	BM
Valparaiso University	B

IOWA

Drake Iniversity	BM
University of Iowa	BM
Iowa State University	BM
University of Northern Iowa	BM

KANSAS

University of Kansas	BM
Kansas State University	BM
Wichita State University	BM

KENTUCKY

University of Kentucky	BM
University of Louisville	BM
Murray State University	BM
Western Kentucky University	B

LOUISIANA

Louisiana State University	BM
Louisiana State University in Shreveport	BM
Louisiana Tech University	BM
Loyola University, New Orleans	BM
McNeese State University	BM
University of New Orleans	BM
Nicholls State University	BM
Northeast Louisiana University	BM
Southeastern Louisiana University	BM
Tulane University	BM

MAINE

University of Maine at Orono	BM

MARYLAND

University of Baltimore	BM
Loyola College in Maryland	BM
University of Maryland	BM
Towson State University	B

MASSACHUSETTS

Babson College	BM
Bentley College	BM
Boston College	BM
Boston University	BM
Clark University	BM
Harvard University	M
University of Massachusetts, Amherst	BM
University of Massachusetts, Lowell	BM
Massachusetts Institute of Technology	BM
Northeastern University	BM
Suffolk University	BM

MICHIGAN

Central Michigan University	BM
University of Detroit-Mercy	BM
Eastern Michigan University	BM
University of Michigan-Ann Arbor	BM
University of Michigan-Flint	BM
Michigan State University	BM
Oakland University	BM

MICHIGAN

Wayne State University	BM
Western Michigan University	BM

MINNESOTA

University of Minnesota	BM
Saint Cloud State University	BM

MISSISSIPPI

Millsaps College	BM
University of Mississippi	BM
Mississippi State University	BM
University of Southern Mississippi	BM

MISSOURI

University of Missouri-Columbia	BM
University of Missouri-Kansas City	BM
University of Missouri-St. Louis	BM
Saint Louis University	BM
Southwest Missouri State University	BM
Washington University	BM

MONTANA

University of Montana	BM
Montana State University	B

NEBRASKA

Creighton University	BM
University of Nebraska-Lincoln	BM
University of Nebraska at Omaha	BM

NEVADA

University of Nevada-Las Vegas	BM
University of Nevada-Reno	BM

NEW HAMPSHIRE

Dartmouth College	M

NEW JERSEY

Rider College	BM
Rutgers-State University of New Jersey- New Brunswick	B
Rutgers-State University of New Jersey- Newark	BM
Seton Hall University	BM

NEW MEXICO

University of New Mexico	BM
New Mexico State University	BM

NEW YORK

Alfred University	B
Bernard M. Baruch College	BM
Binghamton University	BM
Canisius College	BM
Clarkson College	BM
Columbia University	M
Cornell University	M
Fordham University	BM
Hofstra University	BM
New York University-GSBA	M
New York University-CB&PA	B
Rensselaer Polytechnic Institute	BM
University of Rochester	M
Rochester Institute of Technology	BM
St. John's University	BM
State University of New York at Albany	BM
State University of New York at Buffalo	BM
Syracuse University	BM

NORTH CAROLINA

Appalachian State University	BM
Duke University	M
East Carolina University	BM
University of North Carolina at Chapel Hill	BM
University of North Carolina at Charlotte	BM
University of North Carolina at Greensboro	BM
University of North Carolina at Wilmington	BM
North Carolina A & T State University	B

NORTH CAROLINA

Wake Forest University, School of Business and Accountancy	B
Wake Forest University, Babcock School	M
Western Carolina University	BM

NORTH DAKOTA

University of North Dakota	BM

OHIO

University of Akron	BM
Bowling Green State University	BM
Case Western Reserve University	BM
University of Cincinnati	BM
Cleveland State University	BM
University of Dayton	BM
John Carroll University	BM
Kent State University	BM
Miami University	BM
Ohio State University	BM
Ohio University	BM
University of Toledo	BM
Wright State University	BM

OKLAHOMA

University of Oklahoma	BM
Oklahoma State University	BM
University of Tulsa	BM

OREGON

University of Oregon	BM
Oregon State University	BM
University of Portland	BM
Portland State University	BM

PENNSYLVANIA

Carnegie-Mellon University	BM
Drexel University	BM
Duquesne University	BM
Lehigh University	BM
University of Pennsylvania	BM
Pennsylvania State University	BM
University of Pittsburgh	BM
Shippensburg University	B
Susquehanna University	B
Temple University	BM
Villanova University	BM

RHODE ISLAND

University of Rhode Island   BM

SOUTH CAROLINA

Clemson University	BM
College of Charleston	B
University of South Carolina	BM
Winthrop College	BM

SOUTH DAKOTA

University of South Dakota   BM

TENNESSEE

East Tennessee State University	BM
Memphis State University	BM
Middle Tennessee State University	BM
University of Tennessee-Chattanooga	B
University of Tennessee-Knoxville	BM
Tennessee Technological University	BM
Vanderbilt University	M

TEXAS

Baylor University	BM
East Texas State University	BM
University of Houston-Clear Lake	BM
University of Houston-University Park	BM
Lamar University	BM
University of North Texas	BM
Southern Methodist University	BM
Stephen F. Austin State University	BM
University of Texas at Arlington	BM
University of Texas at Austin	BM
University of Texas at El Paso	BM
University of Texas, Pan American	BM
University of Texas at San Antonio	BM
Texas A & M University	BM

TEXAS

Texas Christian University	BM
Texas Tech University	BM

UTAH

Brigham Young University	BM
University of Utah	BM
Utah State University	BM
Weber State University	BM

VERMONT

University of Vermont   BM

VIRGINIA

College of William and Mary	BM
George Mason University	BM
James Madison University	BM
Norfolk State University	B
Old Dominion University	BM
Radford University	BM
University of Richmond	BM
University of Virginia-Darden School	M
University of Virginia-McIntire	BM
Virginia Commonwealth University	BM
Virginia Polytechnic Institute & State University	BM
Washington and Lee University	B

WASHINGTON

Eastern Washington University	BM
Gonzaga University	BM
Pacific Lutheran University	BM
Seattle University	BM
University of Washington	BM
Washington State University	BM
Western Washington University	BM

WEST VIRGINIA

West Virginia University   BM

WISCONSIN

Marquette University	BM
University of Wisconsin-Eau Claire	B
University of Wisconsin-La Crosse	BM
University of Wisconsin-Madison	BM
University of Wisconsin-Milwaukee	BM
University of Wisconsin-Oshkosh	BM
University of Wisconsin-Whitewater	BM

WYOMING

University of Wyoming	BM

CANADA

University of Alberta	BM
University of Calgary	BM

THE BEST GRADUATE BUSINESS SCHOOL FOR YOU

The Graduate Business School market is highly competitive and leaves no room for error. The MBA is a significant personal and financial investment. By applying **experience, intelligence** and **contacts,** you will maximize your opportunity for admission to the best program for you.

The *Business School Network (BSN)* has been founded specifically with this goal in mind.
THE BSN DELIVERS INTELLIGENCE TO MATCH THE NEEDS AND GOALS OF INDIVIDUAL CANDIDATES.

Information includes:

- □ School comparisons by attribute,i.e.,top functional areas, recruiter preferences, international emphasis,etc.
- □ Full descriptions of all career services/resources
- □ Special relationships with employers
- □ List of top Recruiting Employers
- □ Examples of graduates pursuing non-traditional careers
- □ Partnerships with key businesses
- □ Special initiatives with small, emerging and non-traditional employers
- □ Full-time, part-time, executive program comparisons

Services include:

- • Assessment and consultation on MBA programs in the context of intelligent career management.
- • Collaboration in developing precise, marketable applications including essays.
- • Preparation for the application process including research, networking and interviews.

Contact: THE BUSINESS SCHOOL NETWORK
84 Cedar Grove Road, Suite 25, Somerville, NJ 08876
Tel: 908 722-0361   Fax: 908 429-9416

Name: _____   Tel: _____

Address: _____   Fax: _____

I am interested in information on the following schools:

1. _____   2. _____

3. _____   4. _____

I am potentially interested in a meeting in one of the following BSN offices:

□ Philadelphia, PA   □ Somerville, New Jersey
□ New York City   □ Washington D.C.
□ Wilmington, Del.

My single-most important question about the decision to pursue an MBA is...

_____

DR. THOMAS BACHHUBER

Dr. Thomas Bachhuber is a leader in career development and university relations with a national reputation throughout the college market. As author of 5 books including *The Best Graduate Business Schools*, he has developed successful working relationships with colleges/universities across and outside the country.

He is the former Director of the Career Development Center at the University of Maryland-College Park and National Director for University Relations for Career Research Systems, Inc.,where he managed relationships with over 160 major university career/placement offices.

Dr. Bachhuber is the President of *The Business School Network,* which provides services for individuals considering and applying for Graduate Business School. The BSN is a division of Bachhuber & Associates, a career development and university relations company with business ties to outplacement, corporate college recruitment, international foundations, publishing, and sports management.